Pascal
for the

Macintosh™

Henry Ledgard
Andrew Singer

with the assistance of Peg Robbins

Addison-Wesley Publishing Company

Reading, Massachusetts • Menlo Park, California • Don Mills, Ontario • Wokingham, England
Amsterdam • Sydney • Singapore • Tokyo • Mexico City • Bogotá • Santiago • San Juan

Library of Congress Cataloguing in Publication Data

Ledgard, Henry F., 1943-
    Pascal for the Macintosh.

    Includes index.
    1. Macintosh (Computer)—Programming.   2. PASCAL
(Computer program language)   I. Singer, Andrew, 1943-
II. Robbins, Peg.   III. Title.
QA76.8.M3L44   1986   001.64'2   84-24503
ISBN 0-201-11772-X

Macintosh is a trademark licensed to Apple Computer, Inc.

ABCDEFGHIJ-HA-898765

Prelude to Programming

One *The Machine and the Language*

Two *Writing Simple Programs*

Three *Drawing and Using Procedures*

Prelude to Variables

Four *Performing Calculations*

Prelude to Choices

Five *Making Decisions*

Prelude to Repetition

Six   *Repeated Calculations*

Seven   *Programming Techniques*

Eight   *Testing Programs*

Prelude to Types

Nine *Data Types*

Prelude to Arrays

Ten *Arrays and Strings*

Prelude to Subprograms

Eleven *Functions and Procedures*

Prelude to Files

Twelve *Input and Output*

Prelude to Records

Thirteen *Record Structures*

Fourteen *More on Graphics*

List of

Illustrative Programs

Preface

It is a pleasure to see this book come to fruition. With the introduction of the Apple® Macintosh™ computer in 1984, there was an attempt to bring some advanced technology to the marketplace at a relatively low price. Among the technological features of this device were a high-resolution screen, the use of a mouse for cursor movement and for selecting actions, and the use of visual images (icons) to help guide the user.

Uniqueness of Macintosh Pascal

With the release of Apple's Macintosh Pascal software, an interactive environment for the programming language Pascal also became available. Most earlier implementations of Pascal had used the compiler technology to implement programs. With an interactive interpreter for running Pascal programs, there came the ability to step through a program as it was being run and to obtain almost instant information on its status. In this way a Pascal program could take on a life of its own. The programmer could in some sense "see" the program running. For us, using and teaching these aspects has been a pleasure.

All of this technology though was not without another deliberate design goal—ease of use. It has often been the case that programming language implementations have been heaped in a technology of complicated command languages and conventions that programmers need to follow. With the Macintosh and its Pascal, this was clearly not the case. Human engineering was paramount.

General Goals

The most visible goal of this book is to help teach the uninitiated to program in Macintosh Pascal. In this matter this book follows traditional lines. The book introduces the mechanics of using the Macintosh Pascal system, introduces the reader to some simple programs, and then presents a systematic development of the concepts in Pascal. These concepts include syntax, assignment, control structures, data types, procedures, and so on.

In many ways this book follows the CS 1 course of the Association for Computer Machinery's curriculum '78. The goals of CS 1 (see *Communications of the ACM,* October 1984) are (1) to teach methods of problem solving and the writing of algorithms, (2) to teach a particular high-level programming language, (3) to teach programming techniques and methods of style that promote quality. These are certainly the goals in this book.

But this book was also written out of a bit of frustration. I have seen too many books on programming that tend to drag the reader on with an almost exclusive reliance on the syntax of the programming language. Authors tend to think that once the syntax is understood, the rest will follow in due course. This usually leads to an overemphasis on the technical aspects of the programming language, a reliance on syntax equations for teaching, a tendency toward sterile examples, and a general lack of understanding of the deeper issues of programming.

This book is not at all traditional in these aspects. The examples, ideas, and presentation issues in this book have evolved over several years. They have been given a great deal of thought. The hope has been to spark attention and enthusiasm and to motivate excellent work.

Motivation through Problems

At the outset, the design of this book is based on problems, programming problems. It is my belief that programming is understood best when the solving of problems drives the learning process. It is the problems here that introduce the need for a given Pascal construct. These problems have been chosen to help the reader think about programming. Technical details, such as the syntax and semantics of Pascal, are introduced following the problem that motivates their need. After all, ultimately a programming language is used to solve real problems.

Thoughtful Examples

Another philosophy is teaching through examples. An astute and experienced programmer is often guided by many general concepts that come into play at various stages of the programming process. But the student of programming is in a different position. The student must, somehow, discover these concepts. The dilemma is that teaching programming through syntax masks the greater principles involved, but teaching through general concepts often leaves the student at sea in an attempt to understand what the concepts truly imply. So, the approach here is to make frequent use of examples. The examples guide both the teaching of syntax and concepts.

Practice Sessions

The student of programming must also face the task of his or her own work. This can be a sizable jump, from talk to action. For this purpose, there are special sections at the end of each chapter called "Practice." These are not appendages, but part of the text. They attempt to go into detail and challenge the reader to respond. All kinds of issues are addressed in these drills: syntax, finding bugs, the effect of removing parentheses, whether 5.0 can be changed to 5, using pointers, type declarations, using conditions, and more. The goal is to explore the fine print and involve the reader in an active way.

Following the practice sections, each chapter concludes with a selection of programming exercises. These are to be done on the computer. An attempt has been made to avoid toy exercises in favor of more real life problems.

Book Structure

In the structure of this book each chapter or sequence of chapters follows a somewhat general pattern:

1. Motivation
2. Example
3. Technical details
4. Practice

The motivation sections of this book are short Sherlock Holmes dialogues taken from a previous work (*Elementary Pascal,* by Henry Ledgard and Andrew Singer, published jointly by Random House and SRA (student edition), 1982). In each of these dialogues, Sherlock Holmes (the teacher) and Watson (the student) attempt to solve some kind of programming problem. In the course of the narrative, some basic programming principles are presented in an easily readable form. An example, a Macintosh Pascal program embodying the solution to the problem, is presented after each narrative. Then come the technical details, a discussion of the syntax and meaning of features in Pascal. Here the rules of Macintosh Pascal are given and concepts like type declarations and punctuation rules are explored at great depth. These technical matters comprise the bulk of this book. Following these sections are the practice sections.

Reaching Toward Real Programming

The last chapter of this book concludes with a program of some reasonable scale, a program to perform text formatting and layout.

Writing programs like this is not easy for the student, especially the first-time student of programming. But this, in a nutshell, is the objective here: to understand Pascal with sufficient depth to reach the level of programming in the last chapter.

A Spirit of Lightness

The Sherlock Holmes dialogues reproduced here from an earlier general text on Pascal have been slightly edited for compatibility with Macintosh Pascal. I think it is fair to say that they give a lightness and spirit to an area, computer programming, that is often rather dryly presented. But the dialogues have an even deeper purpose: to make the reader think about programming. As in any discipline, some ideas in programming are more important than others. It is these ideas that are presented in the narratives. Thus separated from the technical details of our profession, the fundamental ideas remain simple and readable.

Acknowledgments

This book owes much to the work of Andrew Singer. Several years ago Andrew Singer set as a goal to design and implement a programming system that would bring ease of use and human engineering to the center of design. In the development of Apple's Macintosh Pascal, Andrew Singer was one of the principal architects. It was also Andrew Singer's goal to see that a book be designed around such a product. This book would, he hoped, both set a high standard for programming and be a pleasure to read and use.

Jon Hueras, a special person, provided some key assistance behind the scenes. He is a splendid colleague. A number of people helped contribute to the writing of the predecessor to this book, *Elementary Pascal.* These include Edwina Carter, Steve Chernicoff, Louis Chmura, Karen Herman, Ed Judge, E. Patrick McQuaid, Robbie Moll, Rich Scire, and Holly Whiteside. John Bennison kindly provided a thoughtful review of the manuscript.

Portions of the text contain excerpts from *Programming Proverbs,* by Henry Ledgard, Paul Nagin, and Jon Hueras, copyright 1979, reprinted with permission of Hayden Book Company. The photograph of the Analytical Engine is courtesy of the Crown Copyright, Science Museum, London.

Amherst, Massachusetts
December 1984

To the Reader

This book is about programming. It is meant to teach a person with little computer experience how to write computer programs. The programming language is Macintosh Pascal.

Users of a professionally designed software system like the Macintosh Pascal system expect it to be free of strange quirks. We expect it to be error free, easy to use, and consistent. We expect the computer to respond rapidly. In order to achieve such professional results, many persons are involved. They have to work together, to read each other's programs, to learn what makes one solution to a problem better than another, to think about new releases of software and new features that might be needed. All of this implies that programming is not only a technical activity, but a human activity.

Let us now take a look at the "amateur" programmer, one who probably enjoys programming and most likely works alone. The programs do not have to be sold by Apple; most likely the author is the only one to use them. They don't even have to work properly all the time, for the amateur can grow to understand and tolerate any shortcomings that a program might have. An amateur's programs are relatively small (although occasionally some large ones are written). They usually don't have to fit with other software that someone else may have written. They just have to work, so to speak, most of the time and do something that is fairly useful. It is not the concern of the amateur to write something like the software required for a commercial word processor or a drawing package for children. The world of the amateur is thus quite self-contained.

If something goes wrong, the amateur can probably fix the program easily. Since only one person has written it and probably understands it quite completely, making corrections is a relatively simple chore. As for its behavior when it is run, it doesn't really matter whether the input conventions are convenient or whether the display is pleasant to read. Since no one but the program's designer depends on the program, it probably doesn't even need any documentation to reveal how it works. In short, it's a solo flight.

But now let us look again at the professional. The task of a professional programmer is very different from the amateur's task. The biggest difference is that the program may be used by thousands upon thousands of people. This poses some very stringent requirements. First of all the program had better do something useful or no one will use it or buy it. It is not enough to do the job halfway: a complete task has to be accomplished. The program should work just the way a user would expect it to under all sorts of circumstances. You can bet that all sorts of unusual inputs will eventually be tried. This means the demands on program correctness can be enormous.

Importantly, a professional programmer must work with many other people during the creation of a program. It is not enough for the program to be a private matter between the programmer and the computer. Other people have to deal with this program in intimate ways. Someone else may need to document how the program works. Another person may be called upon to make a change to the program. The program may be large enough so that a whole team of programmers is required to create it and these people must collaborate in intricate ways. The professional certainly does not stand alone.

On top of this, the professional's program may be used for many years, often long after its author has any interest in the program and, usually, after the program's author has moved on to other things. It is quite normal for other people, other programmers that is, to take over the work. Imagine looking at hundreds of pages of a program written by someone else. How would you deal with such a program? What if it is poorly written? What if your taking over is vital to the completion of a project? In the *real* world, this happens! Even something simple, like how the program is laid out on pages of paper, may be critical to someone else. The professional programmer annotates a program with comments describing how it works. To be really useful the comments must be accurate, brief, and informative. This itself is no easy task. And down to the nitty gritty, a programmer has to use names for things in a program. It is not enough to think of names haphazardly, for the meaning needs to stand out to the human reader.

Even something as fundamental as understanding the problem itself is an issue for the professional. It is not enough to conceive what the problem is in broad terms, the professional must spell it out. Ideally a complete written description of what the program is to do should be stated beforehand. This should even include the form in which data is entered by the user, and the exact layout on the screen of any results. The professional can spend an enormous amount of time just trying to understand this one aspect of software.

You see, professional programming is not a simple activity. It is systematic; it is disciplined; it has a large human element. It can be tiring at times to work this way and to take into account the myriad aspects that must be brought into play, but the goal is always the same: a program that is a pleasure to read, update, run, and most important, to use.

In the chapters that follow you will be introduced to the world of Macintosh Pascal and programming in this language. The goal in writing this book is to try to give you the very best ideas we can about this subject.

Prelude to Programming

The Analytical Engine

IN an incoherent and, as I deeply feel, an entirely inadequate fashion, I have endeavoured to give some account of the remarkable career of Mr. Sherlock Holmes as a criminal investigator and consulting detective. As the reader is undoubtedly well aware, my companion's interests were as broad as Nature herself and he often spoke on an amazing variety of subjects as though he had made a special study of each. In my modest chronicles of the cases that I have had the privilege to share with Sherlock Holmes, I have often alluded to his numerous publications, but I have said nothing before of his unparalleled contributions to the development of the Analytical Engine.

My first introduction to the Analytical Engine was in the late spring, shortly after the conclusion of one of the most ghastly adventures we had ever shared, which I have chronicled under the heading of "The Adventure of the Speckled Band." The entire day Holmes was in a mood that some would call taciturn. He was most unsettled, smoked incessantly, played snatches on his violin, sank into reveries, and hardly answered the casual questions that I put to him. We sat through a silent dinner together, after which, pushing his plate aside, he revealed to me the problem with which he was preoccupied.

"You can never foretell what one mind will come up with, Watson, but you can say with precision what an average person will do. Individuals vary, but percentages remain constant; and while we have not yet grasped the results that the human mind alone can attain, it has its distinct limitations. There are only particular individuals on whom we can rely to produce the same chain of logical argument from one occasion to the next."

"I certainly wouldn't argue with you, Holmes," I replied. "But as yet we haven't found a suitable replacement for human reasoning."

"Oh, on the contrary, Watson," he answered nonchalantly. "Have you ever heard of the Analytical Engine?"

"I know of no substitute for the mind of man."

"Have you ever heard of the Analytical Engine?"

Holmes chuckled. "Then you must learn of it. It is an ingenious mechanism, a machine that has displayed a considerable talent for deductive reasoning, far superior to the average logician. You recall my intervention in the matter of that notebook floating in the River Cam last month?"

"I am not likely soon to forget the sight of that bloated face staring up at me, Holmes," I replied grimly, considering the sorry state of mankind that such events should come to pass. "What connection has the late professor with this Engine?"

"Well, as you may remember, my investigation led me to the Cavendish laboratories; and it was there that I had occasion to study the Engine, if only briefly. Since then I have been in correspondence with mathematicians at Cambridge who have been conducting experiments with it. Watson, I do not exaggerate when I say that the Analytical Engine is capable of solving, within minutes, complex numerical problems that would keep five of London's finest mathematicians working for hours. Furthermore, it is adept at logic and has a perfect memory for detail.

"The Engine also has its limits," he continued. "It can only undertake problems whose solutions are spelled out in minute detail and that are presented in its own peculiar language."

"Really, Holmes, sometimes you go too far with my patience!" I exclaimed. "You expect me to believe that this device is capable of solving problems, has a perfect memory, and actually speaks a language of its own?"

"No, no, my dear Watson, you take me too literally. The Analytical Engine does indeed have a language of its own, but communications must be written out."

"Now you tell me it can read?"

"In a sense, yes."

I threw up my arms in a desperate gesture and began to rise from the table.

"I fear I am going too fast for you, Watson. Bear with me for a moment and I shall do my utmost to explain all this to you. Everything I say is true, but let me assure you that the Analytical Engine hardly resembles a human being.

"Its 'language' is actually a highly logical code, designed by mathematicians in order to operate the Engine. This code is not difficult to master, but it does require considerable discipline. It has a very small vocabulary, which is nothing to compare with the English tongue. This vocabulary is arranged into statements according to a limited set of rules.

"The major problem in communicating with the Engine is that one must use the utmost care and precision in giving it instructions, for it has no imagination whatsoever and cannot correct even trivial errors in spelling or punctuation. It is, after all, like other machines in that it has no awareness of the tasks that it performs; therefore it will obey the most unreasonable of instructions. For example, if it is told to print the number zero *ad infinitum*, it will continue to do so for hours on end, until a human being finally causes it to stop."

"But Holmes, how does one give instructions to this Engine?" I asked, scarcely crediting my companion's remarks thus far and wondering whether perhaps his penchant for cocaine had finally betrayed his reason.

"By writing a set of instructions in code and supplying them mechanically to the Engine. Such a set of instructions is called a *programme*, because it is an orderly and precise procedure for solving a problem. The art of writing programmes is called, reasonably enough, *programming*."

"Of what relevance is this strange machine to you, Holmes?"

"I intend to employ the Engine whenever possible in my future criminal cases," he replied. "As you know, I have been rather overburdened with work in recent months, so the Engine's speed and potential accuracy are most attractive to me. It has a great capacity for dealing with large amounts of information as well."

"But, Holmes," I interrupted, "do you truly expect this device, if it is as unimaginative as you say, actually to solve crimes?"

"Not at all, my dear Watson," said Holmes with a laugh. "I daresay it is not clever enough to replace my brain; but it will be useful for storing information, as well as for performing certain repetitive tasks that absorb too much of my time. Of most interest to me is that it will provide a means of expressing my logical methods in a rigorous form, and perhaps be useful in communicating to others my modest attempts at formulating a Science of Deduction."

Chapter 1

The Machine and the Language

The Analytical Engine was indeed the forerunner of today's computers. In the 1830s Charles Babbage and his collaborator, Lady Augusta Ada Lovelace (Lord Byron's daughter), between them worked out most of the fundamental principles upon which modern computing is based.

Holmes's insight into the promises and pitfalls of the computer (in the Prelude to this chapter) is striking. The ability to handle great amounts of data, to remember even the tinest detail, to make extremely accurate calculations, and to obey instructions over and over again are all well recognized.

What are not so well recognized are the pitfalls: the often endless details, the computer's intolerance of error, the annoying idiosyncracies, and the need for unremitting rigor.

A first attempt at programming is likely to be a frustrating experience. The demanding precision to which Holmes alludes is quite unfamiliar to most people. You struggle to piece together a variety of computer instructions, making changes almost randomly and hoping somehow the program will work. You might put a line into your program that says,

Print the answer

and expect the computer to print the correct result. This would be futile. To get a computer to do your bidding, you must tell it precisely what you want it to do in exactly the proper way.

When you do this, you have at your command a kind of modern genie. For example, the manuscript for this book was typed on the Apple Macintosh using Apple's MacWrite™. MacWrite makes it easy to modify the text in small and large ways and then print out revised versions quickly for study and further improvement. When the revisions are finished and the manuscript complete, the text can be transferred to another computer which reproduces it in a form that makes it possible to typeset the book automatically. Babbage would be especially satisfied if he were alive today, for it was his desire to eliminate error from tide tables that led him to develop the Difference Engine from which the Analytical Engine evolved. In fact, this early computer was designed to set type to enable the printing of the tables.

In the chapters that follow, you should find all that you need to know in order to write first-rate computer programs yourself. The present chapter introduces you to the Macintosh environment and Macintosh Pascal. If you are already familiar with the mouse, pulldown menus, icons, and overlapping windows, you may want to skip ahead.

1.1 ● Starting Up and Using the Mouse

The on/off switch for the Macintosh is located on the back of the machine on the left side as you face the screen. When you turn it on, the screen displays an image, or *icon*, of a disk with a question mark flashing. Below the screen under the left side of the front is a knob which controls the brightness of the screen; you may want to adjust the brightness before continuing. The Macintosh Pascal disk contains the system information needed by the machine, as well as the Pascal interpreter. Insert the disk label side up, metal end first. You can hear it snap into place.

When the machine has finished reading the system information it needs, the screen displays an icon of a disk with the disk name underneath it in the upper right corner of the screen, and the trash icon underneath it in the upper right corner of the screen, and the trash icon (a tiny garbage can) in the lower right corner. The command menus appear across the top of the screen. There is also a pointer somewhere on the screen. The location of the pointer is controlled by the *mouse*.

The mouse is the primary means of communicating with the machine. There are four ways of signaling with it.

To *locate* the pointer, roll the mouse on any flat surface. The pointer follows the movement of the mouse. If you are too close to the edge of a table, just pick up the mouse and move it to a new starting point.

To *click* the mouse, press the button on top of the mouse and then release. To *click* an icon or a window, *locate* the pointer on it and *click* the mouse. Clicking an icon or a window causes it to become active. The active item is highlighted to distinguish it. The commands that you choose from the menu will act on whichever item is active.

To *double-click*, press and release the mouse button twice quickly.

The *drag* the mouse, move the pointer to the desired location, push the button down, and hold it down while you move the pointer to the new location, then release the button.

An icon can be dragged to a new position by locating the pointer on the icon and then dragging it to the new location. The icon will stick with the pointer until you release the mouse button.

The pointer, or cursor, is not always an arrow. It is displayed as an Ibeam when choosing edit locations, a plus sign when a program is running, a wristwatch when the computer is busy and you must wait. Regardless of the cursor's chape, its location is always controlled by the mouse.

Each menus across the top of the screen offers several selections. To read the selections on any one of them, locate the pointer on the menu name, press the mouse button and hold it down. The selections displayed in bold type are available. To choose one, drag the pointer down to your choice and then release the mouse button. Notice that some of the selections are followed by a symbol and a letter. These represent keyboard commands that can be substituted for the menu and mouse. The Macintosh screen is shown in Fig. 1.1 with the file menu highlighted.

To open a disk or file, either choose Open from the File menu or double-click the icon. In order for an item to be opened it must be the active item; if the one you want to open is not the highlighted item it can be activated by clicking it. Opening an item causes its contents to be

1.2 ● Menus, Windows, and Icons

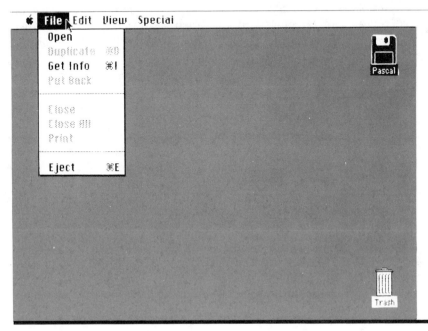

Figure 1.1 ● File menu on Macintosh screen

displayed on the screen in a window. The display will be by Icon, by Name, by Date, by Size, or by Kind depending on which view was last selected for that file from the View menu. To close the window, either choose Close from the File menu or click the white square on the left side of the title bar.

It is not necessary to close one window before opening another; more than one can be displayed at a time. You can tell which window is the active one by looking at the title bar; it will be lined on the active file and clear on the others. When the windows overlap, the active one will always appear at the front. To activate a different window, click anywhere within it.

You may need to rearrange the windows on the screen to suit your needs. To move the whole window, drag it by its title bar. If you want to make it larger or smaller, drag from the size box in the lower right corner. The arrows on the bottom and right borders are for scrolling the screen. Move the pointer to the arrow, then press and hold the mouse button to get the view that you need. You can also change the view by clicking anywhere on the bottom or right border or by dragging the white square on either of these borders to a new position. The position of the square on the border indicates the position of the view in relation to the total document.

The icons displayed in the windows and on the screen tell you what kind of information is contained. Files are represented by file folders, documents by a sheet of paper, garbage by a trash barrel, and so on. These sets of information can be relocated by dragging the icon from place to place. Documents can be moved from folder to folder or disk to folder; files can be moved to the trash barrel, all the documents contained within go with it. They will remain in the trash barrel and can be retrieved until you choose Empy Trash from the Special menu. Once you have emptied the trash, they are gone for good. If you want to save a particular document, drag it to the disk window or to another folder before you move the file folder to the trash. When you have finished moving icons around, choose Clean Up from the Special menu and the macine will straighten out your icon display.

To move information to a different disk, make sure its icon is displayed in a window, then activate the current disk icon and choose Eject from the File menu. Insert the new disk and drag the icon you want to save to the new disk icon. The machine will direct you from that point. A copy is always left behind when a file or document is moved to a new disk.

These filing activities are all part of the Finder, a control system provided by the Macintosh which makes it easy for you to keep your work in order. The information presented here will get you started; for more detailed information on the Finder you should refer to the Macintosh manual.

Figure 1.2 presents a simple Pascal program. This program reads a Fahrenheit temperature, computes its Celsius equivalent and prints the result.

We will discuss the structure of a program in detail in the next chapter. The purpose of the present chapter is to introduce the working environment and the process of entering and running a Pascal program on the Macintosh. You may choose to enter this program into your computer to get a feel for the system. As you enter it, be aware that every detail is important; correct punctuation and spelling are not just niceties here, they are absolute necessities.

When you open a Macintosh Pascal file, you are presented with three windows: *Untitled, Text,* and *Drawing* (see Fig. 1.3).

The Untitled window should show as the active one. When you type in a program, that is where it appears. Drag the window out to the right to give yourself a better view while you are typing. Type the program just as it is printed in Fig. 1.3, but be prepared for some surprises. The entries are automatically formatted as you go along. Certain words become boldface lowercase print. These are *keywords* and will be discussed in the next chapter. Alignment is performed as soon as each statement is accepted by the machine. Some line changes are automatic, but you can use the carriage return to create blank lines and to put the comment (the sentence enclosed by curly brackets) on a line by itself.

1.3 ● Entering, Editing, and Running a Program

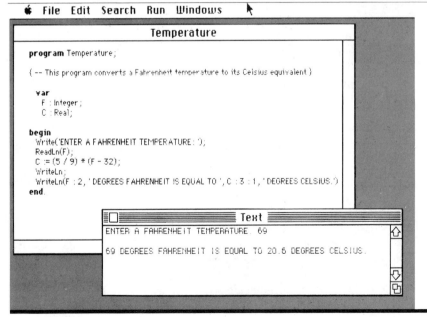

Figure 1.2 ● Program Temperature

Figure 1.3 ● The three windows on the Macintosh screen

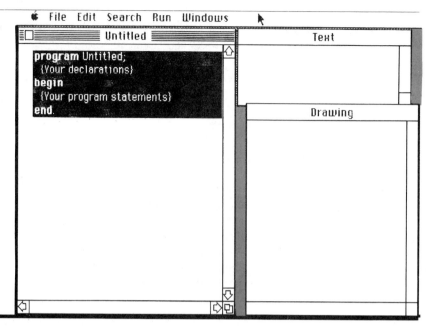

There are several options available for making changes and corrections. The simplest way to correct a mistake is to use the Backspace key. The Backspace key will erase as it goes and new data can be entered immediately.

Another tool available is the Edit menu. The cursor location tells the machine *where* an operation is to be performed, and the Edit menu tells it *what* is to be done.

You can change the location of the cursor by using the mouse to move the Ibeam to the desired location and then clicking or dragging. Clicking selects a location; dragging selects a section of text, which becomes highlighted. A whole word can be highlighted by double-clicking it. To highlight several words or several lines of text at once, place the Ibeam at one end of the section and drag directly to the other end of the section; everything between will become highlighted. Pressing the Backspace key will clear the entire highlighted area. Entering new text will also clear the highlighted area; the new text will replace it.

Once you have placed the cursor, you have several choices available to you from the Edit menu. You can *Clear* the highlighted area from your program, *Copy* it onto the clipboard, or *Cut* it out of its present location and *Paste* it into a new spot. When you Cut or Copy, the text is put onto the clipboard, replacing whatever was there before.

If you have any doubt about what the clipboard contains, go to the Windows menu and select Clipboard. This causes the clipboard window to be displayed on the screen, allowing you to view the contents. The Windows menu also offers the choice Type Size. Choosing small type allows more of the program to be displayed at one time.

Once the program is entered correctly, it is important to save it. The File menu has a Save As command and a Save command. You choose Save As first to name your program. When the dialog screen appears, type the name of your program and then click the Save button. If you make changes later, choose Save to have the changes saved on the disk. Up until you Quit the program you have the option of reverting to the last saved version; choose Revert from the File menu to discard the most recent changes.

Always save your program before you run it. Don't take a chance on losing it; this can happen if something in the program causes a problem for the machine.

There is one more thing to think about before running a program. Consider the location of the program's output. You will probably want to activate the Text window for this program. The output is written to the Text window whether it is active or not; the purpose of activating it is to make it visible. If you did not cover it completely when you enlarged your program window, you can activate it by clicking in the visible portion. If it is completely covered, either shrink the program window or go to the Windows menu and select Text.

Now choose Go from the Run menu to start the program. When you see Pause appear on the menu line, the machine is waiting for data from the keyboard in order to continue. You have the option of choosing Halt from the Pause menu or entering the needed data. For the example program, the data needed is an integer representing a Fahrenheit temperature. As soon as you enter an integer number followed by a space or carriage return, the program will continue its run. Step will run one line of the program at a time. The finger in the left margin points to the next step that is to be executed. Step-Step activates the pointer to show which step is being executed, but does not stop after each statement.

There comes a time when a printed copy of the program or the output is needed. To print only the program, activate the program window, turn on the printer, and choose Print from the File menu. This will cause a dialog box to appear requesting certain instructions: the quality of print, the page range, the number of copies, and the type of paper being used. Once these choices have been made, click the OK box and printing will begin. To print the output of the program, you must follow the instructions for printing the contents of the screen. Hold down the "Command" key (the wide key to the left of the space bar) and the "Shift" key while you type the number "4." This will cause the contents of the active window to be printed. If the "Caps Lock" key is also down, the contents of the whole screen will be printed.

The information in this chapter will get you started using your Macintosh and Macintosh Pascal; as you continue to use the computer, refer to the menu commands summarized in Appendix A.

1.4 ○ Practice

Operating the Macintosh

The best way to become proficient at using the Macintosh is, of course, to sit down and use it. This section should be read at the computer as you experiment with some of the options. If the disk you are using has previously been used by someone else, there may be some differences from what is described below. Do the best you can.

Experiment first with opening and closing the disk icon and the trash barrel. Choose different Views and note the arrangement of the information with each view. Next, open the system folder. Inside the system folder there should be an icon marked Empty Folder. Duplicate the empty folder. What is the name given to the new folder?

● ● ●

A new folder icon should have appeared next to the original and should be labeled Copy of Empty Folder. Once a duplicate folder has been created, it can be moved onto another window or into a folder or disk. The name can be edited whenever the icon is displayed. Move the folder to the disk window and then choose Clean Up from the Special menu to keep the desktop neat. Edit the name on the folder so that you can use it to store your work. Do this before you continue.

● ● ●

Now that you have a folder for storing programs, it would be nice to have something to put in it. Entering the text of a program may not be the most enjoyable part of the programming process, but it is important that you become proficient at it. Fortunately, Macintosh Pascal assists you in this operation. Open the Macintosh Pascal application now and enter the example program Temperature. Run it through a Check and make whatever corrections are required. Do not save it yet. Choose Quit from the File menu. What happens?

● ● ●

The Macintosh usually sounds a warning when you may be making a mistake or when your intentions are unclear. The dialog box that appers on the screen requires your attention before you can continue. It is a reminder that you have not saved your program. Choose Save. You will be asked for a name for your document; enter the name Temperature, then click the Save button in the dialog box. What happens?

● ● ●

Now the computer can act on your original Quit command; it will return to the Finder. When returning to the Finder, whichever windows were open when you left the Finder will still be open. Find the icon for the program you just entered and saved and put it into your folder. You can do that either by dragging the document icon to the folder icon, or by dragging the document icon onto the folder window.

● ● ●

Open program Temperature. Now close the windows using the Close choice from the File menu. Clicking the white box on the menu bar does not accomplish what is desired here; when you are in the Pascal application, clicking the disappear box *does* make the window disappear from the screen, but it *does not* close the file. Choosing Close closes the present program but does not return to the Finder. Note that the disk icon and the trash barrel are not on the screen. The Pascal application is still open. Check the File menu now. What are the new choices available?

● ● ●

Two additional choices are now available, New and Open. Choosing New creates a blank program window for a new program. Choosing Open puts up a dialog box listing the available files. We need program Temperature again. There are two ways to open it. What are they?

● ● ●

The dialog gox shows the names of the available files along with an Open choice, a Cancel choice, and an Eject choice. A file can be opened by clicking the file name and then the Open button, or by double-clicking the file name.

Run program Temperature at least once using Go. Run it again by holding down the fan key and typing "G." Note that the Pause menu lights up when the computer needs data from the keyboard. Now Step through the program; either choose Step or use the fan key and "S." There are several things to note as you step through.

1. The finger points to the line that is to be executed next; that line is executed when you choose any Run command.

2. The Pause menu does not light up when you are using Step; however, note that the cursor appears on the text screen when data is needed.

3. If you try to advance beyond the Read statement without entering needed data, a warning is sounded.

● ● ●

Using the Search menu, change All Occurrences of "F" to "FTemp" and "C" to "CTemp" everywhere in the program. Do not Save. Run the edited version. How does the output change?

● ● ●

All Occurrences means exactly what it says. The "F" in the word "Fahrenheit" and the "C" in the word "Celsius" are replaced with "FTemp" and "CTemp" producing a very strange sentence.

Revert to the previous version of the program. Print the program using the Print choice from the File menu. Run the program and print the output screen.

● ● ●

Save the program under a different title (use Save As). Return to the Finder. The right side of the title bar shows the Space Available on the disk. Note the amount. Now, move the new version of the program to the trash barrel. How much does the space available change? Empty the trash. Again, how much does the space available change?

● ● ●

Moving a file to the trash barrel does not remove it from the disk; therefore, the space available on the disk does not change. However, once the trash has been emptied, the space is available for other use. Removing program Temperature creates 1K more of disk space. Notice that when you choose Empty Trash, no warning beep is sounded. Always be aware of what is in the trash barrel before you empty it. When in doubt, open the window and check. You will be warned if you try to empty something the computer needs, such as the system folder.

Open the Control Panel (keep looking, it's there somewhere) and adjust the speaker volume by dragging the knob up or down. Open program Temperature and change the Type Size to small. Now quit the application, eject the disk, and turn off the machine. Restart the disk. What happened to the speaker volume? What happened to the type size?

● ● ●

Each time the Pascal application is opened, the default conditions are active. Changes are maintained when going from one program to another, but returning to the Finder deactivates them. The system changes, on the other hand, which are set at the Control Panel, are recorded on the disk and remain active until changed again.

● ● ●

Try the review exercises below. You should be off and running now.

Fill in the Blanks

1. A file can be opened by choosing _____ from the _____ menu, or by _____ the file icon.

2. Clicking the _____ causes the window to disappear.

3. To name a file, choose _____ from the _____ .

4. To change the name of a file, the _____ must be displayed.

5. To shrink or stretch a window, drag from the _____ corner.

6. To print the contents of a window as displayed on the screen, hold down the _____ key and the _____ key and press the number _____ .

7. The control panel is found in the _____ menu.

8. When the Macintosh application is active, the contents of the clipboard can by displayed by choosing _____ from the _____ menu.

True or False

1. Choosing GO from the RUN menu causes the cursor to move.

2. Some menu selections are in boldface print, some in light print. The lighter selections must be double-clicked.

3. If you type "help" on the screen, the computer will tell you what mistake you have just made.

4. You cannot see through a Macintosh window.

5. Macintosh Pascal is easy to use.

6. In order to erase the letter you just typed, press the Backspace key.

7. The Command key is marked "C."

8. Saving the file causes the contents of the screen to be copied to the internal memory of the Macintosh.

9. Instead of choosing from the RUN menu, you can type "run."

10. The contents of the trash barrel can never be retrieved.

In order for you to check your own weak spots, the answers for the True/False and Fill in the Blanks exercises are given in the following paragraphs. If you feel reasonably comfortable with your results, continue on. As you begin writing and running your own programs, you'll get plenty of practice using the Macintosh.

There are two ways to open a file. It can be opened by activating the icon with a single click and then choosing OPEN from the FILE menu or by DOUBLE-CLICKING the icon.

When a window is active, the title bar at the top of the window shows a set of horizontal lines. The lines are interrupted on the left side by a small white box. Clicking the WHITE BOX ON THE LEFT SIDE OF THE TITLE BAR causes the window to disappear.

To name a file, choose SAVE AS from the FILE menu. This causes a dialog box to appear. Type the name into the space indicated. This causes the computer to set aside a location on the disk for that particular file and to associate the given name with that location. To change the name later, go to the window containing the FILE ICON. Activate the icon by clicking it, then edit the name using the cursor to erase the old name or make corrections.

A window can be stretched or shrunk by dragging the LOWER RIGHT corner to a new location.

It is possible to print the contents of a single window or the contents of the whole Macintosh screen. To print only the active window, hold down the SHIFT key and the COMMAND key and type the number "4." To print the whole screen, first press the Caps Lock key, and then the fn, Shift, and 4.

At the top of the screen, in addition to the menu names, there is an apple. Press and hold on the apple and a list of choices including the control panel is displayed.

When using the Finder application, the clipboard can be viewed by choosing Show Clipboard from the Edit menu. In the Macintosh Pascal application, that choice is not available in the Edit menu. However, there is a choice labeled CLIPBOARD under the WINDOWS menu, which causes the contents of the clipboard to be displayed.

Let's take a look at the True/False questions. Number 4 is obviously true. Number 6 is also true. As far as number 5 goes, to each his own. The others are false.

The movement of the cursor is always controlled by the mouse. However, the form that the cursor takes depends on what activities are being performed. When a program is running, the cursor appears as a plus sign.

Some menu choices appear in boldface print, others are light. Only those in boldface print are available. Trying to choose one that is in light print has no effect.

If you type the word "help" on the screen, all you will get is the word "help" on the screen.

The Command key is located at the bottom of the keyboard to the left of the space bar and is marked with the picture of a fan.

When a file is Saved, it is written to the disk.

Typing "run" at the keyboard does not cause a program to run. However, a program run can be initiated by holding the Command key down and typing "G" at the keyboard. Command "S" will run one line of the program; this may be a little quicker than using the mouse and menu if you are running several lines.

Don't empty the trash until you are sure you do not need the contents. Until it is emptied, you can retrieve whatever is there by dragging the icon back to the screen. However, once the can is emptied, it is gone for good.

1.5 ○

Programming Exercises

1.1   Entering a Program

Entering the text of a program is a task in itself. It is important that you become proficient at it. Fortunately, Macintosh Pascal gives you a good deal of assistance. The following program is to be entered word for word. If you make mistakes, they must be corrected. Once the program is entered, run it through Check and Go.

```
program WriteName;
  var
    Name : string;
begin
  WriteLn('What is your name? ');
  ReadLn(Name);
  WriteLn('Thank you, ',Name, '.')
end.
```

Note: If you enter this program correctly, the text screen will first show a request for your name. Enter your name by a return. The response line should appear, properly punctuated with a comma following the "Thank you" and a period at the end.

1.2   Running a Program

Enter the following program and then run it several times, successively using the following values as inputs for I:

   0   5   25   25,000   25.25

Can you explain the outputs?

```
program Square;
   var
      I : Integer;
begin
   Read(I);
   Write(I * I)
end.
```

1.3   Read and ReadLn

When a Read statement is encountered in a program run, the cursor begins flashing on the text screen, indicating that data is expected. If the statement is a ReadLn rather than a Read, the run does no continue until a return is encountered. Change the Read in the program of the previous exercise to ReadLn and run the program again with the same set of input values. When you enter the 25.25 what happens to the decimal portion?

1.4   Write and WriteLn

Write and WriteLn are related in a way similar to Read and ReadLn. With Write, the data is written to the screen, and then any further data is continued on the same line. With WriteLn, new data is written to a new line. Enter the following program and then try to find ways to improve the output.

```
program NewYear;
begin
   Write('HAPPY NEW YEAR');
   Write('HAPPY NEW YEAR')
end.
```

1.5   Calculations

Enter the following program:

```
program Calculate;
   var
      X : Integer;
      Y : Real;
begin
   Write('Enter an integer number: ');
   ReadLn(X);
   Write('Enter a real number: ');
   ReadLn(Y);
   WriteLn((X + Y) : 4 : 1);
   WriteLn((X - Y) : 4 : 1);
   WriteLn((X * Y) : 4 : 1);
   WriteLn((X / Y) : 4 : 1)
end.
```

This program is a little trickier to enter than the previous one. Watch out! The : 4 indicates that the value of the expression in parentheses shall be written using not less than 4 spaces. The : 1 indicates that 1 decimal place will be displayed . Using the values given below as inputs, make whatever changes are necessary to ensure that the output appears in a column that is right justified; that is, the right hand edge must be even. Here are the values:

        X =   2   Y =   4.0
        X =   10   Y = 30.0
        X = 555   Y = 33.3

Chapter 2

Writing Simple Programs

The following programming application demonstrates how a simple Pascal program is written. It gives an example of the steps from problem to printout. With the information contained in this chapter, you will be able to write some simple programs of your own.

You have an opinion on what temperature is comfortable for a study room. You may think of the temperature in degrees Fahrenheit and might find it useful to relate room comfort to degrees Celsius. When you think of a particular Celsius temperature as being related to comfort, instead of thinking of it only as the equivalent of some Fahrenheit temperature, it becomes more meaningful. To do this, let us consider a simple program to display three temperatures along with their comfort levels. The problem is defined as follows:

to read in 3 Fahrenheit temperatures defined by the user as too cold, comfortable, and too hot,

to compute the Celsius equivalent of each of them, using the formula $C = (5 / 9)(F - 32)$,

to display the results with the following format:

TEMPERATURE SUMMARY

F		C
?	Too Cold	?
?	Comfortable	?
?	Too Hot	?

The question marks stand for the given temperatures.

2.1 ● The Concept of an Algorithm

Of all the topics discussed in this book, the most fundamental is the concept of an algorithm. The rigor demanded by a computer algorithm is the essence of programming, no matter which special language you are working in. Let's quickly review the properties of an algorithm, for this gives us the key to all that is taken up in later pages.

Generally, an *algorithm* is a sequence of instructions given to solve some problem. Any algorithm must have the following characteristics:

1. *It must be organized properly.* An algorithm reflects some sequence of instructions carried out in the real world. Accordingly, the instructions must be arranged in some meaningful way in order to solve the problem at hand.

2. *It must go step by step.* Each instruction in the algorithm must be some form of imperative statement, or command, to carry out a given step in the problem solution. After each step, the next step in the solution must be unambiguous.

3. *It must be precise.* The instructions given in an algorithm can leave no room for ambiguity. Thus it must be possible to interpret the instructions in only one way.

4. *It must make the data explicit.* Each item we choose to include in our algorithm must be clearly identified. For example, if an algorithm has something to do with temperatures, and these are calculated during the course of the algorithm, then these items need to be described explicitly.

5. *It must contain no irrelevant information.* There can be no loose ends, no extraneous instructions, no frills. The algorithm must state only the relevant instructions needed to be carried out.

6. *It must be correct.* An algorithm is always directed toward its single goal—to establish results that will be known upon its completion. The results must be exactly what you want.

All of these features are things that we often take for granted. In an algorithm, we must be rigorous to the last detail.

For our problem we first need to request some data, the three temperatures, from the user. When the machine reads these three numbers, it assigns them to particular variables, so we must have a name or identifier for each one. The program is easier to read if the names are descriptive of the value being entered, so we have chosen to use TooCold, Comfortable, and TooHot.

Once we have the three values, we can apply our formula to each of them in turn; we assign each temperature to F, calculate the Celsius equivalent, and store the result as C. Each time we assign a new value to F or C, the assignment causes the previous value to be discarded, so each value must be printed before the next one is calculated. Before we print the temperatures, however, we want to print a title and heading.

When all of these steps are put into the proper order, we arrive at the algorithm shown in Fig. 2.1.

The corresponding program is shown as Fig. 2.2. Notice here that the Celsius temperature required for the output is a two-digit integer; however, our formula returns a decimal number, so we have added one more step to give us the type of number that we need for our summary.

        C := Round(RealC);

The additional step creates a need for an identifier for the intermediate value of C. Since it has to be declared as a Real number we have chosen to name it RealC. We will explain more details as we proceed.

Now we have a working model of a typical Pascal program. As you have probably already observed, the writing of programs requires that you know a number of sometimes odd conventions. Let's start by examining the major components of our example program.

2.2 ● General Program Structure

```
program TemperatureSummary;
    -- declarations
begin
    -- statements
end.
```

Figure 2.1

Definitions:
    TooCold   :   degrees Fahrenheit entered by user
    Comfortable: degrees Fahrenheit entered by user
    TooHot   :   degrees Fahrenheit entered by user
    F: Fahrenheit temperature
    C: Celsius temperature

Algorithm:
    Request degrees Fahrenheit for each comfort level
    Read temperatures for TooCold, Comfortable, and TooHot
    Write headings
    For each temperature do the following:
        set F to temperature
        apply formula $C = (5/9)(F-32)$
        write: F, comfort level, C

All programs begin with the word **program** followed by the name of the program, in this case TemperatureSummary.

Following the program heading are definitions for all of the objects in a program. Each definition is called a *declaration*. In Pascal, this rule must be followed strictly. Every name used by the programmer must be defined in a declaration. For example, "F" is the name that stands for a

Figure 2.2 ● Program
TemperatureSummary

```pascal
program TemperatureSummary;
{ -- This program reads 3 Fahrenheit temperatures entered by the user, }
{ -- calculates the Celsius equivalents, and prints the results. }
  var
     TooCold, Comfortable, TooHot : Integer;
     F,C : Integer;
     RealC : Real;
begin
{ -- Request temperatures }
   Write('Enter 3 Fahrenheit temperatures: too cold, comfortable, too hot: ');
{ -- Read Fahrenheit temperatures }
   ReadLn(TooCold, Comfortable, TooHot);
{ -- Write headings }
   WriteLn;
   WriteLn;
   WriteLn('TEMPERATURE SUMMARY');
   WriteLn('----------------------');
   WriteLn(' F              C ');
{ -- Calculate celsius equivalents and write results }
   F := TooCold;
   RealC := (5 / 9) * (F – 32);
   C := Round(RealC);
   WriteLn;
   WriteLn(F : 2,' Too Cold ', C : 2);

   F := Comfortable;
   RealC := (5 / 9) * (F – 32);
   C := Round(RealC);
   WriteLn;
   WriteLn(F : 2,' Comfortable ', C : 2);

   F := TooHot;
   RealC := (5 / 9) * (F – 32);
   C := Round(RealC);
   WriteLn;
   WriteLn(F : 2,' Too Hot ', C : 2);
end.
```

Fig. 2.2 continued

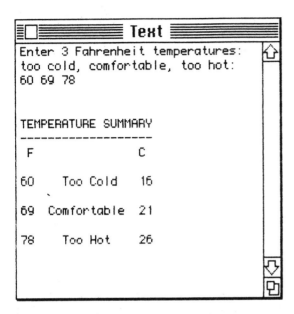

```
▤□�e═══════ Text ═══════
Enter 3 Fahrenheit temperatures:
too cold, comfortable, too hot:
60 69 78


TEMPERATURE SUMMARY
-------------------
 F                  C

60     Too Cold    16

69   Comfortable   21

78     Too Hot     26
```

Fahrenheit temperature. This name must be declared, as in

> F : Integer;

This declaration means that the name F will hold integer values during the course of the algorithm portion of the program. The three temperatures entered by the reader; TooCold, Comfortable, and TooHot will also hold integer values. We want to display an integer value for the Celsius temperature also; that must be declared. However, when we apply the formula, $C = (5 / 9)(F - 32)$, the calculation will produce a real number; therefore, we must assign the result to a variable that has been declared as Real, as in

> RealC : Real;

Next we come to the algorithm portion of the program. An algorithm is written as a series of *statements.* There are several kinds of statements in Pascal. Each of them specifies some action to be carried out by the computer. For example, consider the assignment statement,

> RealC := (5 / 9) * (F − 32)

The symbol := is read as "becomes"; it assigns the value of the expression on the right to the variable on the left. During the course of the program, F takes on three different values. When a new value is assigned to the identifier, it replaces the existing one, which is discarded. Therefore, we print out the F and C values in each case before starting the next calculation.

Other statements in Pascal cause a series of actions to be performed. For instance the statement

WriteLn(F : 2, '   Comfortable   ', C : 2)

is actually a procedure call. It calls the procedure WriteLn, which causes the machine to print the integer value for F using two digits, print the character string enclosed by the parentheses, print the integer value for C using two digits, and then move to the beginning of the next line.

A program always ends with the word **end** followed by a period.

All of these points will be taken up in greater detail in later chapters. For the remainder of this chapter, however, let's take a closer look at the individual components of a program.

2.3 ● The Units of a Pascal Program

At the most elementary level, a Pascal program consists of a sequence of symbols. The possible symbols are listed in Table 2.1. The arrangement of symbols is subject to numerous and sometimes complex conventions that you will have to learn as you go along. Here we pin down a few of the more primitive conventions, including the rules for writing names, numbers, character strings, and comments.

Identifiers

An *identifier* is a name created by the programmer. It consists of one or more letters, digits, or underscores, but the first character must always be a letter. An identifier can be up to 255 characters long, but cannot contain any spaces. The identifiers we have used are

F   C   TooCold   Comfortable   TooHot   RealC

Macintosh Pascal accepts the use of the underscore in an identifier, therefore we can, if we choose, use

TOO_HOT

instead of

TooHot

In identifiers, uppercase and lowercase letters are treated as being equivalent, which means that the identifier

COMFORTABLE

is the same as

Comfortable

Keywords

Table 2.1 also lists the 38 keywords in Pascal. A keyword is a special identifier that tells the computer what to do. For example, the keyword **program** introduces a program. Other keywords have more ubiquitous meanings. For example, the keyword **end** marks the end of something—the end of a sequence of statements, for instance, or the end of the program.

You don't have to memorize all the keywords. The important point is that each has a specific role. Furthermore, the keywords in Pascal are said to be "reserved," meaning that you may not use them as identifiers in your program. For example, if we wished, we could change the name TooCold to Chilly, but we could not change it to Program or Array because these are reserved.

Table 2.1 ● Macintosh Pascal Symbols

Digits

0 1 2 3 4 5 6 7 8 9

Letters

a b c d e f g h i j k l m
n o p q r s t u v w x y z
A B C D E F G H I J K L M
N O P Q R S T U V W X Y Z

Special Symbols

+ − * / = < > [ ] ' ( ) @ $
. , : ; ^ >= <= <> : = .. { }

Keywords

and	else	label	packed	until
array	end		procedure	uses
			program	
		mod		var
begin	file		record	
	for	nil	repeat	while
case	function	not		with
const			set	
	goto	of	string	
div		or		
do	if	otherwise	then	
downto	in		to	
			type	

Numbers

Suppose you wish to compute the number of feet to the scene of a crime, or an amount of money embezzled in a series of bank transactions. Pascal, like any other programming language, has a rather fixed set of conventions for writing numbers.

The first kind of number you can write is an *integer*, which means a whole number. An integer is represented by a sequence of digits, possibly preceded by a plus or a minus sign:

0	10
1776	+10
100000	−10

Negative numbers can be used to represent things like a temperature of minus 10 degrees or a bank balance that is "in the red."

The second kind of number you can write in Pascal is a *real number*. A real number must have either a decimal point, a letter "E" followed by a scale factor (which means "times ten to the power of"), or both. For example, you may write the numbers,

```
12.34
1234E−2
0.1234E2
0.1234E+2
```

both of which stand for the same real number.

The E notation (often called scientific notation or floating point notation) is especially useful for very large or very small numbers, which might arise if you are trying to calculate the distance between two planets or the weight of a molecule. Instead of writing,

```
123000000000000
0.0000000000000456
```

you can write,

```
1.23E+14
4.56E−14
```

This saves you from counting zeros to find how large or small a number is.

These are the only conventions you can use for writing numbers. Be careful, for as much as you would like, you cannot write numbers like the following:

```
2.        { you must write 2.0 }
.3        { you must write 0.3 }
1,000     { you must write 1000 }
$123      { you must write 123 }
```

With both integer and real numbers there is a limit to the number of digits that the machine will accept. If you are using an integer greater than 32,767 or less than −32,767 it must be declared as LongInt instead of Integer. Real numbers are limited to 8 decimal digits; however if greater accuracy is needed, they can be declared as Double or Extended. Whatever number you have in mind, you must declare it as either an integer, long integer, real, double, or extended number. Normally you use integers to represent thing you can count (the number of degrees Fahrenheit or the scheduled time of a train arrival, for example) and real numbers to represent things you measure or calculate that cannot be determined exactly (the number of feet to the scene of a crime or the result of a division problem, for example).

Character Strings

Often when you use a computer program, you want your program to print messages telling you what is going on. You can do this with character strings, such as

'Enter a Fahrenheit temperature:'

To print a character string, you simply include it in a Write or WriteLn statement, just like

WriteLn('TEMPERATURE SUMMARY')

in our example program.

A character string consists of a sequence of characters enclosed by single quotes. You might have expected that a character string would be enclosed by double quotation marks("); so be careful, as a single quotation mark, an apostrophe('), must be used.

Any characters that the computer recognizes can be put into a character string, even such characters as $ and %. If you would like to have an apostrophe itself as part of a character string, just type two apostrophes in a row, and it will output as a single apostrophe. Thus we may have

'THE BOY''S HAIR IS BROWN'
'NOTE THE PAIR OF SINGLE QUOTES ABOVE'

'STRINGS MAY CONTAIN SPECIAL CHARACTERS'
'LIKE $ AND %'
'as well as lowercase letters'

Comments

One of the most useful features of programming languages is the ability to annotate your program with *comments*. Completely ignored by the computer, comments are there entirely for the enlightenment of a human reader. For example, in the sequence

```
{ -- Calculate Celsius equivalents and write results }
F := TooCold;
RealC := (5 / 9) * (F - 32);
C := Round(RealC);
WriteLn;
WriteLn('F : 1,'    TooCold    ', C : 1);
```

the first line is a comment.

A comment consists of any sequence of characters enclosed by curly braces. The text of the comment may include anything you like except a right curly brace (}).

```
{ -- If you include a carriage return in your comment, }
{ -- a right brace will be automatically entered to end the line, }
{ -- and a left brace will be entered at the beginning of the next line. }
```

Comments may be placed between lines of the program or at the end of lines. If they are entered within a line of program text, they will be moved to the end of the line.

As far as running the program is concerned, the comment will have no effect and will be treated just as if it were a blank space.

If you, choose, you can enclose comments with the symbols (* and *) instead of curly braces; for example,

```
(* -- Write headings *)
```

No matter which symbols you use, be sure to close off each comment with its terminating *) or }. If you do not, all the program text following the comment will be treated as part of the comment itself.

2.4 ● Syntax Issues

Much of the formatting of a program is done for you in Macintosh Pascal. Each statement is started on a new line. Indenting is performed automatically. You do have the use of blank lines and spaces at your disposal, however. For instance, it is much easier to read,

```
{ -- Request temperatures }
  Write('Enter 3 fahrenheit temperatures: ');
  ReadLn(TooCold, Comfortable, TooHot);

{ -- Write headings }
  WriteLn;
  WriteLn;
```

than

```
{Request temperatures}
  Write('Enter 3 fahrenheit temperatures:');
  ReadLn(TooCold,Comfortable,TooHot);
{Write headings}
  WriteLn;
  WriteLn;
```

The only difference between the two examples is the use of spacing. The computer will ignore blank spaces and blank lines, but the human reader will not. In fact, the proper spacing of programs can go a long way in making your intended purpose clear.

There are a few restrictions on the placing of blank spaces and blank lines. These restrictions need not concern you very much, as they are reasonably obvious. For example, you may not put blank spaces between the characters of an identifier or between the : and the = of a :=. And, of course, at least one blank must be inserted between adjacent words (for example, between **program** and the program name).

Finally, the end of a line is treated as if it were a blank space, at least as far as the computer is concerned. All of these rules follow common intuition, and generally speaking, you may insert blank spaces and blank lines wherever convenient.

Now we come to the rules for the placement of semicolons. The first rule is simple. A semicolon is required at the end of a program heading, as in:

program TemperatureSummary;

As we shall see later, the same rule applies to procedure and function headings.

The second rule is just as simple, but a bit more embracing: a semicolon is required after each declaration. For example, a semicolon is required after the variable declaration,

RealC : Real;

and after each declaration of a list of variables, as in

TooCold, Comfortable, TooHot : Integer;

Things begin to get a bit more sticky when we come to the algorithm part of a program. A semicolon must be placed between the statements in a sequence of statements. In effect, in a simple sequence of statements a semicolon is required after each statement except the last. When we get to structured statements, there will be more details to remember, but this will suffice for now. If you have any doubts about the placement of semicolons, refer to Appendix B, which summarizes the formation rules for writing programs in Macintosh Pascal.

Following the practice section, there are suggestions for some programs that you should be able to write with the information covered so far.

2.5 ● Practice

Consider the program shown in Fig. 2.3, which prints a replica of the letter H. Certain properties of this program are shared by all other Pascal programs, short or long.

Syntax

Figure 2.3 ● Program BigH

```
program BigH;
  { -- This program prints a replica of the letter H, }
  { -- printed with 14 lines of H's. }
  begin
    WriteLn('HH          HH');
    WriteLn('HH          HH');
    WriteLn('HH          HH');
    WriteLn('HH          HH');
    WriteLn('HH          HH');
    WriteLn('HH          HH');
    WriteLn('HHHHHHHHHHHH');
    WriteLn('HHHHHHHHHHHH');
    WriteLn('HH          HH');
    WriteLn('HH          HH');
    WriteLn('HH          HH');
    WriteLn('HH          HH');
    WriteLn('HH          HH');
    WriteLn('HH          HH')
  end.
```

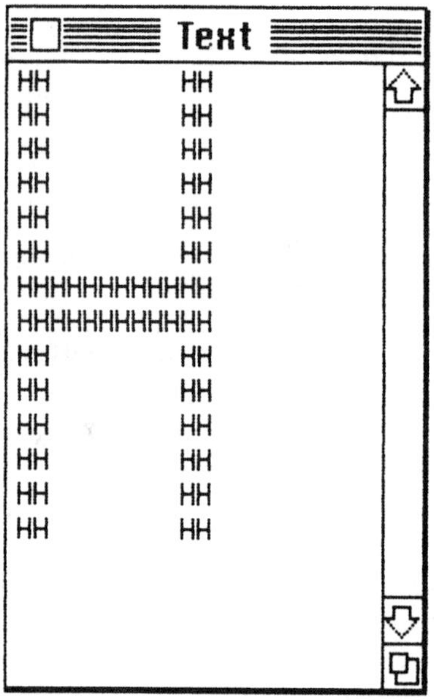

```
======= Text =======
HH          HH
HH          HH
HH          HH
HH          HH
HH          HH
HH          HH
HHHHHHHHHHHH
HHHHHHHHHHHH
HH          HH
HH          HH
HH          HH
HH          HH
HH          HH
HH          HH
```

1. The program starts with the word **program.**

2. The program has a name, in this case BigH.

3. The program name is followed by a semicolon.

4. The statement part of the program starts with the word **begin.**

5. The program ends with the word **end** followed by a period.

Some other factors in this program also deserve mention. The word WriteLn means "Write a Line"; it causes each string to be printed on a line by itself. Each WriteLn is followed by a character string contained within parentheses. The character strings are enclosed by single quotes. There are 14 of these statements separated from each other by 13 semicolons. Two characters are used, the letter "H" and the blank space. There are 8 blanks used between the H's on 12 of the statements. Since the output font has a fixed character width, the letters will line up nicely.

You may have noticed in reading program BigH that it has no declarations part, although it is a valid program. Most programs will make use of names or identifiers, and each of these identifiers must be declared in the declarations part of the program. The identifiers we have used so far have all been variables; that is, the value of the identifier can change during the course of the program. When declaring variables, it is necessary to state the identifier and its type.

Some of the following are valid identifiers and some are not. Make your choices before you read on.

1. Item2
2. Item2.2
3. NEWITEM
4. Two3rds
5. 2 Thirds
6. Input
7. R2D2
8. file
9. If_Then_Else
10. TenDivTwo

All identifiers share the following characteristics:

They start with a letter.
They contain only letters, digits, and underscores.
They are less than 255 characters long.

Numbers 1, 3, 4, 6, 7, 9, and 10 are all valid identifiers. Number 2 can not be used as an identifier because it contains a decimal point. Number 5 is disqualified for two reasons: it starts with a number, and it contains a space. Number 8 is a reserved word.

Following are items that might be included in a mortgage calculation program. Each item needs an identifier. If they are to be read from the keyboard or calculated during the program, they must be declared as variables. In addition, they must be declared to be of type Integer, LongInt, Real, or string. How would you declare each of them?

1. Total amount of mortgage

2. Interest rate

3. Monthly payment

4. Amount of monthly payment on the principle

5. Amount of monthly payment on the interest

6. The address of the property

7. The account number

● ● ●

The identifiers for these items should be as descriptive as possible without being overly long; your choices may differ from ours. There may be some matter of opinion on the other choices also, depending on the concept of the finished program. Here are our suggestions.

Identifier	Type
1. MortgageAmt	LongInt
2. IntRate	Real
3. MonPayment	Real
4. MonPrinPayment	Real
5. MonIntPayment	Real
6. Address	string
7. AccountNum	LongInt

The mortgage amount may or may not be over 32767, the maximum that can be declared as Integer. LongInt is certainly safer here. The account number also may be small enough to be Integer; but since we don't know, it is safer to use LongInt. Items 2, 3, 4, and 5 will be dollar values with accuracy to two decimal places. When dealing with very large mortgages, it may be necessary to use Double for 3, 4, and 5. Let's hope that interest rates will never require a number that large! The address is declared as a string; it contains both numbers and letters, and no arithmetic calculations will be performed on it. It may be desirable to break the address down into StreetAddress, City, State, ZipCode.

Details are very important in any kind of programming. The following program has a fatal error. See if you can find it before you continue.

```
program Double
{ -- This program reads in a number N and }
{ -- prints twice its value. }
    var
        N : Integer;
begin
    Read(N);
    Write((N+N)
end.
```

● ● ●

The placement of semicolons is very important in Pascal. The program just shown is missing the semicolon following the program name and will not run. An error message will result.

- A semicolon must be placed after the program name, after each declaration, and between statements.

Below is a series of statements concerning some details of Pascal. Some are true, some are false. Use the True/False quiz and the following Fill in the Blanks to check your understanding.

True or False

1. The first nonblank character in a program must be the **p** in **program.**
2. The last nonblank character in a program must be a period.
3. The identifier **Record** may be used as the name of an integer value.
4. A semicolon can be placed after every statement.
5. The following sequence of characters is a well-formed comment:

    { The symbols { and *) may be used in comments. }

6. The Pascal number 2.0 is an integer.
7. Spaces may be inserted between any two characters in a program.
8. Two statements, for example,

    Write('THIS');   Write(' AND THAT')

    may appear on a single line.

9. The parentheses in

    Write('THIS')
    may be omitted.

10. A declaration always ends with a semicolon.

● ● ●

Fill in the Blanks

As you continue with Pascal, the information in this chapter will become second nature. Try filling in the blanks in the following statements to see how much you have already retained.

1. Before beginning to write the program, you should write an

    _____.

2. Each variable in a program must be given a name; this name is known as its _____.

3. The two parts of a program are the _____ part and the _____ part.

4. A program ends with _____.

5. Identifiers can be constructed using letters, digits, and _____.

6. The whole number 32,776 should be declared as a _____.

7. Character strings are enclosed by _____.

8. Keywords cannot be used as _____ in a program.

9. Comments are useful to improve a program's _____.

10. A _____ is required after the word **program**.

● ● ●

The following paragraphs contain the answers for the True/False (T/F) and Fill in the Blanks (FB) questions. If you have done well, then you have been paying close attention to details. This characteristic will serve you well as you continue expanding your programming skills.

Before beginning to write a program, always write an ALGORITHM. This will force you to define the problem carefully, and will keep you from wandering off on a tangent while writing the program itself (FB1).

A program always starts with the word **program** and ends with the word **end** followed by a period (FB4). However, comments can be placed before the word **program** and after **end**, so the answer to the first and second True/False questions is actually "False." The program can start with the letter "p" or a left hand curly brace and can end with the word "end" followed by a period, or a right hand curly brace (T/F1,T/F2).

A program contains a DECLARATION part and a STATEMENT part (FB3). Each declaration is followed by a semicolon (T/F10). Semicolons are also required after the program name and *between* statements in a sequence. Do not get into the habit of thinking that each statement is followed by a semicolon; it will cause confusion later. The answer to the fourth question is "False" (T/F4).

Each variable in a program must be given a name, which is known as its IDENTIFIER (FB2). An identifier is constructed of letters, digits, and underscores (FB5); and must begin with a letter. Keywords cannot be used as IDENTIFIERS (FB8, T/F3). The declaration of a variable gives its name, or identifier, and also tells what type of values the variable will hold during the course of the program. Integer variables can hold values between –32,767 and +32,767. Integers outside this range must be declared as LONGINT (FB6). Numbers containing a decimal part are declared as Real, therefore Record cannot be used as the name of an integer value (T/F3).

Identifiers can also be used for values that remain constant throughout the program. These values may be numbers or character strings. Character strings are enclosed by SINGLE QUOTES (FB7).

A Write statement must be followed by a pair of parentheses (T/F9) enclosing the identifiers whose values are to be written and/or the actual values enclosed by single quotes. The parameters in the list must be separated by commas. WriteLn can be used without the parentheses to simply skip a line.

Most of the formatting in Macintosh Pascal is done automatically. For instance, each statement is placed on a new line (T/F8). Some care is required with blank spaces; however, most of the rules follow the dictates of common sense. A SPACE is required after the word **program** before the program identifier (FB10). Spaces inserted between characters in an identifier are not allowed; and in a Write statement, there may not be a space between the *e* and the beginning parenthesis. Also watch out for any double symbols, such as the assignment symbol (:=) and two single single quotes contained in a character string (T/F7).

Comments are used to improve a program's READABILITY (FB9). A comment begins when the symbol { or (* is encountered, and ends when the symbol } or *) is reached. In True/False question 5, the comment ends in the middle instead of where it is obviously intended to end.

2.6 ◯

2.1   Learning to Use Macintosh Pascal

Learning to use a programming language requires attention to many details. The smallest error can cause your program to stop in the middle of a run or perhaps not even start. So be prepared for the worst, gather your wits about you, and solve the following problem: Write a program to print MY NAME IS followed by your name. A sample output might be

MY NAME IS SUE

2.2   Printing a Checkerboard

Write a program print the initial configuration of checkers on a checkerboard; for example,

```
 B  B  B  B
 B  B  B  B
  B  B  B  B
 _  _  _  _
  _  _  _  _
 R  R  R  R
  R  R  R  R
 R  R  R  R
```

where B stands for black and R for red. Can you make the checkerboard look even nicer?

2.3 Big Z

In the practice section, you read a program to print a big H. Now write one to print a big Z. Remember that the spacing differs from the program screen to the text screen.

2.4   Secret Numbers: Version 1

There are many computer applications where a code number is required. Write a program that requests a number from the user, and then returns to the user a written message containing the number and a warning that the number must be remembered for future use.

Note: This problem is the first in a series of programming exercises involving entry codes.

2.5   Writing a Sequence

When printing numerical values, it is usually desirable to control the spacing. Write a program that reads a number, and then, on a new line, prints the number three times with 5 spaces between.

2.6   Real versus Integer

A variable cannot be declared as both Real and Integer. You may, however, want to print an integer value followed by a decimal point and zeroes. For instance, when dealing with dollar values, it is often better to show the pennies. There is more than one way to solve the problem. Write two different programs that read a number, say 814, and then print it as a dollar amount, say $814.00.

2.7   A Simple Area Computation

Given the radius, the area of a circular surface is found using the age-old formula,

$$A = PI \cdot r^2$$

or in computer notation,

$$A := PI*(R*R)$$

where PI, computed to five decimal places, is 3.14159. Write a program to read in the radius of a circle as a real number and output the corresponding area as a real number. For example, with the input 2.101, the area would be 13.86761. The result can be computed to any number of decimal places.

2.8   Square Roots

There are predefined functions in Pascal that will return the value of a calculation. This is accomplished by simply using the name of the function in a statement, for instance the statement

Write(SqRt(AnyNumber))

will calculate the square root of the identifier in parentheses, and print the result.

Write a program that reads a number and then writes the square root of the number.

2.9   An Average Program
Write a program to find the average of three real numbers. Declare an identifier for each number, for the sum, and for the average. Print the average with two decimal places.

2.10   Mileage
Miles per gallon is calculated by dividing the number of miles traveled by the number of gallons of fuel used. The figures needed here are the mileage showing with a full tank at the beginning of the check; the mileage showing at the end of the check, again with a full tank; and the total number of gallons added during the course of the check.

For this program, assume that fuel has been added four times. The program must read the beginning and ending mileage and the four amounts of added fuel, and print the miles per gallon using one decimal place.

Chapter 3

Drawing and using Procedures

Macintosh Pascal allows access to the Apple QuickDraw library. The QuickDraw routines can be used in a Pascal program to draw both shapes and text on the screen by using predefined procedures and functions stored in the QuickDraw library. Entering the names of the subroutines into a program calls upon the machine to automatically perform a series of actions. For instance, given integer values for the four identifiers Top, Left, Bottom, and Right, the call

FrameRect(Top, Left, Bottom, Right)

causes the machine to locate two horizontal and two vertical lines on the screen, and draw the rectangle enclosed by the intersection of the four lines. Using similar statements one can draw ovals, circles, rectangles with rounded corners, and wedge-shaped sections of circles. These can be either hollow or solid.

This chapter presents some of the basic procedures and functions available. With these routines you will be able to write some interesting programs of your own. Some of them are used in the program of Fig. 3.1. This program puts the temperature chart given earlier onto the drawing screen and puts a frame around it. The two changes are reflected in the revised algorithm shown in Fig. 3.2.

To use QuickDraw efficiently and comfortably one must understand the drawing screen. Imagine the Macintosh screen as divided into very small squares, 72 per linear inch to be precise. These squares are called *pixels,*

3.1 ● Screen Layout

Figure 3.1 ● Program
TemperatureChart

```
program TemperatureChart;
{ -- This program reads 3 Fahrenheit temperatures entered by the user, }
{ -- calculates the Celsius equivalents, }
{ -- and charts the results on the drawing screen. }

  var
      TooCold, Comfortable, TooHot : Integer;
      F,C : Integer;
      RealC : Real;
      Right : Integer;

begin

{ -- Request temperatures }
    Write('Enter 3 Fahrenheit temperatures describing too cold,
                  comfortable, too hot: ');
    Read(TooCold, Comfortable, TooHot);

{ -- Set up for drawing }
    TextSize(12);
    TextFont(4);

{ -- Write headings }
    MoveTo(30,46);
    WriteDraw('TEMPERATURE SUMMARY');
    MoveTo(30,66);
    WriteDraw('F                C');

{ -- Compute Celsius and print }
    F := TooCold;
    RealC := (5 / 9) * (F – 32);
    C := Round(RealC);
    MoveTo(30,86);
    WriteDraw(F : 2,'   Too Cold ', C : 2);

    F := Comfortable;
    RealC := (5 / 9) * (F – 32);
    C := Round(RealC);
    MoveTo(30,106);
    WriteDraw(F : 2,'   Comfortable ', C : 2);

    F := TooHot;
    RealC := (5 / 9) * (F – 32);
    C := Round(RealC);
    MoveTo(30,126);
    WriteDraw(F : 2,'   Too Hot ', C : 2);

{ -- Draw frame }
    Right := 30 + StringWidth('TEMPERATURE SUMMARY') + 5;
    FrameRect(30,25,130,Right);
    MoveTo(25,50);
    LineTo(Right,50);
    MoveTo(25,70);
    LineTo(Right,70)

end.
```

Figure 3.1 continued

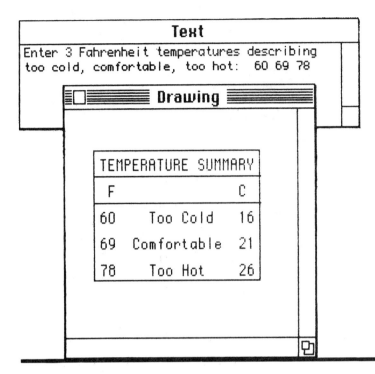

Definitions:
  TooCold, Comfortable, TooHot: Fahrenheit temperatures entered
    by user
  F: Fahrenheit temperature
  C: Celsius temperature
  Right: frame boundary

Algorithm:
  Request 3 temperatures from user
  Set up for drawing screen
  Write headings
  For each temperature do the following:
    set F to temperature
    apply formula C = (5 / 9)(F − 32)
    write: F, comfort level, C
  Draw frame

Figure 3.2 ● Revised
algorithm for Fig. 3.1

short for "picture elements." There are 512 pixels across the screen and
342 down. The squares are part of a coordinate system with its origin at
the upper left corner of the screen. The horizontal or x coordinates
increase from left to right just as they do in the conventional mathematics
coordinate system. The vertical or y coordinates increase from top to

bottom. This is not the conventional coordinate system but corresponds to the way a page of English text is read.

When you address a point on the screen by stating first an x location and then a y location, you are actually designating a pixel that is bounded by four imaginary lines. In Fig. 3.3, the single black square would be addressed as 5,4. It is located between horizontal coordinates 4 and 5, and between vertical coordinates 3 and 4.

When you draw on the screen, you start with a pen which is 1 pixel wide and 1 pixel high. The pen size can be changed by using the standard procedure Pensize. For instance

Pensize(3, 2)

expands the pen to 3 pixels wide by 2 pixels high. The expanded area of the pen always hangs down and to the right. A location designated for the pen corresponds with its upper left pixel. In Fig. 3.3, the pen with size 3,2 when moved to position 5,4 covers the larger shaded area. For the purposes of this chapter, we will use only a pensize of 1,1.

In order to create the desired output, it is necessary to tell the machine exactly where to place each line of text and where to draw the frame. The size of the print influences all of these choices, so that decision must be considered first. Type size is designated in "points," a typographic term meaning approximately 1/72 of an inch. Notice that there are 72 pixels to the inch. Convenient, isn't it? The sizes available are 9, 12, 14, 18, and 24 point. If you are using 12 point text size, 12 pixels will allow room for the letters themselves plus the space above them. This is the size used for the chart in the example program. It is activated by the call

TextSize(12);

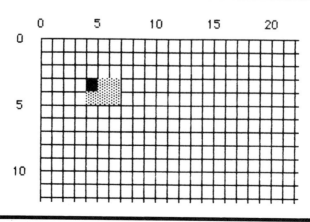

Figure 3.3 • Pen location

The upper left corner of the chart is situated at 25,30; that is 25 pixels to the right and 30 pixels down from the top. This position is a purely arbitrary decision; you can start the chart anywhere you like as long as you allow room on the screen toward the right and down from the starting point.

More space is needed between lines on a chart such as this than what is normally allowed on a page of print, so we allowed 20 pixels for the height of each line; that is, for each new line of text we move down 20 pixels in the y axis. When the machine acts upon a WriteDraw call, it starts writing to the right and up from the location of the pen. A little arithmetic is required here to center the line of text between the dividing lines. The space for the title is 20 pixels high, it starts at 30 and goes down to 50. Since we have chosen to use 12 point type, the printing itself uses 12 of those pixels; that leaves 8 pixels of space. Dividing those 8 pixels gives us 4 spaces above the print and 4 below. You can see at this point that it is useful to plot out the components of the output on a piece of graph paper before you begin to write the program. The output format is part of the algorithm. Shown in Fig. 3.4 are the vertical or y coordinates used for TemperatureChart program.

The x values are plotted in the same way. The left boundary was previously placed at 25. Some space is needed between the frame and the text, so we start the text 5 pixels to the right at 30. If we leave the character strings in our Write statements just as they are, the horizontal spacing takes care of itself. But how do we know where to place the right boundary of our frame? It is necessary to know how many pixels of space the character string is going to use. This can be calculated by the function call

StringWidth('TEMPERATURE SUMMARY')

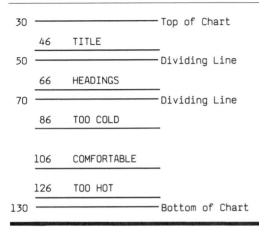

Figure 3.4 ● Vertical (y) coordinates for the program TemperatureChart

The width of the string is calculated for us. It is not really necessary to know the numerical value of this width; our goal is to locate the right boundary for the frame. We can use the identifier Right instead of an integer in a FrameRect statement, and assign a value to Right with the following statement:

Right := 30 + StringWidth('TEMPERATURE SUMMARY') + 5

The 30 represents the start of the text; the 5 is the space between the end of the text and the frame. The layout in Fig. 3.5 shows these *x* locations more clearly.

3.2 ● Calling QuickDraw Procedures

Write and WriteLn are not part of the QuickDraw library. In order to write text onto the Drawing window, we must use one of the following statements instead.

```
DrawChar('A')                              { a character }
DrawString('TEMPERATURE SUMMARY')  { a string }
WriteDraw('The value of X is ', X )        { strings and variables }
```

All of these are QuickDraw procedures which use the drawing screen as the output area. The WriteDraw procedure is the most versatile as it allows the entering of variables and/or character strings between the parentheses.

When the machine starts to write it uses the same type size that is being used for the program unless you have specified otherwise. If you choose to use something different, the statement

```
TextSize(12)                               { Integer }
```

sets the type size. Enter 9, 12, 14, 18, 24, or an integer variable between the parentheses. For changing the font, use

```
TextFont(4)                                { Integer }
```

The integer used will call a text font from the available set. We are using text font number 4 in our program because it has a fixed character width; this allows us to plan our output to appear in even columns.

Figure 3.5 ● Horizontal *(x)* coordinates for the program TemperatureChart

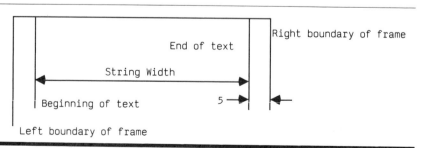

These text size and text font statements must appear before the first Write statement.

For the TemperatureChart program all of the WriteLn statements that we used in our TemperatureSummary are changed to WriteDraw to cause the text to be printed on the drawing screen instead of the text screen. In addition, each WriteDraw statement is preceded by a MoveTo statement to place the pen in position for writing. A MoveTo statement requires two coordinates; for instance,

MoveTo(10,20)   { x coordinate, y coordinate }

On the output layout we determined that the text would start 30 pixels to the right and 46 pixels down; these values are entered into the MoveTo statement,

MoveTo(30,46);
WriteDraw('TEMPERATURE SUMMARY');

We increase the y value by 20 for each new line of text.

When the text is complete, we draw the frame. The values for Top, Left, and Bottom were established on the output layout. In order to get the value for Right we enter the StringWidth expression. Then a single procedure call draws the frame.

Right := 30 + StringWidth('TEMPERATURE SUMMARY') + 5;
FrameRect(30,25,130,Right);

As you see, you can use either integers or identifiers within the parentheses; you could even use an expression, such as $y + 3$. However, you cannot use a variable that has been declared as Real; only integer values will be accepted.

In addition to the StringWidth function that we used in the program, there is a function call that returns the width of a single character.

CharWidth('A')   { a character }

This function returns an integer value just as the StringWidth function does.

There are several ways to draw a line with QuickDraw; we have chosen to use a LineTo statement preceded by a MoveTo. A LineTo statement draws a line to the specified location from wherever the pen is currently located; so we move the pen to the point where we want to begin and then use the LineTo statement to draw a line to the second point. The following four statements draw the two dividing lines.

MoveTo(25,50);
LineTo(Right,50);
MoveTo(25,70);
LineTo(Right,70)

There are two statements similar to MoveTo and LineTo.

Move(dh,dv)   { horizontal distance, vertical distance }
Line(dh,dv)   { horizontal distance, vertical distance }

Instead of moving the pen and drawing a line to a specific coordinate location on the screen, these two statements cause the pen to move a specified distance from the current position. Line draws a line from the current position to the new one. You can use negative values within the parentheses to move to the left or upward, or a zero value for one of the coordinates if you want to move up or down or from side to side. For instance, if the pen is located at 50,75 and you say,

Line(0,–25);

the pen will draw a line from 50,75 to 50,50. This would be a vertical line.

There is one more very efficient way of drawing a line. The call

DrawLine(a, b, c, d)

draws a line from point a,b to point c,d.

The example program calls FrameRect to draw the frame. This call draws the outline of a rectangle. Additional operations that can be performed on rectangles are

PaintRect(T,L,B,R)   — draws a solid rectangle instead of a frame.
EraseRect(T,L,B,R)   — paints the rectangle white.
InvertRect(T,L,B,R)   — changes black areas within the rectangle to white and white areas into black.

These four calls can also be used on ovals. Change the Rect to Oval and what will be drawn is the oval that would fit into the rectangle. Thus the call

FrameOval(20,30,70,150)

draws the oval shown in Fig. 3.6.

Figure 3.6 ● Oval with FrameOval call

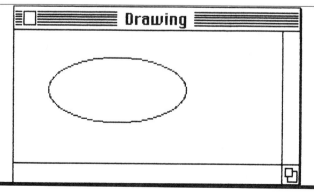

The oval that fits into a square is a circle, so if you describe a rectangle with four sides equal, you will draw a circle, as in Fig. 3.7.

FrameOval(20,20,70,70)

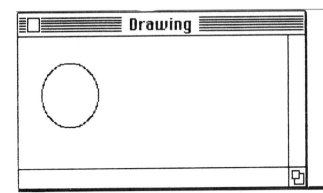

Figure 3.7 ● Circle drawn with FrameOval call

These procedures can also be applied to rounded corner rectangles and to arcs. For the rounded rectangles you will need two more integers describing the horizontal diameter and the vertical diameter of the oval which fits the corner.

FrameRoundRect(20,30,70,150,20,10)

gives Fig. 3.8.

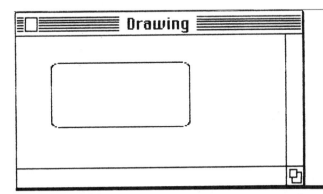

Figure 3.8 ● Rounded corner rectangle drawn with the FrameRoundRect call

Arcs require a little more explaining. The call is written as

FrameArc(Top, Left, Bottom, Right, StartAngle, ArcAngle)

The start angle indicates where the arc begins and the arc angle indicates how many degrees the arc is to contain. Zero degrees is at 12 o'clock and clockwise is the positive direction. Angles are measured relative to the enclosing rectangle. Thus, the call

PaintArc(20,20,70,70,0,90)

draws the sector shown in Fig. 3.9.

Figure 3.9 ● Arc drawn
with the PaintArc call

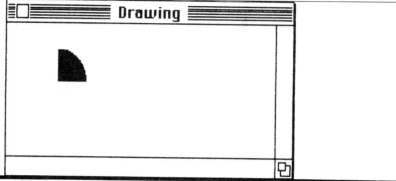

Use care when dealing with arcs. If the enclosing rectangle is not a square, you will be dealing with sectors of ovals instead of circles, but this takes us beyond our goal here.

There are two procedures specifically for circles

PaintCircle(x,y,r)
InvertCircle(x,y,r)

where x and y are the coordinates of the center and r is the radius.

Summary of QuickDraw Procedures

The following list is a summary of the QuickDraw procedures and functions that you should be able to make use of now.

Text Writing

TextSize(Point Size);
TextFont(Font Number);
WriteDraw(Variables, 'Strings');
DrawChar('Character');
DrawString('String');
CharWidth ('Character');
StringWidth('String');

Line Drawing

DrawLine(a,b,c,d);
MoveTo(x,y);
Move(dh,dv);
LineTo(x,y);
Line(dh,dv);
PenSize(Width,Height);

Rectangles

```
FrameRect(Top,Left,Bottom,Right);
PaintRect(Top,Left,Bottom,Right);
EraseRect(Top,Left,Bottom,Right);
InvertRect(Top,Left,Bottom,Right);
```

Ovals

```
FrameOval(Top,Left,Bottom,Right);
PaintOval(Top,Left,Bottom,Right);
EraseOval(Top,Left,Bottom,Right);
InvertOval(Top,Left,Bottom,Right);
```

Round Rectangles

```
FrameRoundRect(Top,Left,Bottom,Right,OvalWidth,OvalHeight);
PaintRoundRect(Top,Left,Bottom,Right,OvalWidth,OvalHeight);
EraseRoundRect(Top,Left,Bottom,Right,OvalWidth,OvalHeight);
InvertRoundRect(Top,Left,Bottom,Right,OvalWidth,OvalHeight);
```

Arcs

```
FrameArc(Top,Left,Bottom,Right,StartAngle,ArcAngle);
PaintArc(Top,Left,Bottom,Right,StartAngle,ArcAngle);
EraseArc(Top,Left,Bottom,Right,StartAngle,ArcAngle);
InvertArc(Top,Left,Bottom,Right,StartAngle,ArcAngle);
```

Circles

```
PaintCircle(x,y,r);
InvertCircle(x,y,r);
```

3.3 ● Writing Elementary Procedures

The procedures discussed in the previous section are *predefined;* that is, they are already stored in memory and can be used by simply including a statement consisting of the name of the procedure followed by a parenthesized list of values or variables. This calls upon the machine to perform the named procedure, using the values indicated in the parentheses. The values given within the parentheses, or the variables representing the values, are known as *parameters.*

There will be a need many times to write procedures of your own, whether for QuickDraw applications or for regular Pascal applications. A brief discussion of writing procedures follows; more detail is presented in a later chapter.

Let's assume that you have a QuickDraw program that draws several squares, and that you also want to draw the diagonals. This can be done by including a procedure. We'll call the procedure DrawDiagonals. The procedure must be declared in the declarations part of the program, as in,

```
procedure DrawDiagonals(Top,Left,Bottom,Right : Integer);
```

The procedure must be given a name, in this case DrawDiagonals. The parenthesized list tells the computer that, when the procedure is called:

four values will be given by the statement; the values will be of type
Integer; the values are to be assigned, respectively, to Top, Left, Bottom,
and Right. Following the heading are the steps that will be taken to draw
the diagonals. This sequence of steps is written just as if it were a
sequence of steps in the program itself. The list starts with the word
begin and ends with the word **end.** The word **end,** in this case, is
followed by a semicolon since execution will return to the next statement
in the program.

The whole declaration of the procedure might look like this:

```
procedure DrawDiagonals(Top,Left,Bottom,Right : Integer);
  begin
    MoveTo(Left,Top);
    LineTo(Right,Bottom);
    MoveTo(Left,Bottom);
    LineTo(Right,Top)
  end;
```

Once a procedure has been declared, the name can be used as a
statement in a program, just as with the predefined procedures. For
instance, the program in Fig. 3.10 draws two squares with their
diagonals.

Note that the names Top, Left, Bottom, and Right that are used in
the header are the same ones used in the program itself. This is not a
requirement; different variables can be used for the parameters of the
procedure. For instance, we could have used the following as the
procedure heading:

```
procedure DrawDiagonals(T,L,B,R : Integer);
```

This heading creates four new variables of type Integer. These
parameters are considered *local* variables. Using these parameters, the
statement part of the procedure reads as follows:

```
begin
  MoveTo(L,T);
  LineTo(R,B);
  MoveTo(L,B);
  LineTo(R,T)
end;
```

The main program would be unchanged. The call

```
DrawDiagonals(Top,Left,Bottom,Right)
```

passes the values associated with Top, Left, Bottom, and Right to the
procedure. The procedure accepts them in order, associating them with
the variables T, L, B, and R. The two sets of parameters must be in the
same order and must be of the same type. In this case, all are
Integers.

```
program Squares;
   var
      Top, Left, Bottom, Right : Integer;
   procedure DrawDiagonals(Top, Left, Bottom, Right : Integer);
   begin
      MoveTo(Left, Top);
      LineTo(Right, Bottom);
      MoveTo(Left, Bottom);
      LineTo(Right, Top)
   end;
begin
   Top := 5;
   Left := 5;
   Bottom := 50;
   Right := 50;
   FrameRect(Top, Left, Bottom, Right);
   DrawDiagonals(Top, Left, Bottom, Right);

   Top := Top + 50;
   Left := Left + 50;
   Bottom := Bottom + 50;
   Right := Right + 50;
   FrameRect(Top, Left, Bottom, Right);
   DrawDiagonals(Top, Left, Bottom, Right)
end.
```

Figure 3.10 ● Program Squares draws two squares with their diagonals

The new program reads as shown in Fig. 3.11.

You should be able to write simple procedures now, but the subject is discussed fully in Chapter 11.

3.4 ● Example Program

We should have all the tools we need now to build a program that will draw a bar graph. Consider the following problem.

Write a program to draw a bar graph showing the number of puppies enrolled in AKC in 1983 by breed using the following figures:

Cocker Spaniel	172,291
Collie	45,337
German Shepherd	129,621
Labrador Retriever	117,221
Poodle	184,297

Figure 3.11

```
program Squares;
var
    Top, Left, Bottom, Right : Integer;
    procedure DrawDiagonals(T, L, B, R : Integer);
    begin
        MoveTo(L,T);
        LineTo(R,B);
        MoveTo(L,B);
        LineTo(R,T)
    end;
begin
    Top := 5;
    Left := 5;
    Bottom := 50;
    Right := 50;
    FrameRect(Top, Left, Bottom, Right);
    DrawDiagonals(Top, Left, Bottom, Right);
    Top := Top + 50;
    Left := Left + 50;
    Bottom := Bottom + 50;
    Right := Right + 50;
    FrameRect(Top, Left, Bottom, Right);
    DrawDiagonals(Top, Left, Bottom, Right)
end.
```

The graph should have the format shown in Fig. 3.12.

Let us first look at what Pascal features will be required. We need to write text in specified locations. We can do that with

MoveTo and WriteDraw.

Figure 3.12

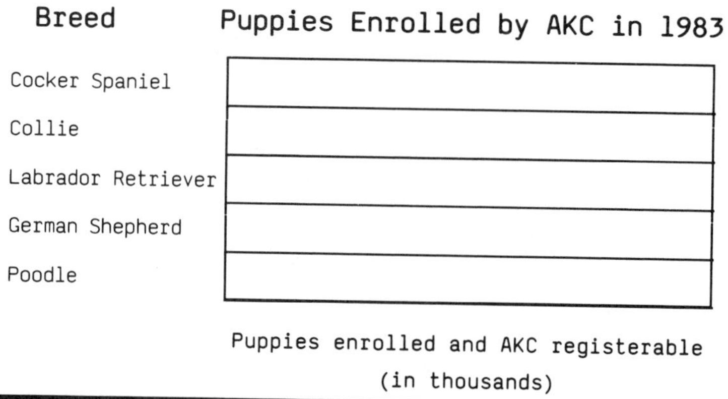

Breed   **Puppies Enrolled by AKC in 1983**

Cocker Spaniel

Collie

Labrador Retriever

German Shepherd

Poodle

Puppies enrolled and AKC registerable
(in thousands)

We need to draw a frame. That we can do with

> FrameRect.

We need to draw the bars, and

> PaintRect

will serve nicely for that. This will draw a solid rectangle.

It looks as if the difficult part of this problem is to determine the locations for the various components of the output. Let's look first at the *x* coordinate, the horizontal distance from the left side of the screen to the beginning of our text, to the beginning of the bars, and to the end of the bars and the right side of the frame. The beginning of the text is easy enough, we just decide where we want the graph to begin on the screen. When we think about where the bars should begin, we run into a problem. We need to allow enough space for the longest breed name, but the space will vary according to what size type we choose. And what if we want to change the type size?

Think about our temperature chart for a moment. If we wanted to change the type size, it would be necessary to go through the whole program very carefully, changing MoveTo and LineTo locations. Not only would this be very tedious, it would also be likely to result in errors. We would like to avoid this potential problem if possible. We can do this by giving names or identifiers to the various values. The ones that do not change in the course of the program can be assigned constant values in the *declarations part* of the program. The type size can also be declared as a constant. That way we can change constant values instead of making changes in the *statements part* of the program. This will not only be easier and lessen the possibility of error, it will also make the program much more readable. The values that change during the program have to be named as variables in the declarations.

We have given the name TextStart to the horizontal location where the text begins. The bars start at BarStart. The title and the label for the bo name TextStart to the horizontal location where the text begins. The bars start at BarStart. The title and the label for the bottom scale can start at the same line as the bars. That still leaves two *x* locations to consider. The right side of each bar shows the number of puppies divided by 1000, so we use a variable named NumPups. The value of NumPups added to the value of the bar start will be equal to Right. The final *x* line, the right boundary of our frame is equal to whatever the upper limit is on our scale. We will name this MaxNumPups.

Now we come to the *y* coordinates, the distance from the top of the screen to the bottom of each line of printing and to the top and bottom of the bars. We can choose the location for the title line, name it TitleLine and then use that as a base for determining the other *y* values. We will decide on a TextHeight, which we can declare as a constant, and will move down by that number of pixels for a new line of text. Each time we add the TextHeight to a present line location, we get a new TextLine. When we look at the bars themselves, we have the height of the bar and the space between bars to consider. Let's name these BarHeight and

BarSpace. We can use these two variables to determine our Top and Bottom boundaries for our rectangle.

We need to think about our frame. The left side lies along the BarStart, which is a constant. The right side is equal to the highest number on the scale, which is also a constant. The top lies along the line where we write "Breed" and the bottom line lies along the bottom of the last bar. Since we will not have the location of the bottom line until we have reached the last breed, we would be wise to store the value for the TextLine "Breed" while we are working in that area. We will store it as a variable named FrameTop.

When we collect these various definitions and determine the steps required to draw the graph, we come up with the algorithm shown in Fig. 3.13. For the corresponding program see Fig. 3.14; the screen that results is shown in Fig. 3.15.

Figure 3.13 ● Algorithm for program BarGraph

Definitions:

NumPups:	number of puppies for each breed in thousands
MaxNumPups:	high limit for number of pups in thousands

Top,Left,Bottom,Right: rectangle specifications

BarStart:	x position for start of bars
BarHeight:	width of a bar in pixels
BarSpace:	space between bars in pixels
TypeSize:	point size of type
TitleLine:	y position for title line
TextLine:	y position for a line of text
TextHeight:	height of text including space in pixels
TextStart:	x position for start of text column
MarkerLength:	length of marker on bottom scale
NumWidth:	width of a number of chosen type size in pixels
StartScale:	x position for start of numbers on bottom scale
ScaleUnit:	increment of numbers and markers on bottom scale
ScaleNum:	number on bottom scale

Algorithm
Write title and column headings
Store frame top
For each breed
   Set bottom
   Set Top
   Set pen for text
   Write breed name
   Set NumPups equal to number of puppies divided by 1,000
   Set Right
   Draw bar
Draw frame
Draw scale markers
Number bottom scale
Label bottom scale

Figure 3.14 ● Program
BarGraph

```
program BarGraph;
   const
      MaxNumPups = 200;
      BarStart = 150;
      BarHeight = 12;
      BarSpace = 4;
      TypeSize = 9;
      TextHeight = 16;
      TextStart = 35;
      TitleLine = 30;
      MarkerLength = 3;
      ScaleUnit = 50;
      NumWidth = 5;
   var
      NumPups : Integer;
      Top, Left, Bottom, Right, FrameTop : Integer;
      TextLine, StartScale, ScaleNum : Integer;
begin
{ -- Write title and column heading }
   TextSize(TypeSize);
   TextLine := TitleLine;
   MoveTo(BarStart, TextLine);
   WriteDraw('PUPPIES ENROLLED BY AKC IN 1983');
   TextLine := TextLine + TextHeight;
   MoveTo(TextStart, TextLine);
   WriteDraw('Breed');

{ -- Store frame top }
   FrameTop := TextLine;

{ -- Draw and label bars }
   Left := BarStart;
   Bottom := TextLine;

   Bottom := Bottom + BarHeight + BarSpace;
   Top := Bottom - BarHeight;
   MoveTo(TextStart, Bottom);
   WriteDraw('COCKER SPANIEL');
   NumPups := 172291 div 1000;
   Right := BarStart + NumPups;
   PaintRect(Top, Left, Bottom, Right);

   Bottom := Bottom + BarHeight + BarSpace;
   Top := Bottom - BarHeight;
   MoveTo(TextStart, Bottom);
   WriteDraw('COLLIE');
   NumPups := 45337 div 1000;
   Right := BarStart + NumPups;
   PaintRect(Top, Left, Bottom, Right);

   Bottom := Bottom + BarHeight + BarSpace;
   Top := Bottom - BarHeight;
```

Figure 3.14 continued

```
    MoveTo(TextStart, Bottom);
    WriteDraw('GERMAN SHEPHERD');
    NumPups := 129621 div 1000;
    Right := BarStart + NumPups;
    PaintRect(Top, Left, Bottom, Right);

    Bottom := Bottom + BarHeight + BarSpace;
    Top := Bottom - BarHeight;
    MoveTo(TextStart, Bottom);
    WriteDraw('LABRADOR RETRIEVER');
    NumPups := 117221 div 1000;
    Right := BarStart + NumPups;
    PaintRect(Top, Left, Bottom, Right);

    Bottom := Bottom + BarHeight + BarSpace;
    Top := Bottom - BarHeight;
    MoveTo(TextStart, Bottom);
    WriteDraw('POODLE');
    NumPups := 184297 div 1000;
    Right := BarStart + NumPups;
    PaintRect(Top, Left, Bottom, Right);
{ -- Draw frame }
    FrameRect(FrameTop, Left, Bottom, MaxNumPups + BarStart);
{ -- Draw scale markers }
    MoveTo(BarStart, Bottom);
    Line(0, MarkerLength);
    Move(ScaleUnit, - MarkerLength);
    Line(0, MarkerLength);
    Move(ScaleUnit, - MarkerLength);
    Line(0, MarkerLength);
    Move(ScaleUnit, - MarkerLength);
    Line(0, MarkerLength);
{ -- Number bottom scale }
    TextLine := Bottom + TextHeight;
    StartScale := BarStart - NumWidth;

    ScaleNum := 0;
    MoveTo(StartScale + ScaleNum, TextLine);
    WriteDraw(ScaleNum : 1);

    ScaleNum := ScaleNum + ScaleUnit;
    MoveTo(StartScale + ScaleNum, TextLine);
    WriteDraw(ScaleNum : 1);

    ScaleNum := ScaleNum + ScaleUnit;
    MoveTo(StartScale + ScaleNum, TextLine);
    WriteDraw(ScaleNum : 1);

    ScaleNum := ScaleNum + ScaleUnit;
    MoveTo(StartScale + ScaleNum, TextLine);
    WriteDraw(ScaleNum : 1);
```

Figure 3.14 continued

```
    ScaleNum := ScaleNum + ScaleUnit;
    MoveTo(StartScale + ScaleNum, TextLine);
    WriteDraw(ScaleNum : 1);
{ -- Label bottom scale }
    TextLine := TextLine + TextHeight;
    MoveTo(BarStart, TextLine);
    WriteDraw('Puppies Enrolled and AKC Registerable (in thousands)')
end.
```

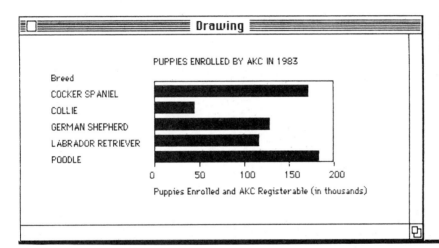

Figure 3.15 ● Bar graph drawn by program BarGraph

3.5 ○ Practice

The drawings shown in Figs. 3.16 and 3.17 are produced by the program shown as Fig. 3.18. This program uses both the text window and the drawing window. The text window is used to request data from the user, and the drawing window is used for the graphics display. The user is asked to enter a number between 1 and 25. That number is then used to control the size of the circle to be drawn.

Notice the boldface words **repeat** and **until** with a sequence of statements between them. This is a repeat loop. The entire sequence of statements enclosed by **repeat** and **until** is repeated, with the diameter of the circle increasing each time, until the diameter finally exceeds 2000. This program demonstrates how easily a moving display can be created with QuickDraw.

The following questions apply to the program Rings.

1. How many variables does this program contain?
2. Can the two lines

Figure 3.16

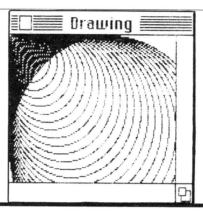

Figure 3.17

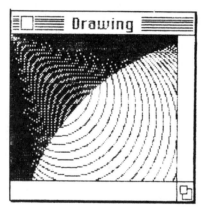

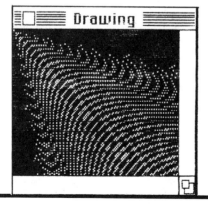

```
program Rings;
    var
        Top, Left, Bottom, Right : Integer;
        Diam, Increase : Integer;
begin
    Top := 0;
    Left := 0;
    Diam := 0;
    Write('Type an integer between 1 and 25: ');
    Read(Increase);
    repeat
        Diam := Diam + Increase;
        Bottom := Diam;
        Right := Diam;
        FrameOval(Top, Left, Bottom, Right)
    until Diam > 2000
end.
```

Figure 3.18 ● Program Rings

Top, Left, Bottom, Right : Integer;
Diam, Increase : Integer;

be combined into one line? How does this affect the program?

3. What happens if the statement

    Write('Type an integer between 1 and 25: ');

is replaced by

    WriteDraw('Type an integer between 1 and 25: ');

4. What happens if the user types a 26 in response to the prompt?

5. How many rings are drawn if the user enters the number 9?

6. What happens if the statement

    FrameOval(Top, Left, Bottom, Right)

is replaced by

    PaintOval(Top, Left, Bottom, Right)

7. How can the drawing be stopped in process to print the screen?

There are two lines following the word **var.** The first line contains four variables and the type description Integer. The second line contains two more variables and the same type description Integer. These six variables could be listed on one line, since they are all of the same type. The line would read,

Top, Left, Bottom, Right, Diam, Increase : Integer;

Don't forget the semicolon after the word Integer; declarations always end with a semicolon. The execution of the program is not affected at all by combining the two lines into one. The difference is in readability. The first four variables are used to define the enclosing rectangle; the second two pertain to the circle. Notice that the first two statements after the **repeat** could also be combined to read

Bottom := Diam + Increase;

This would be a legal statement; however, the separation makes the steps a bit clearer.

Write is used to enter text on the Text screen. WriteDraw would put the output on the Drawing screen. Not only would this use space that we want for the display; but, also, we have not given any instruction regarding where to place the pen. Before writing on the drawing screen, it is necessary to move the pen to the desired location.

The prompt for the user asks for a number between 1 and 25; however, nothing in the program itself checks to see if that request is being honored. The user could enter any number up to 32,767; a number larger than that would be outside the range for Integer and would cause an error. Of course, with very large numbers nothing would appear on the screen.

If the user enters a 9, Diam becomes 9 the first time the loop is executed, 18 the second time, and so forth. On the 223rd loop, Diam becomes 2007 and execution proceeds to the next statement, in this case to **end**.

PaintOval fills a circle rather than drawing the circumference. If PaintOval is used instead of FrameOval, the blackness spreads in a curve from the upper left corner, covering the screen and leaving no white areas showing. The speed with which the darkness spreads is dependent upon the number entered by the user.

When a program is running, a Pause menu appears to the right of the existing menus. To stop the program during the run, move the plus sign over the Pause menu and press the mouse button. The run will stop for as long as you hold the button, and will continue its run when you release the button. To stop the run for a longer time, pull down to the Halt, and then release. The run will stop and you can print the screen. When you are ready to go on, choose Go again, the run will continue where it left off.

The screen dumps in Fig. 3.19 show the display with the user entering a different number.

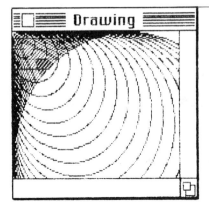

Figure 3.19

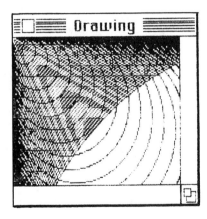

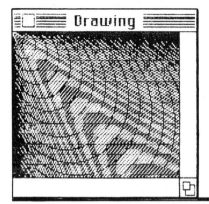

True or False

1. The text screen and the drawing screen can both be used as output in the same program.

2. A pixel is a round dot on the Macintosh screen.

3. WriteDraw is used to draw on the text window.

4. Line(x, y) causes the pen to draw a line from the present pen location to the position x, y on the screen.

5. To draw a line you must use two calls, MoveTo and LineTo.

6. To draw an oval you must describe a rectangle.

7. There are lots of poodles in the United States.

8. It is helpful to sketch the output on graph paper.

9. Bar graphs can only be drawn horizontally with QuickDraw.

10. WriteLn causes the pen to move down a distance equal to the text size.

● ● ●

In program TemperatureChart and program Rings, you have seen that the text and drawing windows can indeed be used in the same program.

A pixel is actually square rather than round. It is a square area on the screen which is bounded by four imaginary lines.

To write on the text window, you must use Write or WriteLn. WriteDraw is for writing to the drawing window.

Number 4 is true.

Although a line can be drawn using MoveTo and LineTo; it can also be drawn using the single call DrawLine(a, b, c, d); therefore, the answer is false.

Numbers 6-8 are all true.

Bar graphs can certainly be drawn vertically with QuickDraw. We leave it to you to write a program for doing exactly that.

The pen is tied to the drawing screen. WriteLn is a procedure call that is used when outputting to the text screen. It causes the computer to write the data designated and then reset to the beginning of the next line. The answer is false.

Fill in the Blanks

1. The Macintosh screen is 512 pixels wide and _____ pixels high.

2. The y coordinate increases as you move from _____ to _____ on the screen.

3. The statement

> Move(8,20)

causes the pen to move _____ pixels down and _____ pixels to the right.

4. In the procedure call

> PaintArc(10,20,80,90,30,60)

the integer 60 describes _____.

5. The call InvertRect(T,L,B,R) causes the black pixels within the described area to _____ and the white pixels to _____.

6. The five shapes predefined in QuickDraw are _____, _____, _____, _____, and _____.

7. Values that change during the course of the program must be declared as _____.

8. Using identifiers for constant values makes it easier to _____.

● ● ●

The Macintosh screen is 512 pixels wide and 342 pixels high.

The y coordinate increases as you move from the TOP to the BOTTOM on the screen. If you are used to using the standard coordinate system, you need to adjust your thinking when you use QuickDraw. Think of the screen as a page of text, which is read from left to right and from top to bottom.

The statement Move(8,20) causes the pen to move 20 pixels down and 8 pixels to the right. The horizontal location is always given first.

In the procedure call PaintArc(10,20,80,90,30,60), the integer 60 describes the SIZE OF THE ARC. Since the arc starts at 30 and continues for 60 degrees, it ends at 90 degrees.

The call InvertRect(T,L,B,R) causes the black pixels within the described area to BECOME WHITE and the white pixels to BECOME BLACK.

The five shapes predefined in QuickDraw are RECTANGLE, OVAL, ROUNDED RECTANGLE, ARC, and CIRCLE.

Values that change during the course of the program must be declared as VARIABLES.

Using identifiers for constant values makes it easier to MODIFY THE PROGRAM. In most cases, it also makes it easier to read and understand the program. Any of these answers is correct.

3.6 ○

3.1   Drawing a Figure

Here is a fun program for you to start with. Draw a snowman. The minimum requirements for this snowman are: a body, a head, two eyes, a mouth, and two arms. Add as many other things to the picture as you like.

3.2   Enlarging the Circle

Cartoons are created by changing the drawing in each frame just slightly, and then displaying the frames one after the other very quickly. Using this principle, write a program to create a circle which appears in the center of the drawing screen and grows larger.

3.3   More Big Letters

Drawing big letters, similar to the Big "H" in Chapter 2, is easily accomplished on the drawing screen as well as the text screen. However, remember that WriteLn does not work on the drawing screen.

Rewrite BigH to output to the drawing screen. Use MoveTo only at the beginning; thereafter, use Move.

3.4   A Simple Procedure

The program from the preceding exercise would be very useful as a procedure. Make the necessary changes to accomplish this. Then write a second procedure to print a big I. A program to write a big word HI anywhere on the drawing screen now requires only four additional statements. Write it.

3.5   Drawing a Box

A box can be represented in two dimensions by drawing two rectangles and connecting the corresponding corners with a line. Write a program to draw a box.

3.6   Positioning Circles

When the 15 balls for a game of pool are racked, they form a triangle with 5 balls in one row, 4 in the next, then 3, 2, 1. Write the program to draw this stack of pool balls.

Note: Before you begin, realize that the second row of balls nests into the first row; some calculation is necessary here.

3.7   Graph Paper

For various kinds of visual displays it is necessary to draw a grid on the screen. For this exercise, write a program that divides the drawing screen into one inch squares.

3.8   Temperature Chart

The outdoor temperature varies during the course of a day. Draw a line graph showing the temperature for a 12-hour period. The program should print a request for the temperature for each hour. The output should show the temperatures on the vertical axis and the hours on the horizontal axis. Draw a connecting line from each reading to the next.

3.9   Drawing Road Signs

Using only Move and Line, a fine stop sign can be drawn. Of course a MoveTo is required at the beginning to set the location. Write a procedure to draw a stop sign. Use the procedure in a program showing the location of the two stop signs at a four-way intersection. Label the streets and include an arrow with an "N" indicating which way is north.

3.10   A Better Checkerboard

A checkerboard can be drawn by using lines only, or by placing squares next to each other. Your problem is to write a program to draw a checkerboard on the drawing screen. This is not as easy as it first appears. Remember that the squares are two different colors; this can be represented by using black and white, or by marking every other square in some other way. If you are really adventursome, add the checkers.

Prelude to Variables

The Adventure of the Bathing Machine

THE summer following the little matter of the Vatican cameos was made memorable by three cases of interest, in which I had the privilege of being associated with Mr. Sherlock Holmes and of studying his methods in the use of the Analytical Engine. In glancing over my somewhat jumbled notes of these cases, I find they brought him the fewest personal opportunities in his long and admirable career. Each, however, did provide him with a chance for testing out the Engine's varied capabilities, including a telegraphic arrangement he made at considerable expense for communicating with the Engine over great distances. To Holmes the cases were of themselves of only secondary interest; and although he saved Scotland Yard a good deal of embarrassment in the first of these, the official police took full credit for concluding the affair.

Upon attending one of my new patients one fine June morning, I returned to Baker Street to find Holmes packing his valise in those high spirits that told me he was off on some new adventure.

"You are preparing for a trip," I remarked, eager to display my own deductive faculties.

"Yes, Watson," replied Holmes. "And perhaps your native shrewdness can deduce my destination?"

I studied his packages for a moment. "Off on some scholarly pursuits, I see. Perhaps to Cambridge and the Analytical Engine."

"There is such a delightful freshness about you, my dear Watson. You've really done very well indeed."

I was immensely pleased.

"It is true, however," he continued, "that you have missed everything of importance. As it happens, I leave this afternoon for the Yorkshire coast. Now, Watson, would you care to join me?"

I hesitated for a moment, and then replied. "Indeed I would, Holmes. There is a lull in my practice just now and I could benefit from a change of scene. You have a case, then?"

"A small matter, but not without points of interest," replied Holmes. "We can consider it on the train. Can you meet me at King's Cross at noon?"

"Yes of course, Holmes."

Holmes departed, and I hurried away to pack my bags for a few days by the sea.

As our train lurched northwards, Holmes was deep in thought. Framed in his ear-flapped travelling cap, he hardly spoke until we had passed well out of London. As the grey of the city turned to the green of the countryside, he proceeded to sketch for me the events in an extraordinary matter which had become a topic of conversation the length and breadth of England.

"I take it you are familiar, Watson, with this matter of the disappearance of the Baroness of Whitelsey?" asked Holmes.

"Only what I have learned from what the *Telegraph* and the *Chronicle* have had to say."

"He proceeded to sketch for me the events."

"Well then," he began, "let us review what the papers have reported thus far. It seems that the Baroness was spending a few days at the seaside resort of Scarborough and was daily taking the healthful waters of the North Sea. On each occasion she was taken down to the water's edge in a hired bathing machine, and on each occasion she was accompanied by the same attendants. At her request they would retire to the beach side of the machine while the Baroness dipped into the waters. Now, on the morning of the third of July, the attendants, at the conclusion of this minor ritual, hauled the machine back over the beach only to find it empty. A quick search of the shore revealed nothing, and the matter was placed in the hands of the local police. Needless to say, the Baroness has not been seen since."

After a brief pause, I casually remarked that the accusing finger of the law would certainly point in the direction of these attendants.

"Yes, Watson," he answered. "Our dear Inspector Lestrade has been called in by the local police and he naturally suspects foul play on the part of these fellows, all of whom were detained. Of course he does not have a shred of evidence, but remains adamant about a conviction. The family of one of these unfortunate attendants has asked me to look into the matter."

"Isn't it possible," I suggested, "that the Baroness met with an accidental end and that the attendants tried to conceal her drowning?"

"Possible, yes, and highly probable," replied Holmes. "But it is a capital error to theorize before one has collected one's data. However, as Lestrade has already settled upon this theory, it is up to me to look for an alternative."

With that Holmes lapsed into silence for much of the remainder of our journey, sinking into that deep concentration that some might think morose but that I knew to be a sign that he was pondering a most difficult case.

We arrived without incident and took furnished rooms in the hotel at which the Baroness had been staying. I found the trip fatiguing, but Holmes left immediately to pursue his investigations without so much as unpacking his bag. I dined alone and retired early. Lulled by the seaside air and a single glass of port, I slept late into the next morning.

I awoke to find that Holmes had already breakfasted and gone out again, leaving behind this note:

> Watson—I've gone to Whitby, some 20 miles up the coast. Kindly establish a connection with the Analytical Engine through the local telegraph office.
>
> Holmes

The director of the local telegraph office was most helpful, but in spite of this, I was occupied with filling this request for most of the morning.

When Holmes returned, he appeared elated. "A most profitable morning, Watson. The mystery of the Baroness of Whitelsey is solved to my satisfaction, but we need to resolve one final point. This provides us with an admirable opportunity for testing our new telegraph arrangements for communicating with the Engine.

"Now, the one bit of information we need to determine is the state of the tide at the time that the Baroness vanished. Let us establish this as a problem for the Engine.

"As you know, Watson, tides vary according to a 12 hour and 25 minute cycle. Since high tide today is at 11.00 A.M., tonight it will occur at 11.25 P.M. Let us define the problem in terms of what we know, what is given, and what we wish to determine:

The knowns: Tides recur every 12 hours and 25 minutes.

The givens: It is now July 28, and high tide is at 11.00 A.M.
The Baroness disappeared on July 3, at 9.00 A.M.

To find: The state of the tide at the time of the mysterious disappearance.

"Well, Watson, this begins to define the problem. Let me present my algorithm for solving it. First I will explain generally how the algorithm works and then explain some key ideas illustrated by it."

Holmes then presented his simple algorithm, which I have reproduced in Fig. 4.1.

"First, we express the time for a complete tide cycle in minutes."

"But why in minutes, Holmes?" I asked.

"That is due to a limitation of the Engine, Watson. It cannot work directly with dates and times the way we can. For example, it is inconvenient to read in a date and time such as July 28th, 11.00 A.M.; thus in my algorithm all dates and times are converted to minutes. As you will see, in dealing with dates we can readily express them in terms of the total number of minutes that have elapsed since the beginning of the month.

"We read in TodaysDate as the number 28, representing the 28th of the month. The TideHr is read as 11, for 11.00 A.M. Similarly, the EventDate and EventHr are read in as 3 and 9, respectively, representing July 3rd and 9.00 A.M., the last time the Baroness was seen. In order to do our computations, we must first convert our dates and times to minutes that have elapsed since the beginning of the month. Thus our first calculation is:

Set MinsToHighTide to (TodaysDate − 1) * MinsPerDay

Today's date is 28, but only 27 full days have gone by this month. Thus we subtract 1 and multiply by the number of minutes in a day. This gives the number of minutes in the 27 complete days that have elapsed since the beginning of the month.

Definitions:

— Express the knowns
MinsPerHr is 60 minutes
MinsPerDay is 1440 minutes
MinsPerTideCycle is 745 minutes

Algorithm:

— Obtain the givens:
Read TodaysDate, TideHr, EventDate, EventHr

— Convert times to minutes since the beginning of the month:
Set MinsToHighTide to (TodaysDate – 1) * MinsPerDay
Set MinsToHighTide to MinsToHighTide + TideHr * MinsPerHr

Set MinsToEvent to (EventDate – 1) * MinsPerDay
Set MinsToEvent to MinsToEvent + EventHr * MinsPerHr

— Find elapsed time:
Set ElapsedTime to MinsToHighTide – MinsToEvent

— Find the number of elapsed tide cycles:
Set TideCycles to ElapsedTime / MinsPerTideCycle

— Output the result:
Write TideCycles

Figure 4.1 ● Holmes's algorithm for calculating tides

"We must also consider the 11 hours between midnight and high tide today. So we use a second calculation,

Set MinsToHighTide to MinsToHighTide + TideHr * MinsPerHr

to add the number of minutes that have gone by today to our previous total. We now have the total number of minutes from the beginning of the month until high tide today.

"Next, we follow an identical procedure to arrive at a figure in minutes for the time of the swim and subsequent disappearance."

"But Holmes, why do you calculate from the beginning of the month?"

"That is arbitrary, Watson. I need some date as a reference, and the first of the month is convenient since it allows us to express our input in terms of days of the month.

"We now have the time of today's high tide and also the time of the disappearance, expressed in minutes. We subtract one from the other,

Set ElapsedTime to MinsToHighTide – MinsToEvent

to find the elapsed time in minutes.

"The rest is simple. We divide the elapsed time by the number of minutes in a complete tide cycle, thus giving the number of tide cycles that have taken place in the interim. In this way, our final answer will be expressed in terms of high tide as a reference point.

"Watson, this algorithm demonstrates several key ideas about programming that I would like to explain to you, if you will hear them."

"Of course."

"Very well," Holmes continued. "The first thing to understand is the idea of a *variable*. Each variable we use in the program will have a name that we give to it. Think of a variable as a piece of information that can vary as the program progresses, such as the depth to which the parsley had sunk into the butter that hot day when the dreadful business of the Abernetty family was first brought to my attention."

"But what will cause the variables to change in value?" I asked.

"We will set and change the values of all the variables by the way we write the program," Holmes replied. "They will be completely under our control. Look again at the algorithm for our problem. Here you see several variables, for example, the variables named TodaysDate and TideCycles.

"Next, we have the idea of an *expression*. An expression is a formula for computing a value. You can see some examples in my algorithm. Consider the statement:

Set MinsToHighTide to (TodaysDate − 1) * MinsPerDay

Here MinsToHighTide is a variable whose value we are trying to establish. We use the expression

(TodaysDate − 1) * MinsPerDay

to express the fact that we want the Engine to subtract 1 from TodaysDate and multiply the result by the number of minutes in a day."

"Does it not strike you as curious, Holmes, that the asterisk should represent multiplication?"

"Not at all, Watson. The Engine would have difficulty in sorting out the letter 'x' from the usual multiplication symbol."

"A statement used to set a variable based on an expression is termed an *assignment*, because it assigns a value to a variable. You can think of an assignment as establishing a fact about a variable. In the algorithm, all assignments have the form:

Set *variable* to *expression*

That is, an assignment consists of an expression to be computed and a variable that is to take on the value of the expression.

"It is very important to notice, Watson, that the values of variables may change as the program progresses. We use assignments to elaborate progressive states of knowledge about the data. Consider, for example, the two statements from my algorithm:

Set MinsToHighTide to (TodaysDate − 1) * MinsPerDay
Set MinsToHighTide to MinsToHighTide + TideHr * MinsPerHr

The first we have already discussed. When it is evaluated, the variable MinsToHighTide will be given a value consisting of the number of minutes from the beginning of the month until midnight last night. In the second assignment, the variable is revised to include also the number of minutes that have elapsed today. Notice especially that the expression in the second assignment contains the variable MinsToHighTide, the same variable whose value is to be changed.

"Here," he said, pushing a sheet of paper my way, "I have already written out my algorithm in the language of a Pascal programme. You shouldn't find it at all difficult to decipher."

I studied it for a moment. It was quite a short programme, and I have replicated it here as Fig. 4.2.

"I take it that this curious symbol that resembles a colon followed by an equal sign denotes assignment in the Pascal language?"

"Precisely," replied my companion. "In Pascal we need only say:

MinsToHighTide := (TodaysDate − 1) * MinsPerDay

"I must admit, however, that the elements of originality and enterprise are not too common to the scientific world. The symbol is, indeed, distinctly unimaginative."

"Now, Watson, let us enter the data to the programme by using this telegraph arrangement. We shall soon have our answer."

It was a brisk walk in the bracing sea air to the telegraph office. In a matter of minutes our connections were established. Holmes then carefully telegraphed the numbers

28   11   3   9

representing

July 28   11.00 am   July 3   9.00 am

After a few minutes the results of his programme came clacking back at us over the telegraph. He began scribbling down numbers on a small pad of paper and finally tore the sheet loose.

"Precisely what I had expected," he exclaimed. "There have been nearly forty-eight and a half tide cycles between today's high tide and that fateful episode. This means, Watson, that the tide then differed by roughly half a cycle, which places the mysterious bathing machine well out of reach of the sea. Low tide, Watson! We can turn this little bit of information over to Lestrade and save these poor attendants from any further humiliation."

"But how does this possibly remove them from suspicion?" I asked.

"Elementary, Watson. If the attendants had drowned her, the incoming tide would have washed her body onto the shore to be discovered later. But it was not discovered. No, Watson, there is more to it, as her family has suggested privately. The Baron Whitelsey is known as a cruel man who abused his wife; I venture to say that the Baroness swam out to sea and made good an escape with the help of a confederate. Let us wish her well in her new life. I doubt that she will be seen on these shores again."

Figure 4.2 ● Program Tides

```
program Tides;
{ -- This program reads in the day of the month and the hour of }
{ -- high tide, as well as the day and hour of some earlier event. }
{ -- Times must be given in 24-hour form; for instance }
{ -- 3 p.m. is given as 18. }
{ -- The program computes the number of tide cycles during the }
{ -- elapsed time. }
   const
      MinsPerHr = 60;
      MinsPerDay = 1440;
      MinsPerTideCycle = 745;

   var
      TodaysDate, TideHr : Integer;
      EventDate, EventHr : Integer;

      MinsToHighTide, MinsToEvent, Elapsed Time : LongInt;

      TideCycles : Real;
begin
   Read(TodaysDate, TideHr, EventDate, EventHr);
   MinsToHighTide := (TodaysDate – 1) * MinsPerDay;
   MinsToHighTide := MinsToHighTide + TideHr * MinsPerHr;

   MinsToEvent := (EventDate – 1) * MinsPerDay;
   MinsToEvent := MinsToEvent + EventHr * MinsPerHr;

   ElapsedTime := MinsToHighTide – MinsToEvent;
   TideCycles := Elapsed Time / MinsPerTideCycle;

   Write('The number of tide cycles is', TideCycles)
end.
```

Chapter 4

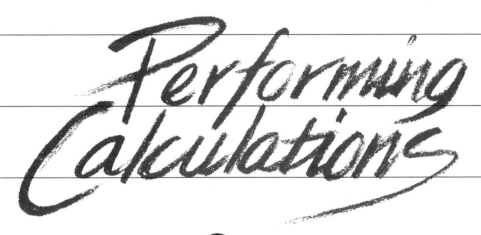

Central to all programs is the notion of a variable and the related concept of assignment. A variable is a name for a piece of information that varies as the program progresses. An assignment is an action that changes this information.

The use of names to refer to values needed in the course of the computations is a characteristic of all computer programs. For example, we may have

4.1 ● Variables and Assignment

```
TodaysDate – 1      { the value of TodaysDate minus 1 }
2 * Velocity        { 2 times the value of Velocity }
Sin(Pi / 4)         { the sine of the value of pi divided by 4 }
```

In each of these forms a piece of information (for example, some number of days) is associated with a name (for example, TodaysDate). This piece of information is called a *value*. This value is not given directly (for example, the value may be 28), but instead is referred to by a name (for example, TodaysDate). This name is called a *variable*, since the value associated with the name will be established or changed during the course of the program.

An *assignment* is the means by which we establish or change the value of a variable. For example, we may have

```
NumSuspects := 0
NumSuspects := NumSuspects + 2
MinsToHighTide := (TodaysDate – 1) * MinsPerDay
```

77

In the first case, the value of NumSuspects is set to zero. In the second case, the value of NumSuspects is incremented by 2. In the third case, the value of MinsToHighTide is set to the value computed by the given formula.

The point of all of these assignments is identical. At each step in our program we have established certain facts about the state of our knowledge. An assignment reflects the fact that we have established a new state of knowledge.

The general form for writing all assignment statements is simple:

variable := expression

When this statement is acted upon by the computer, it means the following:

1. Compute the value of the expression
2. Then associate this value with the variable

While the rules are simple, you must be careful to obey them precisely.

Consider the following sequence of assignment statements, where the variables MyScore and YourScore have initially unspecified values.

```
MyScore    := 0;
     { value of MyScore is 0, YourScore is unspecified }
YourScore := 1;
     { value of MyScore is 0, YourScore is 1 }
MyScore    := 2;
     { value of MyScore is 2, YourScore is 1 }
YourScore := MyScore;
     { value of MyScore is 2, YourScore is 2 }
YourScore := 2 * MyScore
     { value of MyScore is 2, YourScore is 4 }
```

We see here that each statement in the sequence is executed step by step. Furthermore, each assignment establishes a new value for only one variable.

The assignment

```
NumSuspects := NumSuspects + 2
```

given before perhaps deserves a little special attention. Here the variable whose value is being set also occurs in the expression given on the right side of the statement. This causes no problems. First, the value of the expression is obtained; then this value is assigned to the variable, just as before. This statement has exactly the same effect as the following sequence:

```
Value        := NumSuspects + 2;
NumSuspects := Value
```

In both cases, the value of NumSuspects has been incremented by 2.

Macintosh Pascal, like all programming languages, has a number of strictly applied rules regarding the use of variables. One such rule is that all variables used in the program must be stated in a *declaration*. A declaration is a statement of some fact that will be true throughout your program. For variables, the declaration states the name of the variable and the type of information it represents.

For example, consider the following declaration:

NumSuspects : Integer;

This declaration introduces a variable named NumSuspects, and specifies that the information it represents will be an integer number. This last fact is particularly important. It means that whenever you attempt to give the variable a value, the computer will check that the value is indeed an integer number. If you try to assign the variable some other type of value, the computer will complain. Do not be alarmed by this fact—it should be precisely what you want. If the computer does not complain, you can be assured that whenever you refer to this variable, it will stand for an integer number. In Macintosh Pascal, *Integer* values must not exceed ±32,676. In order to use a whole number outside of this range, the variable must be declared as a long integer (LongInt).

Consider next the following declaration:

TideCycles : Real;

This declaration is just like the declaration above except that here the variable TideCycles is specified as Real. This means that the value of the variable will always to a real number.

Real numbers, in Macintosh Pascal, can have up to 8 decimal places. If greater accuracy is required, the variables can be declared as *double* (up to 16 decimal places) or *extended* (up to 20 decimal places).

The variables NumSuspects and TideCycles are said to have different *types*. We will have more to say about types later on, but for now we make the following points. A type tells the computer what kind of value a variable can hold. Once the type of a variable has been specified, it is only possible to assign values of the same type. Thus you cannot assign a real number to an integer variable; that is, you cannot say,

NumSuspects := 12.6   { erroneous assignment }

This is quite reasonable, since 12.6 is a rather unusual number of suspects. When we get to other types of data, we will see that this rule is rigidly enforced.

Pascal, however, allows you one exception. You can write,

TideCycles := 10

and Pascal takes this to mean the following: the integer 10 is converted to an equivalent real number, and this real value is assigned to the variable TideCycles. Note that this is the same as saying,

4.2 ● Declaring Variables

TideCycles := 10.0

As good practice, it is best to assign explicit real values to real variables, just as you must assign explicit integer values to integer variables.

When arithmetic operations are performed on Integer numbers, the results are returned as LongInt. These results can be assigned to Integer variables as long as they fall within the range for integers. Similarly, results of arithmetic operations on real-type numbers are returned as Extended numbers; but the results can be assigned to Real or Double variables provided they fall within the acceptable range for real and double numbers.

In most programs you will have many variables, and many of these will be of the same type. Pascal lets you declare several variables at one go by simply giving the list of variables followed by their common type. For example, we may write,

TodaysDate, HighTideHr, ElapsedTime : Integer;

which declares three variables of type Integer.

One last rule. In Pascal, all of the declarations for variables must be grouped together before the statement part of the program. Further, all of the variable declarations must be preceded by the keyword **var**. Thus, a complete list of variable declarations for a program might look like

```
var
    TodaysDate, HideHr : Integer;
    EventDate, EventHr : Integer;
    MinsToHighTide, MinsToEvent, ElapsedTime : Longint;
    TideCycles : Real;
```

4.3 ● Declaring Constants

While a variable is a piece of information that varies as a program progresses, we often have pieces of information that are known before the program is started and that do not change as the program progresses. Such known facts can be stated with a *constant declaration*.

Consider the following constant declaration.

MinsPerHr = 60;

This declaration specifies a constant named MinsPerHr, whose value is fixed at 60. The constant declaration establishes the association between the name MinsPerHr and its value. Obviously we will not be wanting to change the number of minutes per hour during execution of the program.

More generally, a constant declaration can be used to name any value that is known when the program is written. Just as for variable declarations, all constant declarations must be preceded by a keyword, in this case, the keyword **const**. For example, we may have the constant declarations:

```
const
    MinsPerHr = 60;        { the number of minutes per hour }
    Unknown  = 0;          { standard value for unknown items }
    Pi = 3.14159;          { the value of pi }
    MaxTaxRate = 70.0;     { the maximum rate of tax }
```

In all of these constant declarations, a name is associated with a simple integer or real number. Throughout the program the name and the number can be used interchangeably.

Just as for declared variables, the name of a constant has a defined type. A constant's type is simply that of the value given in the constant declaration. For example, MinsPerHr is of type Integer and Pi is of type Real. The group of constant declarations for a given program must precede the group of variable declarations.

Before going on, one other point. Character strings can also be given a name using a constant declaration, as in

```
const
    Blank = ' ';
    HisName = 'Mycroft';
```

These names can be used in Write statements, such as

```
Write('His name is', Blank, HisName)
```

which prints

```
His name is Mycroft
```

just as you would expect.

4.4 ● Expressions

In every program we want to compute some results. To do this we need to write expressions. An *expression* is a formula for computing a value.

Consider the very simple expression

```
TodaysDate – 1
```

This expression subtracts one from the existing value of the variable TodaysDate. In this expression, we have a subtraction *operator* and two *operands*, TodaysDate and 1. Next, consider the expression

ElapsedTime/MinsPerTideCycle

Here we have a division operator and two operands, ElapsedTime and MinsPerTideCycle. The value of the expression is the real number that is the quotient of the two values.

Both of these expressions illustrate properties that are common to all expressions. First, an expression can contain some special symbols like + and / called *operators*. Second, the operators are applied to the values of the *operands*. The operands may be numbers, variables, constants, or parenthesized expressions. Third, when an operator is applied to operands, a result is computed and this result has a given type. In the first of the two preceding expressions, an integer-type result is computed; in the second, a real-type result is computed.

Table 4.1 lists all of the arithmetic operators in Pascal, along with the types of their operands and the type of the result. With

$$+ \quad - \quad *$$

you may combine integer-type values with real-type values. The type of the result will be an extended number if either of the operands is a real-type number, and a LongInt number otherwise. For example,

Pi + 2

is the same as

Pi + 2.0

Table 4.1 ● Arithmetic Operations in Macintosh Pascal

Operations with Two Operands

Operator	Operation	Type of Operands	Type of Result
+	addition	Integer-type or Real-type	LongInt or Extended
−	subtraction	Integer-type or Real-type	LongInt or Extended
*	multiplication	Integer-type or Real-type	LongInt or Extended
/	real division	Integer-type or Real-type	Extended
div	integer division with truncation	Integer-type	LongInt
mod	remainder after integer division	Integer-type	LongInt

Operations with One Operand

Operator	Operation	Type of Operands	Type of Result
+	identity	Integer-type or Real-type	LongInt or Extended
−	sign inversion	Integer-type or Real-type	LongInt or Extended

In both cases, the result is an extended number.

The operators **div** and **mod** deserve a special note. The operator **div** gives the integer part of the result when one integer is divided by another. The operator **mod** (for modulo) gives the corresponding remainder. For example, we may have:

    7 **div** 2   { value is 3 }
    7 **mod** 2   { value is 1 }

These little operators are quite handy. For example, suppose you are standing in a train station and the time on the clock is 1432. In more familiar notation, you take this as 2 hours and 32 minutes p.m. How would you get this in Pascal? You would write something like

    Hours   := TrainTime **div** 100;
    Mins   := TrainTime **mod** 100

This determines the number of hours and the number of minutes in the given train time. Furthermore, if you know that the number of hours is greater than 12 (for example, 14), you can write,

    PmHours := Hours **mod** 12

to compute the corresponding p.m. hours.

As indicated in Table 4.1, plus and minus may be used with a single operand. This is allowed only at the beginning of an expression, as in

    XCoordinate := −10.0;
    YCoordinate := +10.0

Of course, you will often want to write expressions with several operands and operators, just as you do in conventional arithmetic. For example, you may wish to write,

    (TodaysDate − 1) * MinsPerDay

or

    TotalCash + Deposits − Withdrawals − Embezzlement

To do things like this you have to remember a few rules. The rules are

- Parenthesized operands are evaluated before unparenthesized operands.
- The operators *, / , **div**, and **mod** are applied before − and +.
- Otherwise, evaluation proceeds in textual order from left to right.

These rules are intended to make the writing of expressions easier. Thus if you write,

1 + NumWidgets * 2

and NumWidgets is 3, the result is 7 (which is what you want) and not 8.

To make sure that you have these rules straight, consider the following pairs of expressions. The expression on the left will give the same value as the expression on the right.

1 + 2 + 3	(1 + 2) + 3	{ value is 6 }
1 – 2 – 3	(1 – 2) – 3	{ value is –4 }
1 + 2 * 3	1 + (2 * 3)	{ value is 7 }
1 * 2 + 3	(1 * 2) + 3	{ value is 5 }
– 1 – 2 – 3	((–1) – 2) – 3	{ value is –6 }

This may look a bit tricky, but in normal practice you should have no problem. With proper spacing you can write your expressions like

1 + NumWidgets*2

rather than

1+NumWidgets * 2

so that you and the reader will have no doubt as to what you mean.

Furthermore, when there is a problem, just put parentheses in your expressions to make your intent exactly clear. For example, it is probably not a good idea to write something like

060   – A – B – C

You can make things look a lot better simply by writing

– (A + B + C)

which leaves no mystery for the reader.

Using Predefined Functions as Operands

Consider the expression:

Sqrt(5.0) + 1.0

This expression adds 1.0 to the square root of 5.0. Our interest here centers on the Sqrt in

Sqrt(5.0)

In mathematical parlance, Sqrt is called a *function*, in this case a function to compute the square root of its argument. In Pascal there are a number of such functions that are predefined in the language. For example, you can compute the absolute value of a number or its mathematical sine. A list of all of these functions is given in Table 4.2. To use these functions, you simply write the name of the function followed by its argument enclosed in parentheses, as shown above. All of this works just as you would expect and should cause no problems.

Table 4.2 ● Predefined Arithmetic Functions

x denotes an expression whose whole value is either integer or real, unless stated otherwise.

Odd(x)   True if the value of x is an odd number, and false otherwise. The value of x must be an integer.

Abs(x)   The absolute value of x. If the value of x is an integer, the result is an integer; otherwise, the result is a real number.

Sqr(x)   The square of x. If the value of x is an integer, the result is an integer; otherwise, the result is a real number.

Sqrt(x)   The positive square root of x, where x must be nonnegative. Result is a real number.

Sin(x)   The sine of x, where x is expressed in radians. Result is a real number.

Cos(x)   The cosine of x, where x is expressed in radians. Result is a real number.

Ln(x)   The natural logarithm of x, where the value of x must be greater than zero. Result is a real number.

Exp(x)   The value of the base of natural logarithm raised to the power of x. Result is a real number.

Arctan(x)   The principal value (in radians) of the arctangent of x.

Trunc(x)   The value of x (which must be a real number) truncated to its integer part. For example, Trunc(4.6) is 4 and Trunc(–4.6) is –4.

Round(x)   The value of x (which must be a real number) rounded to the nearest integer. For example, Round(4.62) is 5 and Round(–4.6) is –5. If x is zero or positive, Round(x) is equal to Trunc($x + 0.5$); for negative x, Round(x) is equal to Trunc($x - 0.5$).

Before going on, we must mention two important rules that you have to remember when you write an expression. The first is that if you use a variable in an expression it must already have been assigned a value. If it has not, the computer will not know what to do; and, most likely, your program will come to a stop or give bizarre results. For example, if you write

NumSuspects + 1

and you have not already given a value to NumSuspects, the result will be trouble.

Second, you must be careful when writing expressions containing both integer and real number values. For example, if IntValue is an integer variable and RealValue is a real variable, then

IntValue + RealValue

will give a real result. Watch out for this, for you cannot say,

IntValue := IntValue + RealValue { -- erroneous }

If you want to assign a real value to an integer variable, you have to use one of the functions Trunc or Round given in Table 4.2. Thus you can say something like

IntValue := Trunc(IntValue + RealValue)

to truncate the real result computed by the addition of IntValue and RealValue.

4.5 ● Reading and Writing Information

In almost every program you write, you are going to want to read in some data and print some results. Doing this is easy. Consider the statement

Read(TodaysDate, TideHr, EventDate, EventHr)

When the computer executes this statement, it will ask you for four values. You may give it something like

28   11   3   9

or something like

28   11
3   9

When you give it these values, the four variables will be assigned the values that you typed in. This is exactly the same as writing,

TodaysDate   := 28;
TideHr   := 11;
EventDate   := 3;
EventHr   := 9

in your program. That is, reading data is exactly the same as assigning values to variables.

The general rule for reading data is thus quite simple. You simply use the name Read followed by the parenthesized list of variables whose values you want to read.

For printing your results, the process is just the opposite. For example, consider the statement

Write(TideCycles)

When the computer processes this statement, it will simply print the value of TideCycles. If you want, you can say,

>   Write('The number of tide cycles is', TideCycles)

In this case, your program will write the characters "The number of tide cycles is" followed by the value of the variable of TideCycles.

More generally, you may print out any character string or the value of any expression, provided that each of these items is separated by commas. Thus all of the following statements are acceptable:

>   Write('SOME INTRODUCTORY MESSAGE')
>   Write('YOU CAN PRINT CHARACTERS LIKE $ AND +')
>   Write(OneVariable,Another,AndAnother)
>   Write('PI divided by 4 is ', PI/4)

There is an old computer adage: you read variables and write expressions. It really is just about that simple.

Some closing details. When you use Read, the computer will ignore any line boundaries and keep reading until it gets the input values it wants. When you use Write, the computer will print the output values so as to put several values on a line. The computer has its own way of printing your data, and the results may not always be nice to look at.

If you want to control the situation a bit more, you can also use ReadLn and WriteLn. With

>   ReadLn(TodaysDate, TideHr);
>   ReadLn(EventDate, EventHr)

the computer will expect EventDate and EventHr on a new line, and then advance to the next line before reading any more data. With

>   WriteLn('The number of tide cycles is', TideCycles)

the computer will print the message and value on a single line, and then advance to the next line before writing any more results.

One handy little detail. If you say,

>   Write('Number of suspects is', NumSuspects)

the computer will normally print the value of NumSuspects right justified in a 9-digit field. Thus your output may look like

>   Number of suspects is   4

To make things nicer, you can say,

>   Write('The number of suspects is', NumSuspects : 2)

The 2 in

>   NumSuspects : 2

tells the computer that two spaces are to be used for printing the value of NumSuspects. Thus your output will be

The number of suspects is 4

For printing real numbers, if you say,

Write('The number of tide cycles is', TideCycles)

the computer will print something like

The number of tide cycles is 4.8e+1

However, if you say,

Write('The number of tide cycles is', TideCycles : 6 : 2)

the computer will print,

The number of tide cycles is 48.48

The 6 in 6 : 2 means the value will occupy six character positions. The 2 in 6 : 2 means two digits will be given to the right of the decimal point.

We will take this up in much greater detail in Chapter 12, but this should suffice for most cases.

4.6 ○ Practice

Calculations

Many of the ideas presented in this chapter are illustrated in the program of Fig. 4.3. This program reads in 6 integer values, representing the number of pennies, nickels, and so forth, and prints the value of the coins in dollars and cents. This program, like all of the others in this book, was written with a great concern for the reader. You see that when programs are carefully written, they can be read and understood without a great deal of concern for the many detailed conventions of Pascal.

This program contains several variables. All of the variables are declared in the declarations part of the program. The declaration states the name of the variable and its type. In this particular program all of the variables are of type Integer.

As you read the program, notice that the only variable that actually holds different values during the course of the program is TotalChange. However, NumPennies, NumNickels, and so forth must be declared as variables because their values are initially undefined; they change from an undefined value to a specific value read from the keyboard. It is important to understand here that "undefined" does not mean that they have no value. If you were to put an undefined variable into an expression, the computer would take whatever value existed in the location assigned to that variable and would use that value in your calculation. The result would be trouble. In the first assignment

```
program CountChange;
{ -- This program reads in six integer values, respectively }
{ -- representing the number of pennies, nickels, dimes, quarters, }
{ -- half-dollars, and silver dollars in coinage. }
{ -- The program outputs the total value of the coins }
{ -- in dollars and cents. }
   var
      NumPennies, NumNickels, NumDimes, Num Quarters,
            NumHalves, NumDollars : Integer;
      TotalChange, Dollars, Cents : Integer;
begin
   TotalChange := 0;
   Write('Enter the number of Pennies, Nickels, Dimes, Quarters,
         Halves, Dollars:');
   Read(NumPennies);
   TotalChange := TotalChange + 1 * NumPennies;
   Read(NumNickels);
   TotalChange := TotalChange + 5 * NumNickels;
   Read(NumDimes);
   TotalChange := TotalChange + 10 * NumDimes;
   Read(NumQuarters);
   TotalChange := TotalChange + 25 * NumQuarters;
   Read(NumHalves);
   TotalChange := TotalChange + 50 * NumHalves;
   Read(NumDollars);
   TotalChange := TotalChange + 100 * NumDollars;
   Dollars := TotalChange div 100;
   Cents := TotalChange mod 100;
   Write('Change is ', Dollars : 1, 'dollars and ', Cents : 2, 'cents .')
end.
```

Figure 4.3 ● Program CountChange

statement in CountChange, what is the value assigned, and to which variable is it assigned?

● ● ●

During the course of the program the total amount of money for each type of coin is added to the total amount of change giving a new value for TotalChange. Since TotalChange is used as part of the expression that calculates the new value, it is important to guarantee that it starts out with a zero value; therefore, it is assigned a zero value before any calculations are performed. This is a practice that must become second nature for you. Before any variable is used in an expression, a value must be assigned to it. Quite often, the value initially assigned will be zero.

In the program to count change, find the statement that initially assigns a value to each of the other variables listed in the declarations.

● ● ●

For the number of coins of each denomination, the value is assigned when the Read statement is performed. This statement causes the computer to read an integer value from the keyboard and assign it to the integer-type variable shown in the parentheses following the Read. The first and only values for Dollars and Cents are assigned in the two statements preceding the final Write statement.

Can you think of a shorter way to assign these values?

● ● ●

The parentheses following a Read can contain more than one variable. Several variables can be listed separated by commas. As each value is read from the keyboard, it is assigned to the next listed variable. One Read could cause the number of coins of each denomination to be assigned to their prospective identifiers, as in the following:

    Read(NumPennies, NumNickels, NumDimes, NumQuarters, NumHalves,
        NumDollars)

There is always more than one way to write a program. For instance, the program for counting change could have made use of constants, such as PennyValue, NickelValue, and so forth. Where would these values be declared?

● ● ●

The identifiers used in a program must be declared in a particular order. Constants must be declared before variables. Since the value of a coin does not change, these values could be declared as constants; for instance,

    NickelValue = 5;

The identifier would then be used in the assignment statement, as in

    TotalChange := TotalChange + NickelValue * NumNickels

Once identifiers have been declared, you will most likely want to use them in expressions. The following expressions are written in familiar arithmetic notation. Using Tables 4.1 and 4.2, write them as they would appear in a program. For example,

$A^2 + B^2$

would be written as

Sqr(A) + Sqr(B)

or as

A*A + B*B

(a) $B^2 - 4AC$

(b) $PI \cdot r^2$

(c) square root of $A^2 + B^2$

(d) 1000

(e) one million

(f) 6%

(g) ½ Base · Height

(h) (A + B) / (C + D)

(i) $sin^2(X + 1)$

(j) $|A - B|$

(k) $25,000

(l) $X^2 / 2Y$

Many of the arithmetic notations familiar to us are not recognized by Pascal. The following expressions are correct Pascal:

Sqr(B) – 4 * A * C.

Actually, 4AC looks more like an identifier than an expression. However, it doesn't fit that category either, since it begins with a number.

Pi * Sqr(r) or Pi * (r * r)

Sqrt((A * A) + (B * B)) or Sqrt(Sqr(A) + Sqr(B))

1000

1000000 or 1.0E+6

depending on whether an integer type or real type number is desired.

0.06

(Base/2) * Height

(A + B) / (C + D)

This expression is correct as originally written.

Sqr(Sin(X + 1))

(A – B)

25000

(X * X) / (2 * Y)

In dealing with computer languages, we must be careful of the order in which expressions are evaluated and the value of the result.

Assuming that A, B, C, and so forth are variables of type Integer, state what values are assigned to them.

```
A  := 1 + 1;
B  := 1 + (1 – 1);
C  := 2 * 3 * 4;
D  := 2 * 3 div 4;
E  := 2 * (3 div 4);
F  := 2 div 3 * 4;
G  := (–2) * (–5);
H  := 4 – 3 + 2;
I  := – 2 * 5 + 1;
J  := Trunc(30/7/2);
K  := Round(31.4 * 95.3 * 1.1)
```

● ● ●

You may have noticed as you calculated the preceding values that some of the expressions produce real numbers when they are evaluated. D, E, F, J, and K must be declared as variables of type Real; otherwise, an error results. Remember that real numbers and integers are output differently by the computer. Here are the correct answers assuming that the real numbers are to be output using two decimal places.

```
A  := 2
B  := 1
C  := 24
D  := 1.00
E  := 0.00
F  := 0.00
G  := 10
H  := 3
I  := –9
J  := 2.00
K  := 3292.00
```

If your results are different, try again after reviewing the rules for evaluating expressions. On D, E, and F, you must remember that the word div is special. It does not mean "divided by"; for that you must use the slash (/). **Div** gives only the integer part of the result when one integer-type number is divided by another. Be very careful to say what you mean to say when you use **div** and /.

Like any feature in a programming language, assignment statements have their own peculiar conventions. For each of the following assignment statements, answer True if the statement could be valid in some program, and False otherwise.

(a) A := B

(b) One := One + One

(c) Case1 := –Case

(d) Sum := ((N + 1))

(e) Result := A + B * C mod(X) / 2

(f) –X := A + B

(g) F(X) := 1

(h) Y := SQRT(SQRT(X))

(i) A := (A − (B − (C − (D −(X)))) + 1) (l) P := A div B div C

(j) PlSquared = 3.14159 * 3.14159   (m) I := B * C

(k) 1ROOT := SQRT(X)   (n) X := SquareRoot(Y)

Note: In making your decision, you must consider whether the statement could be valid in any program, no matter how strange.

In reviewing the assignment statements just listed, you must remember that the statement assigns the value of the expression on the right to the variable on the left. Examples i, j, and n do not have valid variable identifiers on the left and therefore could not be used in any program.

In example g, the word SquareRoot is not a predefined function; the name of the function is Sqrt (or SqRt, the capitalization of the letters is not relevant).

Example h would certainly be clearer with some added parentheses; as written it would be evaluated as follows.

Result := A +(((B * C) mod (X)) / 2)

Example m has more than one problem. An equal sign is used instead of an assignment symbol. The numbers contain commas. You and I may assume that the commas were meant to be decimal points; however, the computer does not make assumptions like that.

On questions a-f and k and l you should have answered True.

Fill in the Blanks

1. All identifiers used in a program must be _____ before they can be used.

2. The value of a variable is changed by means of an _____.

3. Constant declarations must be preceded by the keyword _____.

4. Character strings declared as constants must be enclosed by

    _____.

5. Expressions contain operands and _____

6. The asterisk (*) in an expression means that the terms on either side are to be _____.

7. Unless otherwise indicated by parentheses, division is performed _____ addition.

8. Unnecessary parentheses are sometimes added to an expression to improve its _____.

9. Sqrt is a predefined _____.

10. When an integer is subtracted from a real number, the resulting number is of type _____.

11. Using a Write statement, you can print out character strings and _____ of expression.

12. When the statement

    Write(X: 4: 2)

    is executed, the value printed will contain _____ decimal places.

● ● ●

The answers are: DECLARED, ASSIGNMENT, CONST, SINGLE QUOTES, OPERATORS, MULTIPLIED, BEFORE, READABILITY, FUNCTION, EXTENDED, VALUES, 2.

4.7 ○

4.1   A Desk Calculation

In some people's eyes, a computer is just a powerful desk calculator. Sure enough, we can perform common calculations with a computer.

One common application of calculations is the computation of averages. Suppose that you receive quarterly electric bills and wish to compute the average monthly cost. For example, if your quarterly bills in dollars and cents are

170.33   161.42   125.78   147.91

the average monthly cost would be:

50.45

Write a program to read in four real numbers representing quarterly bills and print the average monthly cost. Test your program with the above values.

4.2   Simple Arithmetic

The distributive law of mathematics says that the expression

A * (B + C)

is equivalent to the expression

A*B + A*C

Write a program to test the validity of this law; that is, write a program that reads in values for A, B, and C and then prints the values of both expressions. Can you think of values for A, B, and C where the distributive law will not hold when you run the program? Test your program with these values.

4.3   Unit Pricing

It is now common for supermarkets to compute and display the unit price of items. For example, a 4-ounce item costing 72 cents would be unit priced at $0.18 per ounce, $2.88 per pound.

Write a program to read in

a) An integer representing a given number of pounds (for example, 0)

b) An integer representing a given number of ounces (for example, 4)

c) An integer representing a given price in dollars and cents, where the last two digits give the cents amount (for example, 72 or 072)

and print

a) The unit price per ounce (for example, 18)

b) The unit price per pound (for example, 288).

For simplicity, the unit prices may be given as the integer number of cents per ounce and cents per pound.

4.4   A Very Simple Calculation

Write a program to read in three integers (whole numbers) and print their sum and their average. The numbers should be allowed to have one or more spaces between them. The output should be preceded by the message

THE SUM AND AVERAGE ARE:

For example, with an input of

24   5   0

the output should be

THE SUM AND AVERAGE ARE: 29   14.5

Finally, run your program with input values that are not well-formed number, for example,

2H   5   1.1

or

2,345   3,012   167

Do you think your computer treated you reasonably?

4.5   Metric Conversion

Write a program to convert miles per hour into kilometers per hour. The input value should be the number of miles per hour expressed as a whole number and the corresponding number of kilometers per hour expressed as a whole number. For example, with the input

55

representing 55 miles per hour, the output should be something like

55 MILES PER HOUR = 88 KILOMETERS PER HOUR

There are 1.609 kilometers in each mile.

Note: In order to calculate the number of kilometers per hour exactly, you will have to use real arithmetic. As mentioned earlier, in Pascal, an integer can be converted to a real number by assigning it to a real variable, as in

RealMPH := IntMPH

The calculated number of kilometers per hour (a real number) can be converted to an integer by using the predefined function Trunc, as in

IntKMPH := Trunc(RealMPH * 1.609)

Not very symmetrical, is it?

4.6 B or Better
Assume that an exam has 28 questions. In order to receive a grade of B, at least 80 percent of the questions must be answered correctly. Write a program to determine how many questions you can miss and still earn at least a B.

4.7 Pythagorean Theorem
The Pythagorean theorem states that the square of the hypotenuse of a right triangle is equal to the sum of the squares of the other two sides. Write a program to read the lengths of the two legs and print the length of the hypotenuse.

4.8 Entering a Program
Using the formula

$$A = PI * r * r$$

write a program to read the radius of a circle, draw the circle on the drawing screen, and write the calculated area under the circle. The radius is to be entered in inches and converted to pixels within the program.

4.9 A Price Calculation
Floor covering is sometimes sold by the running foot. The one we wish to purchase comes in a 12 foot roll and costs $11.29 per running foot. There

is a delivery charge of 19 cents per pound, and the carpet weighs 3 pounds per running foot.

For this program, assume a room with a width between 9 feet and 12 feet; the carpet for this room would be cut from a 12 foot roll. Write a program that reads the length of the room and calculates the total price of the delivered carpeting.

4.10   Ordering

Personal computers are quite often called upon to act as handy printing machines, reformatting data into a more useful form. Your problem this time is to enter the following three numbers

    34.60   91.25   101.05

and print them in a chart like the following:

Number	Value
1	34.60
2	91.25
3	101.05

Prelude to Choices

"Y OU see, Watson," remarked Sherlock Holmes, as we sat together one frosty evening considering a recent report that the missing Baroness of Whitlesey had been seen in Vienna, "I attribute much of my professional success to the fact that I regard detection as a science as well as an art; and unlike most of my colleagues, I have never regarded it as drudgery. Detection takes its purest form as deductive reasoning and is comparable only to mathematics in its elegance and intellectual challenge. For this reason, the Analytical Engine, based as it is upon mathematical principles, has seemed a most attractive tool for my labours."

"What is your next plan for using the Engine?" I asked, sensing that my friend was ready to launch some new idea.

"My plan, Watson, is to use this remarkable Engine as a storehouse for some of the minutiae that clutter my mind. Take for instance my monograph, 'Upon the Distinction Between the Ashes of the Various Tobaccos,'" he said, gesturing to a dusty volume that lay before us on the table.

"In this treatise I have described and classified a hundred and forty types of cigarette, cigar, and pipe tobaccos, with coloured plates illustrating the various sorts of ashes. Although I took a special interest in retaining such details as, say, the exact appearance of MacDuffy versus Lunkah cigar ash, most investigators would lack the patience to do so; and I cannot say I blame them.

"The brain is after all like an attic of vast but limited capacity that we fill with whatever matter we deem important for the future. Since the walls of this attic cannot be stretched like India rubber, as we amass more and more information some of the old is jostled out to make room for the new. It would be helpful if we had a device to remember vast quantities of data for us and to supply us with information pertaining to these data whenever we so request. I claim, Watson, that the Analytical Engine is wonderfully suited to this task.

"As an exercise to test my idea, I have prepared a table listing the properties of the ten most commonly smoked cigars in London."

Holmes's table of ash properties is given here.

CIGAR TYPE	TEXTURE	COLOUR	PARTICLES	NICOTINE
Espanada	Caked	Dark	No	++
Heritage	Flaky	Light Grey	No	++
Latino	Varied	Dark	Yes	+
Londoner	Caked	Brown Tint	No	++
Lunkah	Granular	Dark Grey	No	++
MacDuffy	Flaky	Dark Grey	No	++
Old Wood	Varied	Brown Tint	Varied	+++
Top Hat	Caked	Dark Grey	No	++
Trichinopoly	Flaky	Dark	No	++
West Country	Flaky	Light Grey	No	++

While I studied his document, Holmes walked over to the fire and took down a small brass box from the mantlepiece. This he opened, and quietly he smelled the single cigar which it contained.

"I should like to design a programme that would identify the cigars bearing certain specified ash characteristics. Moreover, if the specified characteristics did not match any of these ten cigars, the Engine should indicate this so that I could then research the matter myself."

"I take it, then, that there are particular characteristics of this programme that are of interest?" I queried, for I still had little experience in constructing programmes.

"Precisely, Watson," replied my friend. "The central issue is the need to make decisions and take appropriate actions as the consequence of a given condition. Of course, this is a very common problem in the work of detection.

"There are any number of combinations we can make of the various conditions. We may specify that a certain action be taken under a certain set of circumstances, such as

> if texture is caked then
> — *perform action A*

Another situation that arises is that of two possible actions, with the choice between them depending upon a single condition. For instance,

> if texture is caked then
> — *perform action A*
> else
> — *perform action B*

Finally, we may be faced with a number of possible courses of action, with our choice depending upon one of several conditions:

"He smelled the single cigar which it contained."

```
if texture is caked then
    — perform action A
else if texture is flaky then
    — perform action B
else if texture is granular then
    — perform action C
else (if none of the conditions above are met)
    — perform action D
```

"I understand, Holmes, but how do you solve this problem in terms comprehensible to the Analytical Engine?"

"Simple, Watson," said Holmes. "All we must do is organize the decisions in the form of a consistent algorithm and then translate the algorithm into the machine's language. Here I have listed all the choices of properties for a cigar. Notice that the normal cigar has no particles and has a nicotine content marked with two plus signs. Furthermore, there are two basic kinds of cigar ash. There is Stock 1, which is flaky or caked, and Stock 2, whose characteristics are fluffy or granular."

Holmes's ash classification is reproduced here as follows:

Colour	Dark, Dark Grey, Light Grey, Brown Tint
Texture	Flaky, Caked, Granular, Fluffy
Particles	No, Yes
Nicotine	+, ++, +++
Normal Strength	++, no particles
Stock 1 Cigar	Flaky or Caked
Stock 2 Cigar	Granular or Fluffy

"My strategy," Holmes continued, "is to command the Engine to read a list of properties pertaining to cigar ash. The programme will then determine whether the cigar is of normal strength and whether it is of Stock 1 or Stock 2. With these questions settled, it will then be able to determine whether the cigar is one of the ten types listed in the table. If so, it will name the cigar; if not, it will report this and merely indicate the cigar's strength or class."

Holmes then produced his algorithm, which is given in Fig. 5.1. It seemed entirely clear, and I followed his logic almost instantly.

"They say, Watson, that genius is an infinite capacity for taking pains. It is a bad definition, but it does apply to programming. What relief the Analytical Engine will bring us!" he remarked. "I propose to devote some years to the composition of a text which shall present the whole art of detection and the special uses of the Analytical Engine into a single volume."

"A massive undertaking," I replied. "Surely, Holmes, this will be your greatest contribution to science and humanity."

A flush of colour sprang to my companion's cheeks, and he bowed slightly, like the master dramatist who receives the homage of his audience. The same singularly proud and reserved nature that turned away with disdain from popular notoriety was capable of being moved to its depths by spontaneous wonder and praise from a friend.

As for our study of cigar ash, Holmes applied the programme shown in Fig. 5.2 to test the Engine's performance against his own powers. I have had no keener pleasure than in following Sherlock Holmes in his professional investigations and in admiring his rapid deductions—as swift as intuitions, yet always founded on the same logical basis on which the Engine operated—with which he unravelled the many problems that were submitted to him.

Definitions:
    Texture   :   a texture of ash
    Colour   :   a colour of ash
    Particles :   an indication of particles
    Nicotine :   a result of a nicotine test
    Stock   :   a class of cigar
    Normality :   an indication of particles and nicotine
Alg·ithm:
   Read Texture, Colour, Particles, Nicotine
   If Texture = Flaky or Texture = Caked then
     set Stock to 1
   else
     set Stock to 2
   If Nicotine = ++ and Particles = No then
     set Normality to Normal
   else
     set Normality to Abnormal
   If Normality = Normal and Stock = 1 then
     if Colour = Dark and Texture = Flaky then
       write 'CIGAR IS A TRICHINOPOLY'
     else if Colour = Dark and Texture = Caked then
       write 'CIGAR IS AN ESPANADA'
     else if Colour = DarkGrey and Texture = Flaky then
       write 'CIGAR IS A MACDUFFY'
     else if Colour = DarkGrey and Texture = Caked then
       write 'CIGAR IS A TOP HAT'
     else if Colour = LightGrey and Texture = Flaky then
       write 'CIGAR IS A HERITAGE'
     else if Colour = BrownTint and Texture = Caked then
       write 'CIGAR IS A LONDONER'
     else
       write '***UNIDENTIFIED NORMAL CIGAR OF STOCK 1'
   If Normality = Normal and Stock = 2 then
     if Colour = DarkGrey and Texture = Granular then
       write 'CIGAR IS A LUNKAH'
     else if Colour = LightGrey and Texture = Fluffy then
       write 'CIGAR IS A WEST COUNTRY'
     else
       write '***UNIDENTIFIED NORMAL CIGAR OF STOCK 2'
   It Normality = Abnormal then
     if Colour = BrownTint and Nicotine = +++ then
       write 'CIGAR IS AN OLD WOOD'
     else if Colour = Dark and Nicotine = + and Particles = Yes then
       write 'CIGAR IS A LATINO'
     else
       write '***UNIDENTIFIED ABNORMAL CIGAR'

Figure 5.1 ● Holmes's algorithm to identify cigar ash

Figure 5.2 ● Program
IdentifyCigar

```
program IdentifyCigar;
{ -- This program reads in four properties of cigar ash. }
{ -- The properties are coded as numbers. }
{ -- The program attempts to identify the ash according to the }
{ -- properties, and prints a message giving its findings. }
   var
      Texture, Colour, Particles, Nicotine, Normality : string[9];
      Stock : Integer;
begin
   Read(Texture, Colour, Particles, Nicotine);
   if (Texture = 'Flaky') or (Texture = 'Caked') then
      Stock := 1
   else
      Stock := 2;
   if (Nicotine = 'Plus2') and (Particles = 'No') then
      Normality := 'Normal'
   else
      Normality := 'Abnormal';
   if (Normality = 'Normal') and (Stock = 1) then
      if (Colour = 'Dark') and (Texture = 'Flaky') then
         Write ('CIGAR IS A TRICHINOPOLY')
      else if (Colour = 'Dark') and (Texture = 'Caked') then
         Write ('CIGAR IS AN ESPANADA')
      else if (Colour = 'DarkGrey') and (Texture = 'Flaky') then
         Write('CIGAR IS A MACDUFFY')
      else if (Colour = 'DarkGrey') and (Texture = 'Caked') then
         Write('CIGAR IS A TOP HAT')
      else if (Colour = 'LightGrey') and (Texture = 'Flaky') then
         Write('CIGAR IS A HERITAGE')
      else if (Colour = 'BrownTint') and (Texture = 'Caked') then
         Write('CIGAR IS A LONDONER')
      else
         Write('***UNIDENTIFIED NORMAL CIGAR OF STOCK 1');
   if (Normality = 'Normal') and (Stock = 2) then
      if (Colour = 'DarkGrey') and (Texture = 'Granular') then
         Write('CIGAR IS A LUNKAH')
      else if (Colour = 'LightGrey') and (Texture = 'Fluffy') then
         Write('CIGAR IS A WEST COUNTRY')
      else
         Write('***UNIDENTIFIED NORMAL CIGAR OF STOCK 2');
   if (Normality = 'Abnormal') then
      if (Colour = 'BrownTint') and (Nicotine = 'Plus3') then
         Write('CIGAR IS AN OLD WOOD')
      else if (Colour = 'Dark') and (Nicotine = 'Plus1') and
              (Particles = 'Yes') then
         Write('CIGAR IS A LATINO')
      else
         Write('***UNIDENTIFIED ABNORMAL CIGAR')
end.
```

Chapter 5

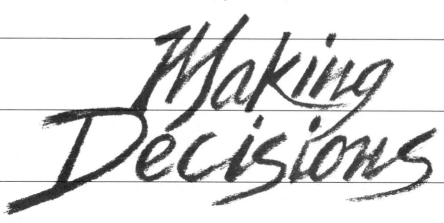

The ability to make decisions is fundamental to programming. It is often necessary to know the result of the next step in order to determine which additional steps are required. Conditional statements provide this option. However, before moving into the area of decision making in Pascal, we pause to make note of a simple but important construct for writing programs.

In previous chapters we have looked at assignment statements as well as statements to read and write data. As you have seen, these statements contain no part that is another statement. In the discussion of decision making to follow, we will encounter new kinds of statements in which a statement may itself contain other statements. In this category we will find, for example, the if statement. Consider the following:

if (Texture = Flaky) **or** (Texture = Caked) **then**
   Stock := 1

This statement, an if statement, contains another statement, an assignment statement. Both the if statement and the assignment statement are considered together as a *single* statement.

    Of course, there are instances where we may want to execute more than one statement after making a decision. This is achieved by means of a *compound* statement. For example, we may write,

if (Texture = Flaky) **or** (Texture = Caked) **then**
  begin
    Stock := 1;

5.1 ● Compound Statements

105

```
        Write('Stock 1 Cigar')
    end
```

A compound statement has the form

```
begin
    statement-1;
    statement-2;
    . . .
    statement-n
end
```

and is itself treated as a single statement. Each statement within the compound statement is executed in sequential order. You will have a great many uses for this simple device as we proceed.

Now let us continue with the means for making decisions in Pascal.

5.2 ● If Statements

The ability to make decisions is fundamental to programming. The basic mechanism for making choices in Pascal is the *if statement*. In its simplest form, there is a condition and one statement, in the following form.

```
if condition then
    statement
```

This statement means

> If the condition is true, execute the given statement; otherwise do nothing.

Normally, an if statement will appear in a sequence of statements. As for any statement, after execution, the next statement is processed. For example,

```
    statement-1;
    if condition then
        statement-2;
    statement-3
```

means

1. Execute statement 1.
2. Execute the if statement; that is, if the condition is true, execute statement 2.
3. Execute statement 3.

Notice here that the if statement is itself considered a single statement. Thus, we may write something like

```
if (Normality = Normal) and (Stock = 1) then
    if (Color = Dark) and (Texture = Flaky) then
        Write('CIGAR IS A TRICHINOPOLY')
```

This should not cause any confusion, for this statement has the following form.

```
if (Normality = Normal) and (Stock = 1) then
    statement
```

In this case the statement following the keyword **then** is itself an if statement.

This ability to include one statement within another has far-reaching possibilities in Pascal. While the basic mechanism is extremely simple, we can produce rather elaborate effects, as in Holmes's program to identify cigar ash.

In the preceding examples, the if statements have a single condition and a single statement. An if statement may also have an **else** part, in the form

```
if condition then
    statement-1
else
    statement-2
```

This simply means

If the condition is true, execute statement 1; otherwise execute statement 2.

For example, we may write,

```
if (Texture = Flaky) or (Texture = Caked) then
    Stock := 1
else
    Stock := 2
```

Here the value of the variable Stock is set to 1 or 2, depending upon the truth or falsity of the condition. As always, after executing the if statement we simply proceed to the following statement.

Finally, we may generalize the ideas just given to include multiple conditions. For example, consider the if statement

```
if (Colour = Dark) and (Texture = Flaky) then
    Write('CIGAR IS A TRICHINOPOLY')
else
    if (Colour = Dark) and (Texture = Caked) then
        Write('CIGAR IS AN ESPANADA')
    else
        Write('*** UNIDENTIFIED NORMAL CIGAR OF STOCK 1')
```

This statement has the form

```
if condition-1 then
   statement-1
else
   if condition-2 then
     statement-2
   else
     statement-3
```

This all means the following:

> If condition 1 is true, execute statement 1;
> If condition 1 is false but condition 2 is true, execute statement 2;
> Otherwise (conditions 1 and 2 are both false), execute statement 3.

Notice here that this statement is really an if statement with an else part, with the same meaning as the if statement given before.

Each of the preceding examples follows the same basic pattern: depending on one or more conditions, a given action takes place. Thus each of the examples falls into one of the following forms:

1. condition   → action A

2. condition   → action A
   else   → action B

3. condition-1 → action A
   condition-2 → action B
   else   → action C

and so on. In all cases, execution continues after the condition-action pairs.

Normally such cascades of condition-action pairs are written in the form:

```
if condition-1 then
   statement-1
else if condition-2 then
   statement-2

   . . .
else
   statement-n
```

For example, we have

```
if (Colour = 'Dark') and (Texture = 'Flaky') then
   Write ('CIGAR IS A TRICHINOPOLY')
else if (Colour = 'Dark') and (Texture = 'Caked') then
   Write ('CIGAR IS AN ESPANADA')
else
   Write ('*** UNIDENTIFIED NORMAL CIGAR OF STOCK 1')
```

This kind of scheme will be used throughout.

Execution of an if statement depends on the truth or falsity of some given condition. We now turn to the rules for writing conditions in Pascal. These rules are analogous to the rules for writing expressions, except that in all cases, evaluation of a condition yields one of the values True or False.

5.3 ● Conditions

The simplest of all conditions is the testing of values to see if they are equal. For example, we may write,

```
if Stock = 1 then
if Texture = 'Flaky' then
if Room[Suspect] = 14 then
if (NumCigars + 1 = MaxNumCigars) then
```

In each of these constructs the condition has the form:

expression-1 = expression-2

These conditions bring up two general rules in Pascal.

1. A condition always evaluates to True or False.

2. The type of the result, True or False, is said to be of type Boolean.

Thus just as we may say the expression

NumCigars + 1

has a numeric value and its type is Integer, we say that the condition

Texture = 'Flaky'

has a value that is either True or False and is of type Boolean. The term Boolean is named after George Boole, the English mathematician who developed symbolic logic.

Testing for the equality of two values is not the only operation we can perform in conditions. Table 5.1 lists several other operators that can be used in forming conditions. For example, to see if one value is less than or equal to another, we may write,

NumCigars <= 10

which tests to see if the value of NumCigars is less than or equal to 10.

The operator <> appears particularly strange. This is the operator for testing for inequality. Thus, while you might be tempted to say,

if Suspect ≠ ColWoodley then   { Illegal! }

which looks perfectly logical, you can not. Instead you have to write,

if Suspect <> ColWoodley **then**   { Legal }

Table 5.1 ● Operators for Writing Conditions

Relational Operators

Operator	Operation	Type of Operands	Type of Result
<>	equality and inequality	Integer, Real, String	Boolean
< <= > >=	ordering	Integer, Real, String	Boolean
in	membership	Left: Integer, Real, String Right: Must be compatible with Left.	Boolean

Logical Operators

Operator	Operation	Type of Operands	Type of Result
not	negation	Boolean	Boolean
end	conjunction	Boolean	Boolean
or	disjunction	Boolean	Boolean

The rationale here is that a $<$ followed by a $>$ stands for "less than or greater than" or "not equal." So much for that.

The operator **in** deserves a special note. This operator allows us to test whether a value is one of a range of values. For example, instead of writing,

if (NumCigars $>=$ 1) **and** (NumCigars $<=$ 10) **then**

we may write,

if NumCigars **in** [1..10] **then**

The notation

[1..10]

stands for the range of values between 1 and 10.

The condition given in

if (NumCigars $>=$ 1) **and** (NumCigars $<=$ 10) **then**

brings up the ability to write compound conditions. A *compound condition* consists of a sequence of relational expressions, separated by the logical operators shown in Table 5.1. For example, we may have the conditions:

(Texture = Flaky) **or** (Texture = Caked)

(Stock = 1) **and** (Normality = Normal)
not (Suspect = ColWoodley)

This use of logical operators is quite natural and should present no problems.

Compound conditions may involve arithmetic operators, relational operators, and logical operators. To write such conditions, the evaluation rules given in the previous chapter need expanding in order to include our new operators. In particular, operators are applied in the following order.

1. **not**
2. * / **div mod and**
3. + − **or**
4. = <> < > <= >= **in**

That is, the operator **not** is applied before the five operators *, /, **div, mod**, and **and**. Then come the three operators +, −, **or**, and so forth.

For example, just as

A + B * C

is equivalent to

A + (B * C)

so too,

A + B = C + D

is equivalent to

(A + B) = (C + D)

Although these examples appear innocent enough, the rules have a few anomalies that you must watch out for. For example, you *cannot* write

if Texture = 'Flaky' **or** Texture = 'Caked' **then**   { Watch Out }

or

if A < B **and** C < D **then**   { Again, trouble }

The reason is that the logical operators **and** and **or** are applied *before* the relational operators. To write such expressions you have to use parentheses, as in

if (Texture = Flaky) **or** (Texture = Caked) **then**
if (A < B) **and** (C < D) **then**

All of this means that you have to be a bit careful in writing complex conditions. One general rule should always help you.

• When in doubt, use parentheses.

If you are still unsure of the rules for writing a condition, you can always refer to Appendix B, which summarizes the grammatical rules for writing Pascal programs.

5.4 • Case Statements

The if statement presented in the preceding section provides a logical method for making decisions based on the truth or falsity of one or more conditions. The *case statement* provides a similar ability for making decisions, but here the action taken depends on the value of an expression.

For example, consider the case statement:

```
case Day of
    1 :  — what to do if Day = 1;
    2 :  — what to do if Day = 2;
    3 :  — what to do if Day = 3;
    4 :  — what to do if Day = 4;
    5 :  — what to do if Day = 5;
    6 :  — what to do if Day = 6;
    7 :  — what to do if Day = 7
end
```

Here we assume the integer variable Day represents the days of the week and thus can take on one of seven values. Each alternative in the case statement determines what to do for a given value of the variable Day. The values given before each colon (:) are called case labels, and must correspond to the possible values of the variable given after the keyword **case.** After each colon, you must give a statement describing the action to be taken when the value of the variable is equal to the corresponding case label.

For example, we may write,

```
case Day of
    1 :  Write('Today is Monday, start on a new case');
    2 :  Write('Tuesday, keep working');
    3 :  Write('Wednesday, take a break');
    4 :  Write('Thursday, see the new client');
    5 :  Write('Friday, summarize the facts');
    6 :  Write('Saturday, try something new');
    7 :  Write('Sunday, take a complete rest')
end
```

Notice here that case labels are given for every possible value of Day. It is not always necessary to cover every individual possibility. An otherwise clause can be added following the list of case alternatives, as in

```
case Day of
   1 :
      Write('Today is Monday, start on a new case');
   6 :
      Write('Today is Saturday, try something new');
   7 :
      Write('Sunday, take a complete rest');
   otherwise
      Write('continue working')
end.
```

If there is no otherwise clause and an unlisted value for the variable is encountered, the program run stops and an error message is issued.

There are a few other things one should know about case statements. First, any statement, including a compound statement, can be used as an alternative. Second, several labels can prefix an alternative. Thus we could write the case alternatives

```
   1 :
      if Date = Holiday then
         Write('Today is a holiday')
      else
         Write('Monday, start on a new case');
```

in which the action is an if statement, or write

```
   2 :
      begin
         Write('Tuesday, prepare the clues');
         Write('and investigate alternatives')
      end;
```

in which the action is a compound statement, or

```
   6,7 :
      Write('Take a long break')
```

in which two alternatives are combined. We can even write,

```
   3 :
      ;
```

to do nothing! This wild-looking alternative is called an *empty statement.* It would look better if we added a comment as

```
   3 :
      ; { do nothing }
```

This may look strange, but sometimes it is just what the programmer wants to do.

5.5 ○ Practice

Conditional Statements

The program in Fig. 5.3 is just about useless; nonetheless, it is simple to understand. See if you can find any errors.

The program GetMaximum is quite straightforward. Actually, it does not contain any errors; it runs nicely just as it is. The first two values are compared and the greater of the two assigned to MaximumValue, which is then compared with the third value. If the third value is greater, it is assigned to MaximumValue; otherwise, the value of MaximumValue remains unchanged. Finally, the actual value associated with MaximumValue is printed.

On many occasions you will look at a program and it will seem just fine. But when you examine the program carefully, you may discover many errors. The program in Fig. 5.4, for instance, contains several errors. Find the errors and make whatever changes are required to make the program work correctly. You might start by thinking of a nautical time for which the program in Fig. 5.3 gives the wrong time.

Notice that the first if statement contains three different conditions to be checked. Should any one of these three conditions be evaluated as True, then the entered time would be considered invalid. So far, so good; now we are assured that the given integer will fall within a certain range. The else part of the statement contains another if statement to distinguish whether the given time is in the morning or afternoon. The difficulty lies in the conversion of the hours right after noontime and right after midnight. The times of day when Hours is equal to 0 and 12 must be considered as special cases. For instance, consider the time 12:45 p.m. Time is read in as 1245. Hours gets 12; Minutes gets 45. Since Hours is less than 12, the output is

12 : 45 A.M.

which is incorrect.

The program in Fig. 5.5 is one way of handling the problem. You may choose to write it a little differently.

There are some fine details that you have to watch for when dealing with conditional statements. In the following examples of conditions, several statements about each are given. Determine which statements are true in each case.

1. **if** $(X<10)$ **and** $(Y>2)$ **then**
   a. You don't need the parentheses.
   b. X must be of type Integer.
   c. The result will be the same if 2.0 is used in place of 2.

● ● ●

```
program GetMaximum;
{ -- This program reads in three numbers }
{ -- and outputs the maximum value given. }

    var
        Value1, Value2, Value3, MaximumValue : Integer;
begin
    Read(Value1, Value2, Value3);
    if(Value1 > Value2) then
        MaximumValue := Value1
    else
        MaximumValue := Value2;
    if(Value3 > MaximumValue) then
        MaximumValue := Value3;

    Write(MaximumValue)
end.
```

Figure 5.3 ● Program GetMaximum

```
program TimeConversion;
{ -- This program reads an integer value representing }
{ -- a nautical time, e.g. 1420, and prints the corresponding }
{ -- value in day-to-day notation, e.g. 2:20 p.m. }

    var
        Time, Hours, Minutes : Integer;
begin
    Read(Time);
    Hours := Time div 100;
    Minutes := Time mod 100;
    if (Time < 0) or (Hours > 24) or (Minutes > 60) then
        Write('NO SUCH TIME FOR ', Time)
    else if (Hours < 13) then
        Write(Hours, ':', Minutes : 2, 'A.M.')
    else
        Write(Hours – 12, ':', Minutes : 2, 'P.M.')
end.
```

Figure 5.4 ● Program TimeConversion

```
program TimeConversion;
{ -- This program reads an integer value representing }
{ -- a nautical time, e.g. 1420, and prints the corresponding }
{ -- value in day-to-day notation, e.g. 2:20 p.m. }

    var
        Time, Hours, Minutes : Integer;
```

Figure 5.5 ● Program TimeConversion

Fig. 5.5 continued

```
begin
  Read(Time);
  Hours := Time div 100;
  Minutes := Time mod 100;
  if (Time < 0) or (Hours > 24) or (Minutes > 60) then
    Write('NO SUCH TIME FOR ', Time)
  else if (Hours = 0) then
    Write('12:', Minutes : 2, 'A.M.')
  else if (Hours in [1..11]) then
    Write(Hours, ':', Minutes : 2, 'A.M.')
  else if (Hours = 12) then
    Write(Hours, ':', Minutes : 2, 'P.M.')
  else
    Write(Hours – 12, ':', Minutes : 2, 'P.M.')
end.
```

Consider how the example would be evaluated if the parentheses were omitted. And is evaluated before the relational operators < and >. We might as well have written

if X < (10 **and** Y) > 2

which makes no sense. When in doubt, use parentheses.

Real numbers can be compared with either real-type numbers or integer-type numbers. However, care must be taken to know exactly what is being compared. Before the comparison is made, both numbers are converted internally to extended numbers. An extended number is represented to 19 or 20 decimal places. An integer is represented with only zeros in the decimal places. When a real number with 7 or 8 decimal places is converted to extended, the extra places are also filled with zeros. A real number with only zeros in its decimal part can be equal to an integer.

Here is another example to consider.

2. **if** Round(X) < 1.0 **then**

    a. X can be of type integer.

    b. If the value of X is 0.5, the comparison will be true.

    c. It would be better to use 1 instead of 1.0.

● ● ●

The function Round is used to round a real number to the nearest integer. X can be an integer, but if it is, the function does not really do anything; it simply returns the same value it is given.

When a number to be rounded is exactly between two whole numbers, as is 0.5, the number with the higher absolute value is chosen; therefore, 0.5 is rounded to 1. This results in the comparison being judged False, since 1 is not less than 1.0.

Consistency is important in programming; therefore, since the rounding function produces an integer number, it is better to use 1 than 1.0.

Let's go to another example.

3. if I*J + 4*K = 6*K + 2 then
   a. You can replace the condition with,
      I*J = 2*K + 2
      and the result will be exactly the same.
   b. You can replace 4*k with 4.0*K and the result will be exactly the same.
   c. The program from which this is taken is probably hard to read.

The two expressions given are identical as far as value goes. In the overall program, there may be a preference for one or the other in order to make the program more readable. Since single letters are used as identifiers, we have no way of knowing what kind of information we are dealing with here.

Replacing 4*K with 4.0*K will have no effect on the result. Here is one more example.

4. **if** (A < 2) **or** (B < –2) **and** (X < 2) **or** (Y < 2) **then**
   a. The condition is true if the values for A, B, X, and Y are 1, 3, 5, and 4, respectively.
   b. The condition has the same effect as
      ((A < 2) or (B < 2)) and ((X < 2) or (Y < 2))
   c. The condition has the same effect as
      (A < 2) and (X < 2) or (B < 2) or (Y < 2)
      That is, rearranging the terms has no net effect.
   d. An error will always result if Y has not been assigned a value.

When in doubt about how an expression will be evaluated, add parentheses to show how the computer will read the expression. **And** is evaluated before **or**; therefore, the expression in example 4 is evaluated as

$$(A < 2) \text{ or } ((B < 2) \text{ and } (X < 2)) \text{ or } (Y < 2)$$

There are three situations here that will result in the condition being evaluated as True. Either A is less than 2, or B and X are both less than 2, or Y is less than 2. When the value of A is 1, the condition is true.

The parentheses shown in statement 4.b change the meaning completely. In order for the result to be evaluated as True, there would have to be two values less than 2; either A or B must be less than 2, and either X or Y must be less than 2.

Adding the correct parentheses to statement 4.c gives

if $((A < 2)$ **and** $(X < 2))$ **or** $(B < 2)$ **or** $(Y < 2)$ **then**

which gives three possibilities: either A and X are both less than 2, or B is less than 2, or Y is less than 2.

As we have said before: when in doubt, use parentheses.

As for statement 4.d, it is asking for trouble to use a variable in an expression when no value has been assigned to it.

Fill in the Blanks

1. A compound statement is bracketed by the words _____ and _____.

2. When comparing two values, inequality is represented by the symbol _____.

3. Compound conditions may involve arithmetic operators, logical operators, and _____ operators.

4. To be sure that complex conditions are evaluated in the correct order, you should add _____.

5. In a case statement, the values given before each colon are called _____.

6. In addition to the stated alternative cases, a case statement can include an _____ clause.

7. A semicolon immediately following the colon in a case alternative, as in

    case Month **of**
       July: ;

means _____.

8. An if statement must also include the word _____.

A compound statement is bracketed by the words BEGIN and END. When comparing two values, inequality is represented by the symbol <>. Compound conditions may involve arithmetic operators, logical operators, and RELATIONAL operators. To be sure that complex conditions are evaluated in the correct order, you should add PARENTHESES. In a case statement, the values given before each colon are called CASE LABELS. In addition to the stated alternative cases, a case statement can include an OTHERWISE clause. A semicolon immediately following the colon in a case alternative, as in

case Month **of**
  July: ;

means DO NOTHING. An if statement must also include the word **THEN**.

5.6 ○

5.1   Secret Numbers: Version 2

This exercise is motivated by automatic teller machines (ATM's), where customers are required to enter a secret code. This is so that someone else does not use your bank card to make withdrawals. In this exercise your program knows your secret code, which you can specify with a constant declaration; for example,

const
  SecretCode = 17;

Your program is to ask the user to enter the secret code. If the user enters the correct code, the computer prints an acceptance message, such as

THANK YOU. HOW CAN WE HELP YOU?

If the code is incorrect, the computer prints a message such as

NO DICE!

You may choose the messages, but the user gets only one chance to guess the code.

5.2   Odd or Even

Many people are afraid of computers. This may, in part, be because they think computers know too much. But you know that the only things a computer knows are what programmers put into their programs.

This is an easy exercise. Write a program that knows about odd and even numbers. The input will be an integer number, say 12 or 271. The output will be a message telling whether the number is odd or even.

Do not make use of the predefined function Odd; pretend it doesn't exist.

5.3   A Change Making Machine

In a certain subway station there is a machine that accepts five-dollar bills and gives the change in coins for each of four possible fares. The fares $0.65, $1.10, $1.75, and $2.10 are indicated by pressing buttons 1 through 4.

Write a program to read in one of the integers 1 through 4 and print the number of each coin given in change on a five-dollar bill. The coins are half-dollars, quarters, dimes, and nickels. For each amount of change, the minimum number of coins is to be used. For example, if your input is

   3

the program should print something like

   6   HALF DOLLARS
   1   QUARTER

You may want to keep an eye on singular (one coin) versus plural (more than one coin).

5.4   Leap Year

Definition: A leap year is a year that is exactly divisible by 4, except centenary years that are not exactly divisible by 400. That's what the dictionary says.

Well, this means that 1948 and 2000 are leap years, but 1900 is not. Write a program to read in an integer and print a message indicating whether the integer denotes a leap year.

5.5   Can You Make a Triangle?

Suppose you had three sticks whose lengths were 2 feet, 3 feet, and 6 feet. You couldn't make a triangle with them. However, if you cut 2 feet off of the long stick, you could.

Three sticks make a triangle if the sum of each pair of lengths is larger than the third. Write a program to read in three numbers and print a message indicating whether they make a triangle.

5.6   Normalized Scoring

In a ten-question, True-or-False quiz, the scores are normalized. That is, the net score is equal to the number of correct responses minus the number of incorrect responses. An unanswered question is ignored in the scoring. Thus with eight out of ten correct responses, one incorrect response and one unanswered question, the net score is 7.

Furthermore, the grade associated with the net score is computed by the following table.

Net Score	Grade
8 – 10	A
6 – 7	B
4 – 5	C
2 – 3	D

A score of 1 or lower results in a grade of F.

Write a program to read in the number of correct and incorrect responses and print the final grade.

Note: You may wish to outguess the problem definition. A case statement may be useful.

5.7   Ordering
Comparing values is one task that can be done easily by computer. This problem assumes that five numbers are to be entered, but only the largest is to be printed out. Write the program and use the following numbers as input.

    14   3   3246   289   1243

5.8   Secret Numbers: Version 3
In this exercise, you are to do the same thing as in Exercise 5.1, except that the customer gets three chances to enter the proper code. You are not allowed to jump ahead here and use loops. The program must be written without loops. Watch out for this exercise; it is harder than it appears.

5.9   Range Check
When long lists of figures are entered into a computer, there is always the possibility of operator error in the entering of the figures. Therefore, accuracy checks are often built into programs. One way of checking for accuracy is to be sure that the entered figure falls into the range that is allowable for the value.

Let us assume that a list of three-digit numbers are to be entered. The numbers are expected to be no lower than 256 and no higher than 516. Write a program to check each value entered and to print a message indicating any entry that is unacceptable.

5.10   Sale Price
Competition has forced some stores into giving an "instant rebate" on selected items. In certain states, a sales tax must be paid on the original price. You are to write a program which will calculate the final price of the item including the sales tax. The program will read the item number and the ticket price. It will print the price less rebate, the tax (figured on the ticket price), and the total due.

To determine the amount of the rebate, the following information is used.

   a) Item numbers consist of six digits.
   b) All items starting with 30 receive a $1.00 rebate.
   c) All items between 203000 and 203049 receive a $3.00 rebate.
   d) All items ending with 99 receive a 50 cent rebate.

Prelude to Repetition

The Adventure of Clergyman Peter

W HAT do you make of this, Watson?" asked Holmes, as he tossed a small telegram in my direction. It read:

Oxford

Must meet with you on a temporal matter of grave concern Will arrive by one o'clock today.

Peter Cowesworthy

"A temporal matter," I replied, studying the message. "I wonder what he could mean by that. I am inclined to think that the man wants your help."

"It's just after twelve now," replied Holmes. "I would say, Watson, that a matter grave enough to carry our mysterious cleric all the way from Oxford to seek my services is more of a corporeal concern than one of the spirit. I should certainly hope that my own little practice is not degenerating into an agency for clergymen to consult me concerning their next sermon. In any event, we shall soon know for certain, for I discern two gentlemen and our landlady ascending the stair."

As he spoke there came a knock on the door, after which Mrs. Hudson admitted two visitors. The elder was a man in priestly attire, a short, birdlike man with thinning white hair and nervous eyes peering from behind gold-rimmed spectacles, and obviously in considerable distress. His younger companion was a tall, lanky fellow with a bulging Adam's apple, protruding nose, and thin lips.

"Gentlemen, I am Sherlock Holmes and this is Dr. Watson, who has been my associate and helper in many matters. How may we be of service to you?"

"Oh my," replied the clergyman, somewhat startled. "This is my Deacon, Mr. Huxtable Penwether."

"Ah, yes, Mr. Penwether, I perceive that you have recently journeyed from the Midlands," observed Holmes.

"Clergyman Peter Cowesworthy."

"Oh, no, you are mistaken, sir," he said. "I have been in London this past week, on errands for the rector."

"Indeed, he has hardly been out of my sight, Mr. Holmes," observed the clergyman.

"Yes, of course," replied Holmes, as he busied himself by filling his pipe. "Well, as Watson can attest, my deductions occasionally miss their mark." With that Holmes bade our visitors over to the basket-chair and armchair beside the empty fireplace.

The clergyman had hardly settled in his chair when abruptly he sprang to his feet and exclaimed, "Mr. Holmes, if your deductions should fail in this matter we must abandon all hope! You are the only man in the whole of England who can help us. The Mazarin Bible has vanished!" With his exclamation concluded, Cowesworthy sank back into his chair.

"Yes, the Mazarin Bible," replied Holmes, "a vellum edition, is it not, a rare Schoeffer type with hand-coloured illuminations? It is a devastating loss, indeed."

Sherlock Holmes had an almost hypnotic power when he wished, and he was an accomplished master at the art of putting a humble client at his ease.

"It was taken from your rooms?" he asked.

"Often it is in my rooms, but I bring it into the church from time to time to inspire the parishioners. It was there last Sunday, but hidden carefully. No one could have known where."

"Rector, I will endeavour to assist you. Please rest assured that Watson and I will do everything within our power to recover your Mazarin Bible. Where are you staying in London, so that we may contact you and report developments as our investigation proceeds?" asked Holmes.

"We have taken two rooms at Anderson's Hotel in Fleet Street."

The next remark astonished me, for Sherlock Holmes was the least romantic of men.

"I commend a walk in Regent's Park to you. It should prove a tonic to your strain, especially on a day as fresh as this one."

When they were gone, Holmes turned to me and said, "Come quickly, Watson, we must get to Anderson's and search Penwether's room. He was surely lying. The discoloration on his boots clearly places him in Birmingham within the past few days."

We proceeded at once to Fleet Street where a sovereign for the hall porter led us quickly to Penwether's door. "I suppose that I am committing a felony," commented Holmes, as he forced the lock, "but it is just possible that I am saving a soul. There we are," he said, pushing open the door. "I don't mind confessing that I have always thought I would make a highly efficient criminal. It is certainly fortunate for society that I have chosen otherwise."

Inside the room no Bible could be found, but the missing volume did not appear to be my companion's chief concern as he occupied himself studying Penwether's soiled clothing.

Back in our rooms at Baker Street, Holmes took me deeper into his confidence.

"An excellent case for the Analytical Engine, Watson. We know that Penwether was in Birmingham and journeyed to London in a total time of four hours. Oxford is on the route, and the fastest transportation from the station there to Cowesworthy's rooms would take half an hour each way. Could Penwether have journeyed from Birmingham to London in four hours with an hour or more in Oxford?"

"But how do you know it took four hours?" I asked.

"His collar and shirt bore the grime of a long journey," said Holmes. "Allowing for an hour stop at Oxford, the amount of railway grime on his cuffs would suggest a four-hour journey. Assuming that this is the case, what do you think of our friend not taking a first-class carriage, a man of his standing?"

"Because he feared being recognised by some fellow traveller?" I suggested.

"Precisely, Watson," he replied. "Now, here I have the timetables for all of London's main-line stations, and I have arranged these in a form that the Analytical Engine can read directly."

Holmes handed me a sheet of paper to which the stations for the Birmingham-to-London timetable had been copied. As examples it had

BI   Birmingham
WA   Warwick
OX   Oxford

I nodded my understanding.

"Now," continued Holmes, "we enter the tables into the Engine according to this organized scheme. Look here and you will see how the stations and times are encoded. The first entry,

Birmingham   5.10

becomes

BI   510

I then studied Holmes's notes and the sample timetable, which are sketched in Table 6.1.

"Now as you recall, our intent is to see whether it is possible to make a four-hour journey from Birmingham to London with an hour's stop in Oxford. To determine this myself, I would carefully examine the schedule for each train, searching through the timetable until I came to Oxford. I would then search for the next train to see if it makes a connection in an hour or more. And even if I found such a train, I would still have to discover how long it took to reach London and so have the length of the total journey. This is a tedious procedure involving much examination and repetitious calculation. Far better to let the Analytical Engine handle it.

"What I want as output is a table where each train is identified by a number, the length of time for a connection at Oxford to the next train, and the total journey time."

A sample sketch of Holmes's output table is given here:

DEPARTING TRAIN	OXFORD CONNECTION	TOTAL JOURNEY
1	255	535
2	50	345

Birmingham to London times, stopping at Oxford

Table 6.1 • Sample Timetable and Input Representation

I. Sample timetable for two Birmingham-to-London trains:
A — means no stop for the given train:

STATION	TRAIN 1	TRAIN 2
Birmingham	5.10	8.05
Warwick	5.30	8.25
Stratford	5.45	8.55
Chipping Norton	6.15	—
Oxford	6.25	9.20
Didcot	6.40	—
Goring	6.55	—
Reading	7.15	10.05
Maidenhead	—	—
London	7.55	10.45

II. City codes:

BI	Birmingham	DI	Didcot
WA	Warwick	GO	Goring
ST	Stratford	RE	Reading
CN	Chipping Norton	MA	Maidenhead
OX	Oxford	LO	London

III. Sample input, with the entries for train 1:

BI	5.10	WA	5.30	ST	5.45	CN	6.15	OX	6.25
DI	6.40	GO	6.55	RE	7.15	MA	—	LO	7.55

"It has never been my habit to hide any of my methods from you, Watson," Holmes continued. "If you will permit me there are some points here that may interest you."

"Proceed, my dear Holmes."

He paused a moment. "What we need, Watson, is a way to tell the Engine to repeat the same sort of calculation over and over again. As you may remember, such repeated calculations are called *loops*. A loop must continue until the answer has been found or until some other condition has been met. Two things are needed: a means of instructing the Engine to perform a series of calculations repetitively and a means of controlling the number of repetitions."

"I say, Holmes, without the second point you would be in much the same situation as the sorcerer's apprentice who knew the magical spell to make brooms fetch pails of water, but knew not the incantation which would make them stop."

"Quite so," replied Holmes. "In fact, that is just the sort of thing that often happens to beginning programmers; and, I might add, even to experienced programmers.

"There are two sorts of loops, depending on which strategy of control one employs.

"A *conditional loop* involves a set of instructions that are to be repeated until some condition is met; for example,

As long as City ≠ London, do the following:
    read City, ArrivalTime

or

As long as Murderer = Unknown, do the following:
    get another clue
    examine the clue

As you can see, Watson, when the first loop is completed, the last city read must be London. Similarly, when the second loop is completed, the identity of our murderer is no longer a mystery.

"There is also a second sort of loop called a *for loop*, involving a set of instructions that are to be repeated some fixed number of times. As an example we might say,

For each of the next nine trains, do the following:
    read the times of the train
    compute the connection and journey duration

When this loop is completed, nine trains will have been processed."

I thought about this for a moment and then asked how he would keep track of how many times the loop had been repeated.

"Elementary, Watson. We have a variable that is identified with the loop and is automatically incremented each time the loop is repeated. You will see an example of this in a moment.

"Here is a sketch of my algorithm for solving our problem," he said. The sketch ran:

Write the result table headings
Read the times of the first train
For each of the next nine trains, do the following:
    read the times of the train
    compute the connection and journey duration
    print the results
Write the caption for the result table

Holmes's algorithm is shown in Fig. 6.1. I did not follow it immediately. "But Holmes," I queried, "what is the significance of the number 40?"

"There are indeed some subtle points here. Our train times are expressed as decimal numbers. Thus the difference of the two train times,

935 − 625

is 310, which is correct; but

920 − 625

is 295, which is not correct for our purposes. In the second case, the answer should be 255, because there is a 2 hour and 55 minute time difference between 9.20 A.M. and 6.25 A.M. If you look at the algorithm, Watson, you will see that in these cases I have subtracted 40 minutes to correct this difficulty. It is simply a question of doing arithmetic with hours and minutes.

"A second subtlety in the algorithm involves preparing for the next train each time the loop repeats. Thus for the second train, we must subtract the time of the first. For the third train, we subtract the time of the second, and so on. Before dealing with the next train, we must save the times of the train we are presently using. Now, Watson, the algorithm should be quite clear."

It was the next day when he produced the final programme, which I offer as Fig. 6.2.

"Holmes," I remarked. "I deduce from your algorithm and programme that this symbol **mod** must be Pascal's way of calculating the number of minutes in a given train time. This is hardly readable."

"My dear Watson, you are such an ideal student and helpmate, a confederate to whom each new development comes as a perpetual surprise; and your grand gift for scientific enquiry makes you an invaluable companion in these endeavours. Let us run the programme and check the output, shall we?"

I was not completely certain how I was to interpret this remark, but I interrupted him no further as he ran the data through the Engine. He sat back while the Engine worked its calculations, but suddenly sprang up in his chair, taking his pipe in his lips, and bounding like an old hound who hears the view-holloa.

"Yes, indeed," he said. "Our friend Penwether most certainly had the opportunity to betray his superior. Let us see how this evidence sits with him, shall we? For now, it remains a matter between the deacon and his creator. We shall give him a short time to decide whether he cares to discuss this with the police."

But our meeting with the deacon was not to be. Within the hour a visit from the Reverend Cowesworthy brought with it the missing Bible and news of Penwether's confession.

"When one tries to rise above Nature," Holmes commented, "one is liable to fall below it. The highest type of man may revert to criminal means if he leaves the straight road of destiny."

Figure 6.1 • Algorithm for calculating train connections

Definitions:

  City   : a code for a city
  TrainNum: the number of a train
  Connection, Journey: intervals of time

  StartTime,   StopTime,   ArrivalTime,
  NextStartTime, NextStopTime, NextArrivalTime: train times

Algorithm:

  — Set up for first train
  Write the result table headers
  Read City, StartTime
  As long as City ≠ Oxford do the following:
    read City, StopTime
  As long as City ≠ London do the following:
    read City, ArrivalTime

  — Handle each connecting train
  Successively setting TrainNum to 2 through 10, do the following:
    read City, NextStartTime
    as long as City ≠ Oxford do the following:
      read City, NextStopTime
    as long as City ≠ London do the following:
      read City, NextArrivalTime

    set Connection to NextStopTime − StopTime
    set Journey to NextArrivalTime − StartTime

    if minutes of StopTime > minutes of NextStopTime then
      set Connection to Connection − 40
    if minutes of StartTime > minutes of NextArrivalTime then
        set Journey to Journey − 40

    write TrainNum − 1, Connection, Journey

    — Prepare for handling the next train
    set StartTime to NextStartTime
    set StopTime to NextStopTime

  Write the caption for the result table

Figure 6.2 ● Program
TrainTable

```pascal
program TrainTable;
{ -- This program reads in a series of train times }
{ -- on the route from Birmingham to London. }
{ -- The program calculates the total time of a journey from }
{ -- Birmingham to London, assuming a stop at Oxford. }
   const
      Oxford = 'OX';
      London = 'LO';
   var
      City : string[2];
      TrainNum, Connection, Journey : Integer;
      StartTime, StopTime, ArrivalTime : Integer;
      NextStartTime, NextStopTime, NextArrivalTime : Integer;
begin
{ -- Set up for first train }
   WriteLn('DEPARTING  OXFORD     TOTAL');
   WriteLn(' TRAIN    CONNECTION  JOURNEY');
   WriteLn('---------  ----------  ------- ');
   WriteLn;

   Read(City, StartTime);
   while (City <> Oxford) do
      Read(City, StopTime);
   while (City <> London) do
      Read(City, ArrivalTime);
{ -- Handle each connecting train }
   for TrainNum := 2 to 10 do
      begin
         Read(City, NextStartTime);
         while (City <> Oxford) do
            Read(City, NextStopTime);
         while (City <> London) do
            Read(City,NextArrivalTime);

         Connection := NextStopTime - StopTime;
         Journey := NextArrivalTime - StartTime;
         if (StopTime mod 100)>(NextStopTime mod 100) then
            Connection := Connection - 40;
         if (StartTime mod 100)>(NextArrivalTime) mod 100 then
            Journey := Journey - 40;
         WriteLn((TrainNum - 1) : 5, Connection : 13, Journey : 11);
{ -- Prepare for handling the next train }
         StartTime := NextStartTime;
         StopTime := NextStopTime
      end;
   WriteLn;
   WriteLn('BIRMINGHAM TO LONDON TIMES, STOPPING AT OXFORD')
end.
```

Chapter 6

Repeated Calculations

The concept of looping is so central to problem solving on a computer that it is hard to imagine any self-respecting computer program that does not contain at least one loop. Looping, in fact, is similar to many everyday situations, as the following informal statements illustrate.

Duplicate the following pattern eight times.

While the cat is away, let the mice play.

Repeat with each ingredient until the mixture thickens.

Search through the trunk until all items are found.

As long as a king has not been crowned, continue advancing forward.

Each of these statements implies a set of instructions to be obeyed repeatedly until a particular condition is met.

We thus see the two basic characteristics of every loop:

1. It has a *body*: the instructions to be executed repeatedly.

2. It has a *termination condition*: an event that must happen to signal the end of the repetition.

In Pascal there are several forms for expressing loops. The choice of a particular form depends upon the problem at hand. These forms are our next topic.

Perhaps the simplest form of loop in Pascal is embodied in the following example.

6.1 ● While and Repeat Loops

while (City <> London) **do**
    Read(City, ArrivalTime)

The body of this loop consists of the single statement

    Read(City, ArrivalTime)

which is executed repeatedly as long as the condition

    (City <> London)

remains true.

It is important to be precise here, for understanding the meaning of even this simple loop is fundamental to all that follows. The loop just shown is called a *while loop*. When this statement is executed, the following takes place:

1. A test is made to see if the value of the variable City is different from London.
2. If the result of the test is positive, the body of the loop (in this case the Read statement) is executed and the whole process begins again from step 1.
3. Otherwise, the loop is terminated.

The net effect of our simple loop is that cities and arrival times at each city are read in successively until the city happens to be London, at which point execution of the loop is complete.

All while loops are statements of the form

while *condition* **do**
    statement

In particular, each while loop begins with a condition. The condition expresses some fact about our data. Each loop also contains a statement. The statement tells which actions are to be carried out repeatedly. As long as the condition remains true, the statement is executed again. Upon termination of the loop, the condition is known to be false. Notice that if the condition is initially false, the statement in the body of the loop is never executed.

The condition given at the head of the while statement has the same form as those given in an if statement. For example, we may have

while (Murderer = Unknown) **do**
    —*what to do as long as the murderer is unknown*
while (NumCigars < 10) **do**
    —*what to do as long as there are fewer than 10 cigars*
while (Time > 1000) **and** (Time < 1200) **do**
    —*what to do between 10 a.m. and noon*

In all cases, the body of the loop is executed repeatedly as long as the condition remains true.

Obviously, there are many cases where we want to specify several actions in the body of a loop. For this we can use the simple device introduced earlier, the compound statement. For example, we may have

```
while (City <> London) do
    begin
        Read(City, ArrivalTime);
        Write('Another city has been read in')
    end
```

Such loops have the general form:

```
while condition do
    begin
        statement-1;
        statement-2;
        . . .
        statement-n
    end
```

Here all of the statements bracketed by **begin** and **end** are processed repeatedly as long as the condition remains true.

In Pascal, there is a very simple variant of the while loop called a *repeat loop*. This loop is a statement of the form:

```
repeat
    statement-1;
    statement-2;
    . . .
    statement-n
until condition
```

Such a loop is executed as follows:

1. The statements in the body of the loop are executed.
2. If the condition is still not satisfied, the process is repeated again from step 1.
3. Otherwise, the loop is terminated.

Notice here that the condition is tested *after* executing the body of the loop. Notice also that the condition is given the other way around; that is, the body of the loop is executed as long as the condition remains false.

For instance, consider the following statements.

```
repeat
    Read(City, ArrivalTime)
until (City = London)
```

This loop tells us to keep reading in cities and arrival times until we find a city whose value is London. This statement has exactly the same effect as

```
Read(City, ArrivalTime);
while (City <> London) do
    Read(City, ArrivalTime)
```

Here we can readily see that the condition used to control the repetitions of the while loop is stated in just the opposite way from that of the repeat loop.

Notice one important difference between a repeat loop and a while loop. The body of a repeat loop is always executed at least once, for the condition is tested at the end of the loop. For the while loop, since the condition is tested first, the body of the loop may not be executed even once if the condition is initially false. Thus a repeat and a while loop will have the same effect only if the condition given in the while loop is initially true.

6.2 ● For Loops

There is yet another form of loop that you can write in Pascal called a *for loop*. Consider the statement

```
for TrainNum := 2 to 10 do
    begin
        Read(City, NextStartTime);
        . . .
        StopTime := NextStopTime
    end
```

Here we have a series of actions that are to be executed exactly nine times. The actions are specified between the **begin** and **end** of the compound statement. Each time the actions are executed, the variable TrainNum takes on a new value. Its first value is 2, its second value is 3, and so forth, up to 10.

Such loops are handy in cases like this where a sequence of actions is to be executed a fixed number of times. For example, we may have

```
for Month := 1 to 12 do
    —what to do for each month
for Column := (FirstColumn + 1) to (LastColumn − 1) do
    —what to do for all medial columns
```

In general, a for loop has the form:

```
for variable := initial-value to final-value do
    —statement
```

The initial and final values given in the heading of the loop determine the number of times the statement is executed. Notice that the statement can be compound, as in the train example sketched previously.

A word of caution: each loop contains a variable in its heading. This variable is called the *control variable,* and conceptually captures the state of the loop's execution. The initial and final values of the control variable are specified by the expressions. In the statement above, if the initial value were greater than the final value, the statement would not be executed. However, it is possible to use a variable of decreasing value with the following form:

> **for** *variable* := *initial-value* **downto** *final-value* **do**
>   —*statement*

The body of a for loop is executed a fixed number of times, starting with the initial value and continuing up or down to and including the final value. On each iteration, the value of the control variable assumes the corresponding value between initial and final values.

Returning to our train example, the body of the loop is executed 9 times; on each iteration, the value of TrainNum takes on one of the values from 2 through 10.

Two other small points are worth remembering. First, within the body of a for loop you should never assign a new value to the control variable. This would only cause confusion—in fact, if you try to do it, you should get an error message. Second, when the entire loop is completed, the value of the control variable is undefined. This means that if you want to use the variable again, you should explicitly assign it a new value.

Summary

There is no question that, as you progress with programming skill, loops become an important problem-solving tool. Repeated calculations are intrinsic to almost any useful computer problem.

Here's a simple strategy for deciding which kind of loop to use. Whenever you want some actions to be repeated until you arrive at some specified result, use a while or repeat loop; whenever you want certain actions to be repeated only a fixed number of times, use a for loop.

One point of caution: since the statements within a loop can include any statement, it is possible to have loops within loops, nested conditional structures within loops, and vice versa. When situations such as this arise, you have to be extremely careful to make the intent of your program clear.

6.3 ○ Practice

Looping

Figure 6.3 contains a program that makes use of some of the concepts contained in the last two chapters. The program MultipleChoice is a quiz reviewing some of the concepts we have covered so far. A case statement and a conditional statement are contained within the repeat loop.

When the repeat loop is performed, one question and the possible answers are printed, then the user's choice of answers is read and compared with the correct answer. If the choice is correct, "Good" is printed, and 1 point is added to the score. If the answer is not correct, "Oops" is written. Next, the question number is increased by 1.

Each time the loop is repeated, the question number is checked. It is the question number that is used as the case label. Each time through the loop, a different case is selected causing a different question to be printed. Notice that each case contains of a compound statement bracketed by the words **begin** and **end**.

The repeat loop continues until the question number exceeds LastQuestionNum, which is given in the constants declarations. Finally, the score is printed and the program ends.

Figure 6.3 ● Program MultipleChoice

```
program MultipleChoice;
{ -- This program presents a series of multiple choice questions }
{ -- on Pascal. The user's score is reported at conclusion. }
   const
      LasQuestionNum = 10;

   var
      Dummy : string;
      QuestionNum, Score : Integer;
      Choice, CorrectAnswer : Char;
begin
   WriteLn('The following is a multiple choice test in Pascal');
   WriteLn('Enter your choice of answers by typing a letter.');
   Dummy := 'cbebdacbbc';
   QuestionNum := 1;
   Score := 0;

   repeat
      WriteLn;
      case QuestionNum of
         1 :
            begin
               WriteLn('Which of the following words need not always');
               WriteLn('appear in a Pascal program?');
               WriteLn('a. begin    b. program    c. identifier');
               WriteLn('d. none of the above');
            end;
```

Figure 6.3 continued

```
2 :
  begin
    WriteLn('The word "integer" is');
    WriteLn('a. the name of a variable    b. the name of a type');
    WriteLn('c. a keyword');
  end;
3 :
  begin
    WriteLn('Pascal was invented by');
    WriteLn('a. Linus Pauling     b. Blaise Pascal');
    WriteLn('c. IBM Corporation    d. Jimmy Carter');
    WriteLn('e. none of the above');
  end;
4 :
  begin
    WriteLn('If a program requests an integer and you type in');
    WriteLn('the letter "K" the computer')";
    WriteLn('a. stops dead     b. beeps a warning');
    WriteLn('c. waits for an integer');
    WriteLn('d. prints an error message and goes on   e. crashes');
  end;
5 :
  begin
    WriteLn('"B" is a');
    WriteLn('a. character     b. letter    c. character string');
    WriteLn('d. 2 of the above     e. all of the above');
  end;
6 :
  begin
    WriteLn('An "if" statement must contain the keyword');
    WriteLn('a. then     b. else    c. or     d. otherwise');
  end;
7 :
  begin
    WriteLn('Which of the following is not a valid identifier');
    WriteLn('a. Number     b. seventeen    c. 8thRow');
    WriteLn('d. FUNCTION6');
  end;
8 :
  begin
    WriteLn('The body of a "repeat" loop will never be executed');
    WriteLn('if the required condition is not met.');
    WriteLn('a. True     b. False');
  end;
```

Fig. 6.3 continued

```
      9 :
        begin
          WriteLn('Declarations must be located');
          WriteLn('a. right after the word "program"');
          WriteLn('b. before the statement section');
          WriteLn('c. right after the word "begin"');
          WriteLn('d. before they are used in the program');
        end;
     10 :
        begin
          WriteLn('Comments are enclosed by');
          WriteLn('a. { }    b. (* *)    c. a or b');
        end;
   end;
   Write('Your choice:   ');
   ReadLn(Choice);
   CorrectAnswer := Dummy[QuestionNum];
   if Choice = CorrectAnswer then
     begin
       WriteLn('Good.');
       Score := Score + 1;
     end
   else
       WriteLn('Oops.');
       QuestionNum := QuestionNum + 1;
   until QuestionNum > LastQuestionNum;
   WriteLn;
   WriteLn('Your score is ', Score : 1);
 end.
```

The following program contains a while loop. Follow it through and determine what will be printed.

```
program FunnyLoop;
  var
    I,X : Integer;
  begin
    I := 0;
    X := 0;
    while (I < 10) do
      X := X + 1;
      Write('THE ANSWER IS ', X)
    end.
```

• • •

The performance of the statement contained in the while loop depends on the truth or falsity of the condition

(I < 10)

Since nothing within the loop ever changes the value of I, it remains 0 indefinitely. Thus, the loop will never be terminated; and the statement following the loop, the Write statement, will never be executed. Nothing will be printed. Care must be taken in writing loops to assure that there is an exit point.

Here is another program containing a while loop. The program works correctly as far as it goes. It reads in a sequence of train times, for example,

1020   1040   1105   1145   1210   1305   –1

and determines whether the times are in order, as they should be for a valid train schedule. The sequence is terminated by typing –1.

When the sequence of numbers shown in Fig. 6.4 is entered, the program works nicely. But what happens when we throw in a few curves? For instance, what if the sequence were as follows?

2140   130   145   210   250   –1

These figures could be valid if the train starts before midnight.

● ● ●

```pascal
program TimeCheck;
  const
    Terminator = –1;
  var
    Time, NextTime, Count : Integer;
begin
  WriteLn('ENTER TRAIN TIMES');
  Read(Time);
  Count := 1;
  while (Time <> Terminator) do
    begin
      Read(NextTime);
      Count := Count + 1;
      if (NextTime = Terminator) or (Time < NextTime) then
        Time := NextTime
      else
        WriteLn('OOPS, CHECK TIME ', Count)
    end;
  WriteLn('ALL ITEMS HAVE BEEN CHECKED.')
end.
```

Figure 6.4 ● Program TimeCheck

With this sequence of times, 2140 is assigned to Time and 130 is assigned to NextTime. Since Time is greater than NextTime, execution passes to the else part of the statement. Notice that in the else part, no new value is assigned to Time, it remains 2140; thus, each new NextTime will be compared to 2140. In each case Time will be greater than NextTime and execution will pass to the else part each time the loop is executed. Each of them will be reported as an "Oops" situation.

Consider the following sequence of times where there is a duplicate.

1020   1020   1105   –1

What will happen on the first pass through the loop?

● ● ●

The time 1020 is assigned to Time before the loop is entered. On the first pass through the loop, NextTime also becomes 1020. The relationship is, therefore, one of equality between Time and NextTime. This is not one of the conditions in the if part of the statement, so execution passes to the else part. This is as it should be, since the train cannot leave two stations at the same time.

In the preceding case, using the program reveals an error in the schedule, but what about the following entries where the numbers are not valid times?

20   99   165   271   –1

● ● ●

Nowhere in the program is there a check for validity of the times entered. As long as the numbers are in order, no error will be reported. Even a negative number can be entered as a time without causing an "Oops."

Let's take a look now at the terminator. The loop continues as long as Time is unequal to –1. If only a –1 is entered, execution passes to the first statement after the loop, and we get the message

ALL ITEMS HAVE BEEN CHECKED

even though no items were entered. What happens with

–1   –1

which is strange to say the least?

● ● ●

Since the execution of the loop depends on Time being unequal to –1, the statements in the body of the loop are never performed, therefore, NextTime is not read at all. Execution passes beyond the loop, and the second –1 is never considered.

How about the situation where the –1 is not entered. What would happen with

        1020   1040   1105

● ● ●

The program instructs the computer to read a number and do something with it, and then to do the same thing again as long as the number read is not equal to –1. Until the terminator is entered, execution continues to return to the beginning of the loop, the Read statement. Execution never reaches the WriteLn statement if –1 is not entered.

There is a moral here. Even these innocently small problems present their little oddities. One of the rules of good programming is to pay special attention to the details. Any of the situations discussed here could arise in a program being used to check a sequence of times. For the program to be really useful, it must address these potential difficulties. As we stated at the beginning of this exercise, the program works fine as far as it goes.

Consider the program in Fig. 6.5. Given the numbers 8 and 6 as input, this program outputs

        THE GREATEST COMMON DIVISOR IS   2

How many times is the loop executed before the result is printed?

● ● ●

Let's follow the values through the loop. When the loop is entered for the first time, the values are assigned as follows:

        Remainder := 2
        HighValue := 6
        LowValue := 2

At the end of the first pass, Remainder is equal to 2, so execution returns to the beginning of the loop. On the second pass the values are as follows:

        Remainder := 0
        HighValue := 2
        LowValue := 0

Since Remainder is now equal to zero, the loop will not be repeated again.

Figure 6.5 ● Program GCD

```
program GCD;
{ -- This program computes the greatest common divisor of two }
{ -- integers. The program uses Euclid's Algorithm. }

{ -- Euclid's algorithm goes as follows: }
{ --   (1) The higher number is divided by the lower. }
{ --   (2) If the integer remainder is not zero, it becomes the }
{ --       next divisor, while the divisor becomes the next dividend. }
{ --   (3) the process repeats until the remainder is zero; }
{ --       the current divisor is the GCD. }
  var
      Num1, Num2, HighValue, LowValue, Remainder : Integer;
begin
  Read(Num1, Num2);
  if Num1 <= Num2 then
    begin
      LowValue := Num1;
      HighValue := Num2;
    end;
  else
    begin
      LowValue := Num2;
      HighValue := Num1;
    end;
  repeat
    Remainder := HighValue mod LowValue;
    HighValue := LowValue;
    LowValue := Remainder
  until Remainder = 0;
  Write('THE GREATEST COMMON DIVISOR IS ', HighValue)
end.
```

Notice that LowValue is now also equal to zero. Since LowValue will always be equal to Remainder at the end of the loop, we could have used

LowValue = 0

as the condition for conclusion. Right?

Wrong! Although the program would work correctly using LowValue instead of Remainder, it would be very poor programming technique. The goal of the loop is to find a divisor that produces no remainder. Although it is important to be aware of all the little details, it is also important to keep in mind the overall purpose of the program.

When writing loops into programs, one of the first steps is to determine which kind of loop to use. Consider the use of a while loop in the Fig. 6.5 program. What happens if the loop is changed to the following?

```
while Remainder <> 0 do
    begin
        Remainder := HighValue mod LowValue;
        HighValue := LowValue;
        LowValue := Remainder
    end;
```

Remember that when a while loop is used, the condition is evaluated before the loop is executed. Look carefully at the program. What is the value of Remainder when the loop is first encountered? If you answered, "I don't know," you are absolutely correct. No value has yet been assigned to Remainder. Before a variable is used, it must be assigned a value, or the results will be unpredictable.

Going back to the repeat loop, what happens if the loop is changed to the following?

```
repeat
    Remainder := HighValue mod LowValue;
    LowValue := Remainder;
    HighValue := LowValue
until Remainder = 0;
```

The ultimate effect of the sequence of assignments shown above is that the value originally associated with Remainder is assigned to both LowValue and HighValue. As you can see, the order in which assignments are made requires careful attention.

Let's consider one more possibility before we leave this program. What happens if Num1 and Num2 are given as –8 and –6?

● ● ●

Right from the beginning we are in trouble here. Since –8 is less than –6, the number with the higher absolute value is assigned to LowValue and the number with the lower absolute value is assigned to HighValue. However, the real problem arrives when the **mod** operator is encountered. Negative numbers cannot be used with the **mod** operator; an error results.

Before we leave you, we reluctantly turn to a discussion of goto's. They say there are two kinds of people: those who hate New York City and those who love it. Well, there are two kinds of programmers: those who believe the goto should be banned forever and those who believe it can be an effective programming tool. This problem will show you why some people would like to ban it.

The goto is a statement that causes a program to continue execution at a specifically named place. Typically, we may have something like

```
    . . .
    goto 25;      { —line A }
    . . .
    goto 25;      { —line B }
    . . .
25 : DoSomethingSpecial;
    . . .
    goto 25;      { —line C }
```

If the program gets to any of lines A, B, or C, execution will immediately continue at the statement labeled 25. The rules for doing this in Pascal are simple.

The first rule is: (1) Any statement in a program can be prefixed by a *label*. For example, we may have

```
10 :   Read(X, Y, Z)
```

or

```
11 :   if NumItems > 100 then
           Write('Too many items')
```

or

```
12 :   X := X + 1
```

As evident above, a label is an integer followed by a colon.

The second rule is a bit strange: (2) All integers serving as labels must be declared. Thus we may have

```
label 10, 11, 12;
```

This line must appear before any constant or variable declarations. Perhaps the rationale here is to make it a bit difficult to use goto's.

Finally, the third rule is obvious: (3) No two statements may have the same label. Otherwise, the computer would not know where to go. For example, it is erroneous to have

```
15 : DoThis;
    . . .
    goto 15;
    . . .
15 : DoThat;
```

That is about all you need, but the power of this innocent-looking statement is enormous, and so is the trouble it can cause.

Consider the program listed in Fig. 6.6. We leave it to you to rewrite this program to eliminate as many goto's and labels as possible, and to make the program as short and clear as you can.

```
program DontGoto;
{ -- This program is a bag of worms. }
   label
      1, 3, 4, 5, 6, 7, 8, 9;
   const
      MaxValue = 99;
   var
      X : Integer;
begin
   goto 3;
1 :
   if X = 0 then
      goto 9
   else
      goto 5;
5 :
   if X > MaxValue then
      goto 6;
   else
      goto 4;
9 :
   WriteLn(X);
   goto 7;
3 :
   ReadLn(X);
   goto 1;
6 :
   X := Round(SqRt(X));
8 :
   X := 2 * X + X;
   goto 9;
4 :
   X := X * X;
   goto 8;
7 :
   WriteLn('ALL DONE')
end.
```

Figure 6.6 ● Program DontGoto

6.4 ○

6.1   Tricky For Loops
Consider the following loop:

```
I := 1;
for N := I to I + 4 do begin
  I := I + 2;
  WriteLn ('N = ', N : 3, ' I = ', I : 3)
end.
```

Even though I is changed within the body of the loop, the loop is executed five times. However, the values printed by the WriteLn statement are

```
N = 1   I =   3
N = 2   I =   5
N = 3   I =   7
N = 4   I =   9
N = 5   I = 11
```

We see that the initial and final values of N are determined before executing the body of the loop.

The following problem is not as simple as it appears. Write an equivalent sequence of statements for any for loop of the form:

```
for variable := expression to expression do
    statement
```

The rewritten sequence must not include a for loop.

6.2   Summing a Long Series of Numbers
If you toss a coin you may get heads on the first toss. But then again you may not. The probability of getting your first heads on the first toss is ½. The probability of getting your first heads on the second toss is ¼. On the third toss ⅛, and so on.

To get the average number of tosses needed to get heads you need to add the series of numbers:

$$1^*(½) + 2^*(¼) + 3^*(⅛) + \ldots$$

Write a program to find the value of this series as the number of tosses approaches infinity. A thousand terms should suffice.

6.3   Secret Numbers: Version 4
It is not clear how many guesses a user should be allowed to make on an ATM; five tries seems reasonable, if we want to be generous we could say 10. This problem is basically the same as Version 3; that is the user gets a certain number of chances to enter the correct code number, which is declared as a constant in the program. This time use loops in the

program, and give the user five chances to enter the correct number. Before the fifth choice is to be entered, the user is to be given a warning, such as

THIS IS YOUR LAST CHANCE

6.4 Monthly Service Charge

Checking accounts at many banks have a monthly service charge but pay interest on your current balance. One possible scheme is as follows:

a) If 10 or fewer checks are cashed, the service charge is $0.10 per check.

b) For the next 10 checks, the service charge is $0.09 per check.

c) For all remaining checks, the service charge is $0.08 per check.

d) If the closing balance is $100 or less, no interest is added.

e) For balances larger than $100, 0.5% monthly interest on the surplus over $100 is credited to the account.

Write a program to read in the number of checks cashed and the closing balance, and print the net amount debited or credited to the account. The closing balance is read in as a real number with a decimal point two digits from the right. Thus 50.64 represents $50.64.

For example, with the input

15
50.64

the output would be something like

DEBIT ACCOUNT BY 1 DOLLAR AND 45 CENTS

With the input

15
1000.00

the output would be

CREDIT ACCOUNT BY 3 DOLLARS AND .05 CENTS

Note: It may be helpful to multiply the closing balance by 100 and do all arithmetic with integer values. You might also wish to comment on the problems of rounding off the results into dollars and cents.

6.5 Accumulated Savings

If a lump sum of money is put into a savings account and left alone, interest is calculated each time on the accumulated amount in the account. That is, interest is paid on the interest as well as on the principle. For this problem, assume that interest is paid only once each year.

Write a program to calculate the total amount in the account after a certain number of years. Assume that the interest rate remains constant through the years. The original amount, the interest rate, and the number of years are all to be entered by the user. The output must show the original amount, the interest rate, the number of years that the savings have been accumulating, and the accumulated amount of savings.

6.6   Paying Your Debts

A debt is said to be *amortized* if it is paid off by a sequence of equal payments at equal intervals. There are four basic quantities to be considered:

P = the principal amount of the debt
I = the yearly interest rate for the debt
N = the number of years for the duration of the debt
M = the constant monthly payment required to pay back the principal P over N years at the interest rate I.

$$M = \frac{P * i * (1 + i)^n}{(1 + i)^n - 1}$$

where

i = $I/12$ = monthly interest rate
n = $12*N$ = number of monthly periods in N years

You are to write a program to compute the average monthly payment to amortize a debt.

Input: The input to this program is a line with the following values,

P I N

where

P = the principal in dollars
I = the percentage interest rate computed to two decimal places (for example, 825 means 8.25 percent)
N = the number of years in integer form

Output: The output from the program is to be the required monthly payment.

Sample input:

20000   800   25

Sample output:

MONTHLY PAYMENT: $154.36

6.7 Roman Numerals

The problem of converting Roman numerals to Arabic numerals lends itself nicely to looping. Write a program to do this. Think this one through very carefully before you begin to write.

6.8   Mailing Labels

Computers generate tons of mailing labels every day. Here's a simple starter.

Write a program that read in an integer stating the number of times you want your own mailing label (name and address) printed. The program should print this label the specified number of times.

Note: If you want to get a bit fancy, buy some sheets of blank mailing labels and try to get the computer to fill them in.

Chapter 7

Programming Techniques

The material so far presented is sufficient for writing programs for solving a wide variety of problems. A word to the wise is in order before continuing, however: Do not be misled by the apparent simplicity of these ideas. True, they are, in and of themselves, very simple. But using them is not.

7.1 ● Problem Solving

When starting a new problem, there are many forces at work that encourage a programmer to abandon thoughtful and effective techniques for unproven shortcuts. Trying to speed up the process results in paying a high price in time and energy later on. Shortcuts sometimes pay off, but for the most part they do not. Starting with an absolutely solid problem definition is one way to get future rewards.

Definition
The place to focus attention at the beginning, as difficult and tedious as it may seem, *must* be on the problem definition itself. If you allow some little detail to escape you, ignore some odd case, or dwell on irrelevant information, you will find yourself playing host to some larger problems down the road.

One of the best techniques is to construct a sample of the input and output for each program before attempting to solve the problem. Among the benefits of this technique are these:

- It forces the programmer to consider the details of the problem.

153

- It can help to uncover any special or annoying cases that will surely turn up later.

- It often forces the programmer to restructure the problem, sometimes ever so slightly, making the program easier to write.

- Above all, it gives a clear idea of the intent of the entire program.

This may sound too obvious; but excellent problem definitions are as rare as excellent detectives, excellent food, or excellent anything. Writing good problem definitions requires plain hard work; there is no way around it. You must take the time to specify the inputs, the outputs, and the exact task the program is to perform. What is needed is persistence and discipline, or as Edison once remarked about genius, it is "one percent inspiration, ninety-nine percent perspiration."

Methodology

Certainly the hardest task in problem solving is developing an overall strategy. There is little sense in pretending that the methods in problem solving are very scientific; nevertheless, there are known psychological techniques to help you over these first crucial steps.

Once you have a problem firmly fixed in your mind, it is a grave mistake to believe that this is the time to start programming. What it is the time to do is to start *thinking*.

Thinking means just that. You need to think about alternative ways to solve the problem. You need to examine various approaches in enough detail to discover the possible trouble spots that may be difficult to program.

Always look for possible errors and provide against them. It is the first rule of programming just as it is the first rule of criminal investigation. You need to polish any proposed solution before attempting to carry on. Remember, it is certainly easier to discard poor thoughts than poor programs.

You may have heard it said before, undoubtedly because it is true: it always takes longer to write a program than it first appears. On the other hand, you can safely assume that the sooner you start writing code, rather than thinking about the problem, the longer it will take to complete the task.

One of the best thinking aids is *analogy*. Presumably the problem being solved is not so unfamiliar that you have not seen anything like it before. Recall solutions to similar problems. You may recognize portions of the problem that have been solved in some similar fashion, or perhaps you have solved a similar problem that had nothing to do with computers. In each of these situations, the point is the same: look to previous solutions, for in them may be the seeds to the solution of the new problem.

In attempting to solve a problem on a computer, there is a tendency to become heavily involved with the oddities of the programming language itself. Although the final solution must be programmed in some language, the best solutions are those for which there is a direct analogy to the world in which the problem is presented. To do this you should attempt to solve the problem without regard to the final computer implementation. Freed from the idiosyncrasies of a programming language, you the programmer can concentrate on the essence of the problem.

Some problems are not at all easy to solve. It has long been an axiom among programmers that in difficult situations two heads are better than one. Working with someone else, customarily known as *brainstorming*, and simply talking about your problem has become a classic programming technique.

Conversations with others are more than idle chatter. In the process of discussing the problem, one often finds inspiration. Do not be afraid to expose the problem at hand and to listen when someone else proposes a solution. It is remarkable how often the simple exposure of an idea can lead to a clearer, better formulated solution.

Of course, if your mind is already made up and your solution is well in hand, you can go right ahead. But take care—supposedly good ideas have been known to show serious flaws when put into action.

Sooner or later you will find yourself in a situation where there appears to be no reasonable solution to a particular problem. You may have tried repeatedly with a given idea, each time finding some new flaw. What should you do when all hope seems lost?

Take a break.

The technique of putting aside a problem for some period of time is generally known as *incubation*. This is a subtle but potentially powerful psychological technique. A complete distraction, a weekend away from a problem, a good night's rest, or some frivolous entertainment can often have far-reaching effects in solving difficult problems.

Our brain is supposedly at work on problems even though we are not consciously aware of it. Rest from a problem is often the predecessor of an inspiration. We have all experienced this in other areas of our lives.

In sum, there are a great many psychological techniques for solving problems. You should use these techniques to improve your problem-solving skills in programming.

Expressing Algorithms

All solutions start from the problem and not from some programming language. Assuming that you have a solid idea of a solution, you must now take your first step toward a concrete program.

A simple device for sketching your ideas is to write out a solution in a very high-level language of your own. The language can be a programming "interlingua," a language somewhere between English and Pascal. This means that you can borrow extensively from English, coining phrases at will, unconstrained by a programming language.

For example, you might write,

Do the following 10 times:
  —*actions to be performed 10 times*

or

Print the values in the table.

On the other hand, the language chosen should be guided by the knowledge that the final program must be written in Pascal. You can, for example, conceptualize a variable, say NumSuspects, and write,

Set NumSuspects to 0

or

If NumSuspects > 4 then
  —*what to do if more than 4 suspects*

In Pascal, the first example can be expressed by an assignment statement, the second by a conditional statement.

The point of this technique is to capture some written form of a solution. This form retains the high level of discourse of the problem domain, yet is specific enough to capture the essence of the algorithm that is being expressed.

7.2 ● Programs as Human Communication

Assume for the moment that you were presented with two computer programs. Each performs the same, presumably very important, task for you. You will have to use one of the programs for the next several years, probably making modifications as time goes on. You are told that the programs, from a performance point of view, are absolutely identical; that is, they perform the same input and output, they run at approximately the same speed, and each has been tested thoroughly and shown to be correct.

You are not allowed to look inside and see the actual programs. The only additional information you have about the programs is that the first one required over a hundred changes in order to make it correct, while the second worked correctly the very first time it was run.

Now the obvious question. Which program would you choose?

This question leads to another: What are the characteristics of a program that would work correctly on its first test? We might conclude that the persons who wrote the program were highly skilled programmers or very lucky. But surely there is more, for there must be some element present in the second program that is lacking in the first. Our only logical conclusion is that the second program was written with such crystal clarity that it allowed its authors to comprehend it as easily as you can read these lines of text. In short, the program must be so transparent that "even a Scotland Yard official can see through it."

In all of the programs in this book, we see an almost obsessive concern for clarity. A program is not just a set of instructions that must be understood by some computer, but a description of an algorithm that must be understood by human beings, especially the person writing and using the program.

The factors that go into making a program well suited for human comprehension are numerous. They include the design of clear algorithms, choice of control structures, the sequence in which operations are performed, and many other issues. But there is a key point mentioned in the quotation above: the choice of names used in a program.

Names

A wise choice of names can make a great contribution to the readability of a program. Let us look at a portion of one of the programs presented earlier:

```
Read(TodaysDate, TideHr, EventDate, EventHr);
MinsToHighTide := (TodaysDate - 1) * MinsPerDay;
MinsToHighTide := MinsToHighTide + HighTideHr*MinsPerHr;
```

Of course, it would be shorter to write,

```
Read(Date1, Hr1, Date2, Hr2);
Mins := (Date1 - 1) * DayLen;
Mins := Mins + Hr1*HrLen;
```

but then we might have to guess at the meaning of Date1 versus Date2 and what units DayLen and HrLen stand for. The difference between the two is that the names in the first fragment have been chosen from standard *English* descriptions of the entities.

Creating good, meaningful names can be difficult, for often it is easy to pick a name with a close but dangerously incorrect connotation. As an example, suppose a programmer decided to represent a file of criminal records, and the record's three fields (the age of the criminal, the criminal's height, and the criminal's shoe size) with the respective names Input, Field1, Field2, and Field3. The name Input might cause a reader to associate an arbitrary file of input data with the name. A better choice would be CriminalFile. Likewise, the data names Field1, Field2, and Field3 are far less clear than Age, Height, and ShoeSize. Even Height may not be so perfect, as it may be better to write HghtInInches or HeightInCm.

A name that is an abbreviation for a longer conceptual unit can also be hazardous, especially when the resulting abbreviation is an acronym that suggests another entity. For example, a programmer who desires a name for a rate of pay entry would be unwise to use the name Rope, which does not reflect the entity's true meaning.

Names like Field1, Field2, and Field3 should be avoided for yet another reason. Suppose the format of the input were changed so that the age became the third field instead of the first, and the height became the first instead of the second field, etc. The name Field1 must be changed to Field3, Field2 to Field1, and so on. Needless to say, it is highly possible that some occurrence of the name Field3 might not be changed to Field1! Finding a mistake like the one just made in the last sentence is another problem with such names.

Another important aspect in choosing names is the effect of abbreviations. The first point to remember is that you should only abbreviate after you have created a full mnemonic name. Second, the chosen abbreviation should not suggest a meaning different from the original name. Let us assume you have created the lengthy name NumberOfCigars and that it suggests the correct meaning. Even though you surely will want to abbreviate the name, you should reject such abbreviations as NumCig or NoCigar, for they may very well be misleading. A name like NumCigars would be preferable.

The choice of appropriate names is seldom an easy matter. Keeping in mind that the main reason for choosing a particular name is so that you (and others using your program) can understand it, it is well worth the effort to invest some thought in the choice of a name. You may not fully appreciate this when first designing your program; but you will, no doubt, appreciate the full value of your labors at some later date when you return to use the program.

Prettyprinting

The use of spacing conventions to illuminate structure is often called "prettyprinting." Prettyprinting is a vital ingredient in reading programs. With good spacing rules, typing errors are much easier to detect and the meaning of portions easier to follow. Most important, the overall intent of the program can be made more transparent to the reader. The conscious use of good spacing conventions can even affect and improve the original code.

With Macintosh Pascal the spacing within a line and all of the indenting are done automatically. The formatting conventions that are used go a long way toward making a program readable. However, there are tools available to the programmer which can make the intent of the program even clearer.

Blank lines are ignored in the processing of a program and can be used freely to set off blocks of information. Skip a line after the declarations section and before and after such things as loops and case statements. When blank lines are used in conjunction with comments even more clarity is gained. Consider the following program:

```
program Temperature;
   var
      F : Integer;
      C : Real;
begin
   Write('ENTER A FAHRENHEIT TEMPERATURE: ');
   ReadLn(F);
   C := (5 / 9) * (F – 32);
   WriteLn;
   WriteLn(F : 2, 'DEGREES FAHRENHEIT IS EQUAL TO ', C
            : 3 : 1, 'DEGREES CELSIUS.')
end.
```

Now read it again with blank lines and one comment:

```
program Temperature;

{ -- This program converts a fahrenheit temperature }
{ -- to its celsius equivalent }

   var
      F : Integer;
      C : Real;
begin
   Write('ENTER A FAHRENHEIT TEMPERATURE: ');
   ReadLn(F);
   C := (5 / 9) * (F – 32);
   WriteLn;
   WriteLn(F : 2, 'DEGREES FAHRENHEIT IS EQUAL TO ', C
            : 3 : 1, 'DEGREES CELSIUS.')
end.
```

The improvement is obvious even on such a simple program as this one. Imagine a longer, more complex program with no blank lines and no comments. Reading it would be a chore to say the least.

Another tool that is very useful in the declarations part of the program is grouping. It is not necessary to include all the identifiers of a particular type in a single declaration; therefore you can say,

```
TodaysDate, TideHr : Integer;
EventDate, EventHr : Integer;
```

instead of

TodaysDate, TideHr EventDate, EventHr : Integer;

This concept of grouping applies to the constants also. Although each will be put on a separate line; they can still be grouped, with the groups separated by a blank line, as in

SideA = 118;
SideB = 78;
SideC = 144;
SideD = 84;

Acre = 43560;

Diameter = 9;
Radians = 82;

These are simple conventions, but like anything else in this book, their implementation requires a great deal of thought.

This brings us full circle to our point of origin—that there can never be a substitute for thinking.

"In solving any sort of programming problem, Watson," Holmes once remarked, "the grand thing is simple, human reasoning. It is a very useful and easy accomplishment, though people do not practice it much. There are fifty who can reason synthetically for one who can reason analytically. I tell you, Watson, we have not yet grasped the results which human reason alone can attain."

7.3 ○ Practice

Program Clarity

There are always a few tricky but interesting questions you can ask about a language. One of these concerns the shortest possible program you can write. Such a program would obviously do nothing when executed. The shortest possible program in Pascal has 18 nonblank characters. Writing it gives you a good chance to review the fundamentals of a Pascal program. Give it a try. The program is shown later in the section.

● ● ●

The program in Fig. 7.1 performs a well-known, simple arithmetic computation. Before continuing, see if you can figure out what that computation is.

● ● ●

In choosing names, the programmer must guard against using identifiers whose relationships are vague, tenuous, or peculiar. The purpose of the

```
program FunnyNames;
   const
      Four = 4.0;
      Five = 2.0;
   var
      Left, Right, Middle, All : Real;
      Left1, Left2, Right1, One : Real;
begin
   ReadLn(Left, Middle, Right);

   Right1 := Four * Left * Right;
   Left1 := Middle * Middle − Right1;
   Left2 := SqRt(Left1);
   One := (−Middle + Left2) / (Five * Left);
   All := (−Middle − Left2) / (2.0 * Left);

   WriteLn(One, ' AND ', All)
end.
```

Figure 7.1 ● Program
FunnyNames

example program in Fig. 7.2 has been deliberately obscured by the use of mnemonic names that appear reasonable at first glance, but that are, in fact, misleading and confusing.

The program in Fig. 7.2 does indeed have a purpose and Inter represents a real quantity. This problem is more difficult than it appears.

● ● ●

Shown below is the shortest possible Pascal program.

```
program P;
begin
end.
```

If you were not able to recognize the intended computation in program FunnyNames, it is considerably clearer in the program shown in Fig. 7.3. The names have been changed, and three steps have been combined into one.

The program in Fig. 7.3 computes the roots of the general quadratic equation

$$ax + bx + c = 0$$

by using the quadratic formula.

Figure 7.2 ● Program
HaveFun

```pascal
program HaveFun;
    var
        Denom, Slope, Inter, Num : Real;
        Row, Col : Integer;
        A : array[1..2, 1..2] of Real;
    begin
        for Row := 1 to 2 do
            for Col := 1 to 2 do
                ReadLn(A[Row, Col]);

        if A[1, 1] = A[2, 2] then
            WriteLn('NO VALUE')

        else
            begin
                Num := A[1, 2] - A[2, 2];
                Denom := A[1, 1] - A[2, 1];
                Slope := Num / Denom;
                Inter := A[1, 2] - Slope * A[1, 1];
                WriteLn('THE ANSWER IS ', Inter)
            end
    end.
```

Figure 7.3 ● Program
BetterNames

```pascal
program BetterNames;
    var
        a, b, c : Real;
        Step1, Step2 : Real;
        Root1, Root2 : Real;
    begin
        ReadLn(a, b, c);
        Root1 := (-b + SqRt(b * b - 4.0 * a * c)) / (2.0 * a);
        Root2 := (-b - SqRt(b * b - 4.0 * a * c)) / (2.0 * a);

        WriteLn(Root1, ' AND ', Root2)
    end.
```

Usually a complex arithmetic computation can be coded as a single arithmetic expression, as it is in BetterNames. However, for the sake of clarity, it is often advantageous to split up a lengthy arithmetic expression and use intermediate variables. In this particular program, it would certainly be useful to check the value of the discriminant of the equation, that is

$$b - 4ac$$

to see if it is a negative number. Since the computer cannot compute the square root of a negative number, an error would be reported if the discriminant is negative. To be useful, the program should contain an if statement which would check for this condition and report it in a Write statement.

We leave you to struggle with program HaveFun for the time being. However, we offer in Fig. 7.4 one possible rewrite of DontGoTo from the last practice section.

```
program WentTo;
   const
      MaxValue = 99;
   var
      X : Integer;
begin
   ReadLn(X);
   if X <> 0 then
      begin
         if X > MaxValue then
            X := Round(SqRt(X))
         else
            X := X * X;
            X := 2 * X + X
      end;
   WriteLn(X);
   WriteLn('ALL DONE')
end.
```

Figure 7.4 ● Program WentTo

Chapter 8

Testing Patterns

Occasionally a program runs correctly and produces the expected output the first time through. However, more often than not, no matter how carefully the program is written, it requires some correction or modification. Choosing Check from the Run menu reveals any syntax or typographic errors. When a mistake is encountered during a Check run, a dialog box appears stating the nature of the error. Three of Apple's Macintosh Pascal dialog boxes are shown in Fig. 8.1

Figure 8.1 ● Dialog boxes

 Either a semicolon (;) or an END is expected following the previous statement, but neither has been found.

 The name "Temprature" has not been defined yet.

 A period (.) is required following the last END of the program but one has not been found.

A pointer in the left margin indicates the location of the error; it can normally be found on the line indicated or on the preceding line. Click the bug to remove the dialog box, make the correction, then choose Check again.

Other errors may be reported during a program run, such as the ones reported in the dialog boxes in Fig. 8.2. The error messages given in Macintosh Pascal are carefully worded to lead the programmer to the cause of the difficulty. Pay attention to them.

A more difficult situation arises when the program is syntactically correct, and has no run errors, but produces output that is unexpected or inconsistent. Sometimes a careful re-reading reveals the source of the difficulty. If that proves unsuccessful, the program has to be checked section by section or possibly line by line.

8.1 ● Breakpoints

Macintosh Pascal provides a simple method for setting breakpoints in any program, allowing one to check and correct a section of the program without running it through to the end each time. The Run menu offers a selection Stops In. This option causes a margin to appear on the left side of the program window. The margin has an icon of a Stop Sign at the bottom. Clicking the margin places a Stop Sign before any line of the program. Each time a stop is encountered during a run, the program halts without executing the line. When any run command is given, execution continues where it left off. To remove a single Stop Sign, click the sign; to remove all of them, choose Stops Out from the Run menu.

If the program has been carefully written, the separate modules should be obvious; setting a Stop Sign for each one and using the Observe

Figure 8.2

An attempt to perform an integer divide (DIV) by zero has occurred.

An incompatibility between types has been found.

A STRING value is too long for its intended use.

window shown in Fig. 8.3 gives an indication of which section is causing the problem.

One or more of the expressions contained in the program can be entered into the Observe window by activating the window, and then typing the expression and a return. Each time a stop sign is encountered, the window is updated to show the current value of the expressions.

Once the problem area is located, stepping through the statements while observing the behavior of variables or expressions can be a very effective way of finding the exact source of the problem. Consider the following simple loop:

```
X := 1;
repeat
    X:= X + 2
until X = 100
```

In such a short loop the error is obvious, but in a complicated program the never-ending loop can be a very troublesome problem. By placing a Stop Sign before the **repeat** and entering X into the Observe window, it is possible to check the value of X before each execution of the loop. As shown in Fig. 8.4, it quickly becomes obvious that X takes on only odd values and will never be equal to 100.

The values of X can be displayed rapidly by choosing Go-Go from the Run menu. Instead of halting before each execution of the loop, the program pauses only long enough to update the Observe window. In the run shown in Fig. 8.4, Go-Go was used until X reached 95, the run was halted by choosing Halt from the Pause menu, and then Step was used to check each line.

To avoid the problem, the condition should read,

until X > 100

Consider the program shown in Fig. 8.5. This program displays for the element radium the percentage of atoms still radioactive after a number of years.

It is interesting to note that, although ActiveAtoms never actually reaches zero, program execution ends when the number becomes too

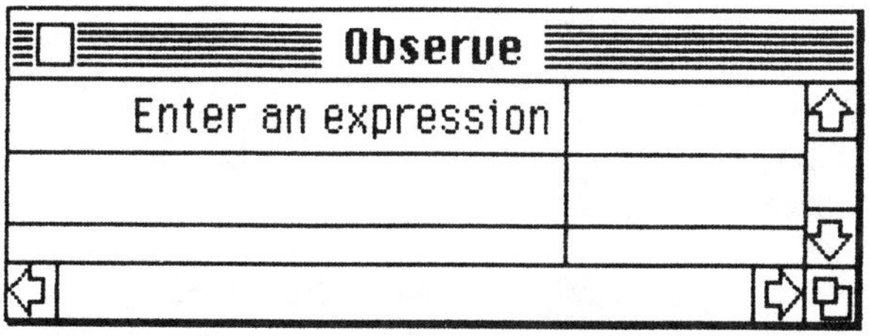

Figure 8.3

small to be within the representable range of Extended numbers. By placing a Stop Sign before the **repeat** line, we can observe the values of YearsPassed and ActiveAtoms. The Observe window is shown in Fig. 8.6 for the first loop, the loops before and after the visible value becomes

Figure 8.4

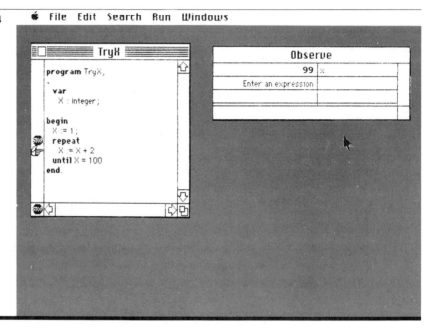

Figure 8.5 ● Program
Radioactivity

```
program Radioactivity;
{ -- This program computes the percentage of atoms still }
{ -- active after each half life for the element Radium. }
    const
        HalfLifeRa = 1620; { years }
    var
        YearsPassed : LongInt;
        ActiveAtoms : Real; { percent }
begin
    YearsPassed := 0;
    ActiveAtoms := 100;
    repeat
        YearsPassed := YearsPassed + HalfLifeRa;
        ActiveAtoms := ActiveAtoms / 2;
    until ActiveAtoms = 0.0;
    WriteLn('After ', YearsPassed : 5, ' years, radioactivity equals zero.')
end.
```

zero, the next to last loop, and the Observe and Text windows at the close
of the program.

Figure 8.6

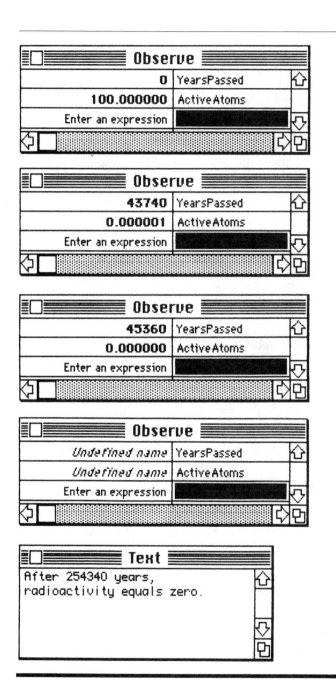

Since ActiveAtoms never mathematically reaches zero, it is better to assign a very low value to be used for comparison. For instance, a constant can be assigned, as in

const
   Epsilon = 1.0e-6;

Epsilon is then used instead of 0.0 as the control value.

A variable that is not shown in the Observe window can be checked by using the Instant window shown as Fig. 8.7.

To enter a statement such as

Write(Identifier);

activate the Instant window (Fig. 8.8), and type in the needed statement or statements. The statements are executed by clicking the Do It button.

The value of a variable can be changed by entering an assignment statement, as shown in Fig. 8.9.

Figure 8.7

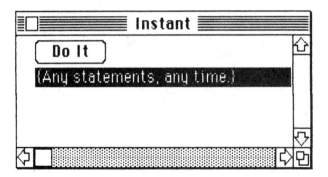

Figure 8.8

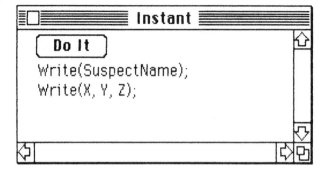

Step and Reset 171

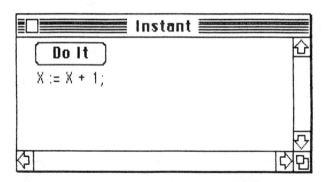

Figure 8.9

Any statement that could be entered into the program can be entered on the Instant window. However, be aware that these newly entered statements do not replace anything already in the program. If the program is halted at a statement such as

Read(Temperature);

and you enter

Temperature := 68;

the Read statement is still executed when the run is resumed; the assignment statement on the Instant window does not satisfy the need for input data dictated by the Read statement.

The Observe and Instant windows are an invaluable aid for getting programs to run correctly. Holmes would surely appreciate the advances that have been made since the days of the Analytical Engine.

8.2 ● Step and Reset

Sometimes the most efficient way to determine the location of the problem is to Step through the program line by line. This is almost like having a Stop Sign on each line. Choosing Step causes only one line of the program to be executed. The pointer indicates which line will be executed next. Go and Step can be used together to speed up the testing. If the mistake is near the end of the program, set a Stop Sign just before the suspected troublespot and choose Go to run the program up to that line; then switch to Step to pinpoint the problem.

The Observe and Instant windows both can be used with Step just as with Go. Expressions entered on the Observe window will be updated as each line is executed. Statements can be entered and executed by means of the Instant window before stepping to the next line.

At any point it may be desirable to go back and do some editing or try different input. Any time the program is halted, choosing Reset returns the program to the beginning.

When all else fails, set the program aside for a while and turn your mind to other matters. Sometimes the harder we look the less we see. Give the problem a chance to incubate; tomorrow the solution may be obvious.

8.3 ○ Practice

Getting Programs to Work

Debugging programs is something that you will certainly get plenty of opportunity to practice. Be aware that a systematic approach is needed for correcting errors, just as for any aspect of programming.

We leave to you the choice of a troublesome program to practice on. If you haven't already created one, you soon will. Perfection in programming is greatly to be desired, but rarely found.

Listed below are some of the steps to follow in getting a Pascal program to work on the Macintosh.

1. Run the program through a Check. This will assure that the typing and syntax are correct.

2. Pay attention to any errors that are reported on the first run. The error messages are there to help you. Quite often they lead you directly to the problem.

If the program checks and runs, but it produces results that are incorrect or inconsistent, or if the program ends prematurely or not at all, then continue with the following steps.

3. Reread the algorithm and the program, watching for errors. If possible, have someone else read them also.

4. Isolate the problem area. The Stop Signs, and the Observe and Instant windows are a big help here. Follow the values of one or more variables whose behavior you should be able to predict. Are the values consistent with your expectations? If not, where do they begin to fail?

5. Step through the problem area. The pointer indicates the next line to be executed. Is the sequence as you expected? If there are if-else choices, make sure that each possibility is tested. You may want to use the Instant window in this case to assign values to the control variable in order to check the sequence of steps.

6. Keep track of any changes you make; random trial and error will only cause you trouble.

7. When all else fails, set it aside for a while. Don't give up; just give yourself a break.

● ● ●

In case you are still struggling with program HaveFun from the previous practice session, here is some help for you. If a line is drawn on a Cartesian coordinate system, and two points on the line are given as x^1, y^1 and x^2, y^2; then, the slope of the line is represented by

$$\frac{y^2 - y^1}{x^2 - x^1}$$

and the point where the line crosses the y axis, the y intercept, is represented by the following formula:

$$y = y^2 - (x^2 * slope)$$

Prelude to Types

An Advertisement in the "Times"

HAD seen little of Sherlock Holmes for many months, and my marriage and my return to practice in the Paddington district having caused us to drift apart. One night in early August, as my way led through Baker Street, I was seized by a keen desire to see Holmes and to know to what use he was making of his extraordinary Engine. I found him lounging upon the sofa, a pipe-rack within his reach and a pile of crumpled newspapers, apparently recent, near at hand. A lens and a number of columns that had been neatly cut from the papers were lying upon the sofa beside him, which suggested he had been in the process of examining them when I entered.

"You are engaged, I see," said I. "Perhaps I am interrupting your work."

"On the contrary, you could not have come at a better time, my dear Watson," he said cordially. "You would confer a great favour upon me should you lend me an ear, for nothing clears up a problem so much as stating it to another person. I think that your time will not be misspent," he continued as he reached for a paper. "This case has its points of interest and, especially, of instruction."

I gave the pile more careful scrutiny and realized that it was largely made up of back editions, for they were yellowed, of the *Times*.

"You are searching for something?" I asked.

"Indeed, Watson. I am searching for a series of trifles," he remarked. "You know my method. It is founded upon the premise that it is usually in unimportant matters that there is a field for observation."

He flipped rapidly through the paper, finally thrusting it under his sofa and taking up another.

"As you know, I customarily read nothing but the criminal news and the personal announcements. I have of late included the advertisements, which are proving instructive."

I waited silently, accommodating my companion's flair for the dramatic, to which I was long accustomed. He lit his pipe nonchalantly and continued.

"You may have read yourself, over the past eight months, of the series of daring burglaries that has been taking place throughout London's most fashionable districts. Scotland Yard is absolutely baffled."

"I have seen what the *Daily Telegraph* and the *Chronicle* have had to say, but not the *Times*," I replied.

"It is theorized that there are two persons involved," he continued, "and although two suspects have been under investigation, the authorities have never been able to establish their presence at the scenes of the crimes. There is nothing more stimulating than a case where everything goes against you. This particular matter is further complicated by the fact that neither suspect ever seems to communicate with the other. Now unless Scotland Yard can prove some means of communication, or better still, determine this means, intercept their messages, and catch them in the act, it is feared that these burglars will remain free. It is necessary to prove that they were indeed conspirators before they can be brought before a magistrate."

"I take it, Holmes, you have come across something in the *Times* linking these two with the crimes that the police have failed to note?"

"Yes, Watson, the *Times* is a paper that is seldom found in any hands but those of the highly educated. Crime is common but logic is rare, and I sense an extremely complex mind behind this. Therefore, it is upon the logic rather than upon the crime that one should dwell. Just when I thought that the criminal mind had lost all enterprise and originality, enter these singularly interesting specialists.

"This is one of those cases where the art of the reasoner should be used for the sifting of details rather than for the acquisition of fresh evidence. This is where Scotland Yard has wasted its energy. I, on the other hand, have considered how I might communicate with a silent partner."

Holmes rose from the sofa and walked towards the hearth rug while scanning the paper he had picked up earlier. I took this opportunity to stretch out in the comfortable armchair which I had occupied so many times before. I looked dreamily up to the mantelpiece, recollecting old adventures we had shared. I started from my reverie as Holmes abruptly pounced upon an advertisement.

"Here!" he exclaimed. "The most recent one, and at the correct time. That accounts for all seven robberies, by my calculations."

He then showed me the item which had arrested his interest.

For Sale: Copies of the Strand *numbering from 23 to 276 with various duplicates. Also, 3 Twybridge carriage wheels in excellent condition. Please enquire: Box 37 GPO*

"I do not recognise the carriage name," I replied, "but some of those issues of the *Strand* have chronicles of your achievements."

"Holmes abruptly pounced upon an advertisement."

"The magazine itself is of little import, Watson, but the numbers of these issues are. The newest volume number minus the oldest volume is a number that fits well into my theory, as is the number of carriage wheels. As for these Twybridge carriage wheels, I can safely attest that there are no such items in existence. I am familiar with forty-two impressions left by carriage wheels, having written a short monograph on the subject.

"I believe the 3 represents three o'clock in the morning, the hour the last burglary took place. Also, is it not curious, Watson, that this carriage, whose name is unfamiliar to us, should have the same name as the street on which the last victim resides?"

Holmes pulled another well-worn newspaper from the stack near him.

"Here is another from last month's paper, offering for sale 209 'Brewster' pigeons; and a robbery did occur on Sunday, July 28th."

I pondered for a moment and asked, "Holmes, I believe you may have something. But about the date, are you sure?"

"Absolutely. If we subtract the lower number from the upper number of the supposed volumes of the *Strand*, we get 253. The 253rd day of the year was September 10th, a Tuesday and the date of the last robbery. July 28th was nearly seven weeks ago. It was the 209th day of the year, a Sunday, and the date of the previous robbery. And, I might add, there are no pigeons of a type called Brewster."

"Amazing, Holmes, but how did you determine the date from just the number?"

"That is the flower that comes from this little seed, Watson. I must take care to explain it to you in detail so that you may appreciate it fully.

"Obviously, Watson, a programme on the Analytical Engine which arrives at the date from the number would be a way to achieve an efficient solution to this problem. The first of January was a Tuesday. If we enter the number

253

the programme will calculate the date

Tuesday, September 10

the date that is the 253rd day of the year. I am sure that these scoundrels just count the days off on the current calendar, but counting is tedious and prone to error. Such a solution lacks elegance and can hardly be considered of broad use."

"There are some other uses you have in mind for this programme?" I asked.

"It is what we learn from the particular construction of this programme that will be of continued use to us, Watson," said Holmes. "We are faced here with finding a means of working on a numerical device with items that have many and varying properties. We are dealing here with a theory of *types*, the representation of things from the real world.

"I have given this notion considerable thought and have taken the trouble of constructing a diagram," he said, handing me a small chart which ran this way (see Fig. 9.1).

"A type, Watson, characterizes a class of objects and the operations that can be performed upon them.

"The current problem has several classes of objects with differing operations possible for them. Consider the days of the week. For us there can only be seven days of the week—Sunday, Monday, Tuesday, Wednesday, Thursday, Friday, Saturday.

"Some of the common operations that we can perform upon them are

1. Computing the day after: Given a day of the week, we can determine the following day, for example,

    DayAfter(Monday) is Tuesday
    DayAfter(Friday) is Saturday

2. Comparison of days: In a given week we can determine if any one day precedes another, for example,

    Monday precedes Saturday
    Monday precedes Wednesday

When we write programmes, we deal with many such types of objects—names, varieties of cigar ash, amounts of money, months, days, and so forth."

Holmes then displayed his algorithm for computing the date from the number of days given in the advertisements. The algorithm is reproduced here as Fig. 9.2. I had no problem in following his simple logic.

"Now for the representation of the problem. When we use the Engine, we have only a small number of commonly used fundamental types at our disposal, for example, integers, characters, Boolean truth

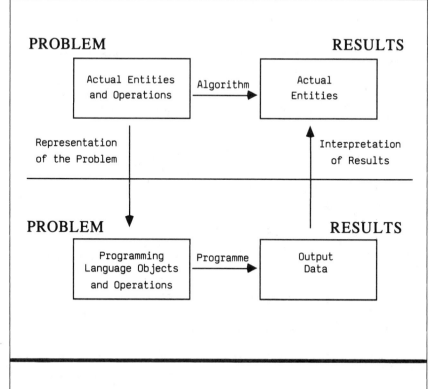

Figure 9.1

Figure 9.2 ● Holmes's algorithm for computing dates.

Definitions:

DayOfWeek : one of the days Sunday through Saturday
Month   : one of the months January through December
DayOfMonth : a number from 1 to 31

CurrentNum : a number from 1 to 365
NumOfDays : a number from 1 to 365

Algorithm:

Set Month to January
Set DayOfMonth to 1
Set DayOfWeek to Tuesday

Read NumOfDays

For CurrentNum set to 2 through NumOfDays, do the following:
  set DayOfWeek to DayAfter(DayOfWeek)

  if DayOfMonth = 28 and Month = February
    set up for new month
  else if DayofMonth = 30 and
          Month = April or June or September or November
    set up for new month
  else if DayOfMonth = 31
    set up for new month
  else
    set DayOfMonth to DayOfMonth + 1
Write DayOfWeek, Month, DayOfMonth

values, and strings. Each of these types has its own special operations defined in the programming language, so we do not have to bother ourselves constantly with defining them.

"For example, we have

addition: We can add two numbers and get their sum.

comparison: We can compare two numbers to see which is greater.

negation: We can negate an integer or a Boolean truth value.

printing: We can print a number or a string.

"Now, Watson," he continued, "the essence of working with any actual type of data is that the objects, such as amounts of money, days of the week, and months, must be defined in terms of the programming language. We must not only choose a particular representation for an object; we must also make sure that operations upon it, as represented in the language, correctly reflect its actual properties.

"For example, we can perform all numeric operations on numeric data; but when the number represents some real entity, like the year 1889, some operations are meaningless. The difference of two years is a useful operation because it is actually sensible to consider the interval of time between two dates. On the other hand, the square root of a year has no useful meaning associated with it. To multiply two years is likewise senseless.

"Specifically, our calendar problem requires us to write an algorithm which correctly depicts the three data types:

> months
> days of the week
> days of the month

The days of the month running from 1 to 31 can easily be represented using integers. The 'day after' DayOfMonth is

> DayOfMonth + 1

Of course, when the value of DayOfMonth is the last day of the month, the day after is not

> DayOfMonth + 1

but 1. This shows that, although we operate on days of the month as integers, they are not really integers; this must be kept in mind or large problems will certainly result.

"Consider also the days of the week. We could represent them as integers: Sunday with 1, Monday with 2, and so forth. Of course, days of the week are not at all numbers; and the special rule for the last day of the week is needed to represent the real world correctly. In a Pascal programme we would have:

```
if DayOfWeek = 7 then
    DayOfWeek := 1
else
    DayOfWeek := DayOfWeek + 1
```

"Simplifying the programme even further, since there are only seven days of the week, we could make each day a named constant,

```
const
    Sunday  = 1;
    Monday  = 2;
    . . .
```

and use the constant names instead of integers, so they would appear as the actual names of the days. Then we would have

```
if DayOfWeek = Saturday then
    DayOfWeek := Sunday
else
    DayOfWeek := DayOfWeek + 1
```

"And now, Watson, for the last step. Pascal allows us to define our own types! We can write,

> **type** DayName = (Sunday, Monday, Tuesday, Wednesday, Thursday,
>   Friday, Saturday);

This is a type with exactly seven values, corresponding precisely to the seven days of the week.

"Just as we can say,

> NumItems: Integer;

to mean that NumItems can take on only integer values, we could instead say,

> DayOfWeek: DayName;

to mean that DayOfWeek can only take on values from Sunday through Saturday.

"To set the current day to Tuesday, we simply say,

> DayOfWeek := Tuesday

Once DayOfWeek has been given a value, we can obtain the day after by saying,

> **if** DayOfWeek = Saturday **then**
>   DayOfWeek = Sunday
> **else**
>   DayOfWeek = Succ(DayOfWeek);

The predefined function named Succ is Pascal's curious way of expressing the value that succeeds another value. Now it is impossible to mix an integer with a day, as one is a number and the other is a different type quite unable to take on a numerical value."

I did not know quite what to say after this great exposition on the theory of types and the days of the week. My silence made it plainly evident that I was hopelessly at sea.

"This should make things clearer, Watson," said Holmes, quickly producing the programme that I have reproduced in Fig. 9.3. The programme was surprisingly easy to read.

"Well, then," I remarked after a while, "it all seems clear to me from here. You plan to anticipate the next theft, unless I am mistaken?"

"Oh, hardly my dear Watson," he replied. "You know that I look upon unnecessary bodily exertion as an extreme waste of energy. This surely is now a matter for the police. After all, Watson, I am not retained by Scotland Yard to supply their deficiencies."

It was one of the peculiarities of his proud, self-contained nature that he was always averse to anything in the shape of public applause, and he bound me in the most stringent terms to publish no account of this matter. Nothing amused Holmes more at the conclusion of a successful problem than to hand over the actual exposure to some orthodox official.

A report in the *Times* a fortnight later described the apprehension of the criminals. Of course, there was no mention of either Holmes or the Analytical Engine. It was, I surmise, his thought that widespread dissemination in the popular press of this remarkable mechanism would naturally come to the attention of the more undesirable elements of the city. How well I recall his once commenting, "I could not rest, Watson, nor could I sit quietly in my chair, if I thought that the Analytical Engine had fallen into the hands of some diabolical mastermind, walking the streets of London unchallenged."

```
program ComputeDate;
{ -- January 1, 1889 was a Tuesday. }
{ -- This program reads in a number named NumOfDays, }
{ -- representing the number of days since January 1. }
{ -- The program prints the corresponding date. }

  type
     DayName = (Sunday, Monday, Tuesday, Wednesday, Thursday,
           Friday, Saturday);
     MonthName = (January, February, March, April, May, June, July,
           August, September, October, November, December);

  var
     DayOfWeek : DayName;
     Month : MonthName;
     DayOfMonth : 1.31;
     CurrentNum : 1.365;
     NumOfDays : 1.365;

begin
  Month :@ January;
  DayOfMonth := 1;
  DayOfWeek := Tuesday;
  Read(NumOfDays);

  for CurrentNum := 2 to NumOfDays do
     begin
        if DayOfWeek = Saturday then
           DayOfWeek := Sunday
        else
           DayOfWeek := Succ(DayOfWeek);
```

Figure 9.3 ● Program ComputeDate

Figure 9.3 continued

```pascal
        if (DayOfMonth = 28) and (Month = February) then
          begin
            Month := Succ(Month);
            DayOfMonth := 1
          end
        else if (DayOfMonth = 30) and
          (Month in [September, April, June, November]) then
          begin
            Month := Succ(Month);
            DayOfMonth := 1
          end
        else if (DayOfMonth = 31) then
          begin
            Month := Succ(Month);
            DayOfMonth := 1
          end
        else
          DayOfMonth := DayOfMonth + 1;
      end;
    Write(DayOfWeek, ' ', Month, ' ', DayOfMonth : 1)
  end.
```

Chapter 9

Data Types

Real-world applications require new ways of describing data that are not intrinsically numeric. Further, we need to deal with items like train schedules and dates that, though numeric in nature, do not behave in the same way as the integers used to represent them. Problems of this sort require careful thought in program design. They also illustrate two essential programming concerns:

- The need to describe objects and their properties with precision and clarity.
- The need to guarantee that the operations over objects do not violate their intrinsic properties.

This brings us to the concept of *types*.

Every constant and variable used in a program belongs to a group of like values, or a type. The declaration

var
    StartTime, StopTime, ArrivalTime : Integer;

states that these three variables are of type Integer. *Integer* is a predefined type containing all the whole numbers between –32,767 and +32,767. If an attempt is made to assign a value outside this range to any of the three variables, an error will result. Real, LongInt, Char, and Boolean are other predefined types that we have already encountered.

Sometimes it is necessary for the programmer to introduce a new set of values. This is done by declaring a type name or *type identifier* and a list

9.1 • Enumerated Types

of the values that are contained within that type. This is known as an *enumerated type*. Consider the following declaration:

type
    DayName = (Sunday, Monday, Tuesday, Wednesday, Thursday,
                  Friday, Saturday, Sunday);

This declaration introduces a type named DayName and seven constants of that type, the names Sunday through Saturday. DayName has now been declared a type identifier. A type name cannot be used as a variable identifier; it would be an error to say,

    case DayName of   { error }

However, just as we can say,

var
    Counter : Integer;

to declare a variable Counter of type Integer, we can now say

var
    Today : DayName;

to declare a variable of type DayName and then say

    Today := Tuesday

Just as a variable of type Integer can take on integer values, a variable of type DayName can take on any of the seven values Sunday through Saturday. In this sense, we say that a type describes a class of values.

For enumerated types, the type declaration explicitly enumerates the class of values. The preceding example illustrates the first basic idea: you introduce a type to describe a class of values needed to solve your problem.

One of the properties of every enumerated type is that the values are ordered. In particular, the values are assumed to be enumerated in increasing order. For the type DayName, the first value is Sunday and the last is Saturday.

A data type consists of a set of values and associated operations. The declaration of an enumerated type specifies the set of values. Just as for integers, the operations on an enumerated type are predefined in Pascal. These include the relational operators for comparing values of the type. Thus, if the variable Today has the value Tuesday, we may have the following comparisons.

    (Today = Friday)   { Comparison is False }
    (Today = Tuesday)   { Comparison is True }
    (Today = Monday)   { Comparison is False }

Assignment is also allowed for enumerated types. For example, we may have

Today := Wednesday

The following examples are not logical, and are erroneous.

Sunday := Monday;   { Only variables can be assigned values }
Today := 1   { 1 is not a DayName }

In the first case, Sunday is not a variable. In the second case, the value assigned to a variable is not of the same type as that declared for the variable.

The position of a value in an enumerated type is known as its *ordinality*. The first value of any noninteger enumerated type has ordinality 0, the next has ordinality 1, and so forth. The function Ord can be applied to any enumerated value, as in

Ord(Wednesday)

and yields the ordinality of the value, in this case 3.

The functions Succ and Pred are two more predefined operations that apply to enumerated values. Their evaluation yields, respectively, the successor and the predecessor of an enumerated value. For a given enumerated type, the first value listed in the type definition has no predecessor and the last value has no successor. For example, we can have the expressions:

Succ(Monday)   { Value is Tuesday }
Succ(Succ(Monday))   { Value is Wednesday }
Succ(Saturday)   { Gives rise to an error }

Notice that if you try to get the successor of Saturday, you will get an error, and *not* the value Sunday as you might expect.

In Pascal, all programmer-defined types are introduced by type declarations of the form:

name = *type-definition;*

The name is a name for the type. The type definition specifies the class of values and, implicitly, the operations defining ways in which the values can be used. Except for subranges of previously defined types (described below), every type definition introduces a distinct type.

With this discussion in mind, we recall the basic definition of a type.

- A type characterizes a class of values and the set of operations that can be performed on them.

In programs, all variables have an associated type, specified when the variable is declared. The operations are defined by the language itself.

One of the key issues in programming is the security with which we can draw conclusions about a program. Consider the following declarations.

```
Today : Dayname;
NewCoin : Coin;
Counter : Integer;
```

where the type Coin has the definition:

```
type
    Coin = (Penny, Nickel, Dime, Quarter, HalfDollar, Dollar);
```

It would be meaningful to have the statements

```
Today      := Tuesday;
NewCoin    := Nickel;
Counter    := Counter + 1
```

but senseless and incorrect to have the statements:

```
Today      := Nickel;           { Nickel is not a Dayname }
NewCoin    := Tuesday;          { Tuesday is not a Coin }
Counter    := Today + 1         { 1 cannot be added to a Dayname }
```

This leads us to the two basic rules for using types:

- A variable may only have values of its specified type
- The only operations allowed on a value are those associated with its type.

As a result of these two rules, we can draw a fundamental conclusion about a program: *The type properties declared by a programmer will not be violated during program execution.* This means that Today will always be a DayName and Counter will always be an Integer. If you try to do otherwise, the computer will complain, and it should.

As mentioned earlier, an enumerated type is defined by listing its values. Such types can be used in many ways as freely as integers and often with great clarity. For example, we may have a loop iterating over the days of the week:

```
for Today := Sunday to Saturday do begin
    —what to do for each value of Today
end
```

Notice the clarity of the loop compared with

```
for DayIndex := 1 to 7 do begin
    —what to do for each value of DayIndex
end
```

Table 9.1 defines a number of enumerated types. The use of such types can add considerably to the clarity of a program.

Table 9.1 ● A Sampler of Enumerated Types

Enumerated Type	Values
DayName	= (Sunday, Monday, Tuesday, Wednesday, Thursday, Friday, Saturday);
Suspect	= (ColWoodley, MrHolman, MrPope, SirRaymond);
CigarTexture	= (Caked, Flaky, Fluffy, Granular, Varied);
Coin	= (Penny, Nickel, Dime, Quarter, HalfDollar, Dollar);
HalfDay	= (AM, PM);
ArmyRank	= (Private, Corporal, Sergeant, Lieutenant, Captain, Major, Colonel, General);
MajorCity	= (London, Oxford, Bristol, Birmingham, Plymouth, Liverpool, York, Manchester);
Shape	= (Triangle, Quadrangle, Pentagon, Hexagon);
Direction	= (North, East, South, West);
Weapon	= (Gun, Knife, Candlestick, Rope, Wrench);
Response	= (Yes, No Unknown);
ReportStatus	= (Unwritten, Drafted, Edited, Completed, InPress, Missing);

9.2 ● Boolean Types

In Chapter 5, we discussed the writing of conditions that give values that are True or False. These values are said to be of type Boolean, and all conditions must yield a value of type Boolean. Moreover, in Pascal you can declare a variable to be of type Boolean just as you can declare a variable to be of an integer type, a real type, or a enumerated type.

Suppose, for example, we wish to write a program to determine which one of a number of suspects matches a given list of characteristics. In searching the list of suspects, we may wish to keep track of whether we have found a match. To do this, we might declare a variable, say:

SuspectFound : Boolean;

Such a variable can only have one of two values, True or False. It is analogous to having the type declaration

type Boolean = (False, True);

At the beginning of our program, since we clearly have not found a match, we can say,

SuspectFound := False

Later in our program we will, of course, change this value to True when a matching suspect is found. The status of a Boolean variable may be used directly as a condition since its value is either True or False; for example,

> **if** SuspectFound **then**
>   *—what to do if a suspect has been found*
> **else**
>   *—what to do otherwise*

Such a statement has the same effect as writing,

> **if** SuspectFound = True **then**
>   *—what to do if a suspect has been found*
> **else**
>   *—what to do otherwise*

The type Boolean thus embodies a very simple but powerful idea. The type has only two values, True and False, and captures the essence of a condition. Furthermore, in any program in which we wish to keep track of a piece of information that can have only two values (for example, on or off, open or closed, known or unknown), we can represent our state of knowledge with a simple Boolean-valued variable.

9.3 ● Character Types

It would certainly be unfortunate if the only types of data that we could read or write were numbers. Suppose we wish to read in the days of the week, a person's name, a message, or two-letter city. What we would really like to do is read the characters directly into our program, rather than think up numeric codes. Fortunately we can do this in Pascal.

We use the Pascal type Char, which is predefined in the language, to work directly with single characters. The values of this type are all the characters you will normally find on your keyboard, and include not only letters or digits but also characters like $, <, and %.

For example, just as you can declare a variable Counter as having an integer type,

> Counter : Integer;

you can declare a variable, say NextChar, of character type

> NextChar : Char;

This declaration, like all variable declarations, specifies a variable whose values will be of a certain type, in this case one of the characters on the Macintosh. Thus if you want to read in a character from the terminal, you can say,

Read(NextChar)

or if you wish to assign a dollar sign to this variable, you can say,

NextChar := '$'

Notice that in programs a character value must always be enclosed by single quotation marks (').

Just as for integer types or enumerated types, you can compare the character values in relational expressions, for example, as in

if (NextChar = '$') then
    —what to do if the next character is a dollar sign
else
    —what to do otherwise

Furthermore, the allowed characters have a given order. For example, the character 'A' is considered to be less than 'B', 'B' is less than 'C', and so forth. Similarly, the characters '0', '1', and so forth are assumed to be in conventional order. The function Ord can be applied to any character to find its ordinality in the character set as in

Ord('*x*')   { *x* = any character in the Macintosh character set }

which yields the ordinality of *x*. The function Chr can also be applied, as in

Chr(*i*)   { *i* = any integer between 0 and 255 }

to yield the character having ordinality *i*.

9.4 ● Subranges of Types

There are many cases where variables have a common type but where the values a variable can take on are known to be within certain limits. For instance, we may know that a person's age will lie between 0 and 100, or we may know a character variable can only denote certain characters. To handle this kind of situation we can use a *subrange* declaration.

For instance, consider the following variable declarations.

```
DayOfMonth   : 1..31
WorkDay      : Monday..Friday
NextCode     : 'A'..'Z';
```

The first declaration specifies a variable DayOfMonth whose values lies in the range 1 through 31. The second declaration specifies a variable WorkDay whose value is one of the weekdays Monday through Friday. The third declaration specifies a character variable NextCode, whose value is one of the letters "A" through "Z."

Subrange specifications are always given in the form

value..value

where each of the values must be an integer, a value from some enumerated type, or a character. The type of such variables is the same as the type of the values in the subrange.

Subranges thus define a restricted sequence of values. The purpose of a subrange type is to control the range of values a variable may take during execution of your program. The bounds given in a subrange definition must belong to the same type (for example, Integer or the same enumerated type) and must be stated in increasing order. Thus, the following range definitions are illegal.

```
1..Penny;        { Error, bounds not of the same type }
Dollar..Penny;   { Error, bounds not in increasing order }
```

Subrange types can be declared just as for other types, by associating a name with a subrange. For example, we may have

```
type
    DayRange       = 1..31;
    WeekDayName    = Monday..Friday;
    Letter         = 'A'.. 'Z';
```

Using these explicit declarations we could alternatively declare our variables above as

```
DayOfMonth  : DayRange;
WorkDay     : WeekDayName;
NextCode    : Letter;
```

A subrange variable behaves much like a variable of the containing type. The only difference is that a subrange variable is constrained during execution to hold only values that belong to the declared range.

While the values of a subrange type are a subset of the containing type, the operations of a subrange type are the same as those of the containing type. Thus, the Succ and Pred functions, comparison operators, and input-output operations apply to subrange values exactly as they apply to values of the containing type. For subrange types whose containing type is Integer, the arithmetic operators apply as well.

In Pascal, there is no type distinction between variables specified as a subrange and those of the containing type. The difference is simply that Pascal keeps track of your constraints on the values. For example, if you say,

```
WorkDay := Sunday
```

the computer will complain, since Sunday is not in the range given for WeekDayName. Similarly, if you say,

```
DayOfMonth := DayOfMonth + 5
```

and the result is greater than 31, an error will arise.

Finally, a note on the operator **in**. You can use this operator to see whether a value is within some set of values. For example, you can say

> **if** NextCode **in** ['A', 'B', 'C', 'D', 'E']

or equivalently,

> **if** NextCode **in** ['A'..'E']

Generally speaking, the value being tested must be either an integer, a character, or an enumerated value. The set of values is specified by listing the members of the set, giving subranges, or both. Thus we may have

> [Monday..Friday]
> [April, June, September, November]
> [1, 3, 5, 7, 9]
> ['0'..'9', '%', '$', '.']

9.5 ● String Types

A sequence of characters can be designated as a *string type*. The declaration of a string-type value can contain a *size* attribute, which sets a limit on the number of characters that can be included. For instance,

> **var**
>   LastName : **string**[10]

declares LastName as a variable that can take on any string-type value containing up to 10 characters. The size attribute of a string type must lie in the range 1 to 255. If no size attribute is given, it is assumed to be 255.

String-type values are enclosed in single quotes, as in

> LastName := 'Watson'

A value of character type can be considered a string type with a size attribute of 1. Thus, the value NextChar can be declared as

> NextChar : Char;

or

> NextChar : **string**[1];

String types have a *length* attribute, which should not be confused with the size attribute. The length refers to the number of characters in the string at any particular time during the program. The size of LastName remains at 10, but the length changes as different names are assigned to it. Consider the following names.

    LastName := 'Smith'   { Length is equal to 5 }
    LastName := 'Milligan'   { Length is equal to 8 }

String variables can be used in Read and Write procedures, such as

    Read(LastName, YrsOfService, TotalCredits);
    AverageCredits := TotalCredits **div** YrsOfService;
    Write(LastName, '–', AverageCredits : 1, ' credits per year.')

The relational operators can be applied to a string-type value to compare it to another string-type value or to a character-type value. The length is very important here since two string values must be of equal length to be considered equal. In the following example, although the values may be equal for all practical purposes, they will be considered unequal and the Write procedure will not be executed.

    LastName := 'Smith';   { Length = 5 }
    OwnerName := 'Smith ';   { Length = 6 }
    if LastName = OwnerName **then**
        Write('Dear Homeowner,')

The value of OwnerName is considered greater than the value of LastName since any character, including a space, is considered higher than no character at all.

In comparing two string-type values, each character of one expression is compared with the character in the corresponding position of the other expression according to the ordering of the characters in the Macintosh character set. Consider the following:

    PresentName := 'Smyth';
    NextName := 'Smith';
    if NextName < PresentName **then**
        List := NextName

In comparing these two names, the individual characters are compared in order. The two "S's" are considered equal and the two "m's" are considered equal. When the third letter is reached, "y" is found to be greater than "i", therefore PresentName is considered greater than NextName.

In addition to the relational operators, there are several predefined procedures and functions that can be used for manipulating strings. The length of a string is obtained by using the function call Length(Str), as in the statement

    Length(LastName)

This call will return an integer equal to the number of characters in the current value of LastName.

Strings can be joined together or *concatenated*. Given the strings

LastName := 'Holmes';
FirstName := 'Sherlock';
Blank := ' '

the whole name can written using the predefined function Concat, as follows.

Write(Concat(FirstName, Blank, LastName))

This will cause the values of the strings Blank and LastName to be added to the end of FirstName.

Other functions are available for inserting strings into other strings at specific locations, deleting sections of strings, copying sections of strings. These make use of the number of characters involved or the Count, and the location within the string or Index. For instance, consider the program segment shown in Fig. 9.4.

This program reads a first name and a last name and stores them as a single string that uses 12 columns for the first name and up to 20 columns for the last name. Blanks taken from a string BlankString are entered after the first name to fill in the field so that the last name will always begin in column 13.

The third statement in the program says,

copy from the string BlankString,
start with the first character,
copy a number of characters equal to FieldWidth1 less the length of
    FirstName,
assign the result to Blanks.

```
program GuestList;
  const
    BlankString = '          ';
    FieldWidth1 = 12;
  var
    FirstName : string[12];
    LastName : string[20];
    Blanks : string[12];
    FullName : string[32];
begin
  ReadLn(FirstName);
  ReadLn(LastName);
  Blanks := Copy(BlankString, FieldWidth1–Length(FirstName));
  FullName := Concat(FirstName, Blanks, LastName)
```

Figure 9.4 ● Program GuestList

The fourth statement says

assign to the variable FullName,
a string consisting of
   the value of the string FirstName
   followed by the value of the string Blanks
   followed by the value of the string LastName.

Other predefined functions and the procedures Delete and Insert are summarized in Table 9.2. Notice that the two procedures actually change the value of the string, whereas the functions return a value without affecting the original string.

Summary

Any programming language comes equipped with certain basic types of data that must be used when writing programs. In Macintosh Pascal, there are several primitive types that are predefined in the language itself. These are

Integer, LongInt
Real, Double, Extended
Boolean
Char
String

In addition to these predefined types, Macintosh Pascal allows you to define your own enumerated types, such as

type
   DayName = (Sunday, Monday, Tuesday, Wednesday, Thursday,
           Friday, Saturday);

Furthermore, Macintosh Pascal allows you to define subranges of integer, character, or enumerated types. For example, you may say

type
   IndexVal = 1..100;
   Letter = 'A'..'Z';
   Weekday = Monday..Friday;

All of these except string type are defined as simple types. Although string type is not considered to be a simple type, it has many of the same characteristics as the simple types and has therefore been included with them. All of the simple types except for the Real group are further defined as *ordinal* types; that is, they are made up of discrete values in ascending order. Table 9.3 summarizes the predefined functions that apply to ordinal and string types.

Values can be compared with one another provided that they are of the same type. Table 9.4 shows the relational operators that can be used for comparing values.

Whatever type of data the program uses, each item must ultimately be represented with one of the predefined simple types, one of the methods for defining your own types, a string type, or one of the structured types discussed in later chapters.

Once a variable in the program has been declared to be of a certain type, it must always have values of that type. This ensures, for instance, that an integer will not be assigned to a character variable or an enumerated value to a real variable.

Table 9.2 ● Predefined Procedures and Functions for Strings

Definitions

Str	= an expression with a string-type value
StrVar	= a string-type variable
SubStr	= an expression with a string-type value
Index	= an integer indicating the position in a string, assuming the first character is 1, the second character is 2, etc.
Count	= an integer indicating the number of characters

The following predefined function calls return a string-type value. The original strings are not affected.

Length(Str)	returns the current length attribute of Str
Pos(SubStr,Str)	searches for SubStr within Str; returns a LongInt value indicating the position of the first character of SubStr within Str; returns zero if SubStr is not found.
ConCat(Str1,Str2, ... Strn)	concatenates all the expressions in the order written; returns the concatenated string.
Copy(Str,Index,Count)	returns a string containing Count characters from Str starting at Index.
Omit(Str,Index,Count)	removes Count characters from Str starting at Index; returns resulting string.
Include(SubStr,Str,Index)	inserts SubStr into Str starting at Index; returns resulting string.

The following predefined procedure calls change the value of StrVar.

Delete(StrVar,Index,Count)	removes Count characters from StrVar starting at Index.
Insert(SubStr,StrVar,Index)	inserts SubStr into StrVar starting at Index.

Table 9.3 ● Some Functions on Ordinal and String Types

Functions

Succ(x)   Computes the successor of x, the value whose ordinal is one greater than x. Taking the successor of the last value is in error.

Pred(x)   Computes the predecessor of x, the value whose ordinal is one less than x. Taking the predecessor of the first value is in error.

Ord(x)   Computes the ordinal value of x in its given ordering. For integers, returns the integer itself.

Chr(x)   Yields the character whose ordinal value is x. The value x must be an integer, and the result is a character.

Note: x is an expression whose value is an integer, character, string, or enumerated type. All such values have a given ordering. For integers, the ordinality is the value itself; for characters, the order is defined by the local implementation; for enumerated types, the values are listed in increasing order. The first value in an enumerated type is said to have the ordinal 0, the second 1, and so forth.

Table 9.4 ● Relational Operations on Simple and String Types

Relational Operations

Operator	Operation	Type of Operands	Result Type
= <>	Equality and inequality	Any simple or string type	Boolean
< <= > >=	Ordering	Any simple or string type	Boolean
in	Membership	Left: integer, character, or enumerated value Right: set of values of same type as left	Boolean

9.6 ○ Practice

Defining Simple Types

The concept of types is a particularly important one, as it makes solving certain classses of problems much easier. Type checking, a plus in any large program, makes it much easier to find small programming errors in Pascal than in a language that lacks it, such as Basic or Fortran. Learning to use types in a program is a must for any Pascal programmer. You could consider it an extra error check that is present at all times in the system.

Following is a list of items, any of which might be included in some program. Write a type declaration for each of them.

1. Name of an employee
2. The suit of a card
3. Current month
4. The number of square feet in a room
5. The number of people waiting in a line
6. Colors in a flag
7. The radio stations in a region
8. The traffic count at a corner
9. The status of a project
10. House pets
11. Absence or presence of a club member
12. Sizes available in a shoe style

● ● ●

The following are all valid type declarations. Of course, styles differ; your answers may be perfectly acceptable although different from ours.

```
Employee = string[40];
Suit = (Spades, Hearts, Clubs, Diamonds);
CurrentMonth = (Jan, Feb , Mar, Apr, May, Jun, Jul,
          Aug, Sep,  Oct, Nov, Dec);
RoomSize = Real;
QueueSize = Integer;
Color = (White, Red, Yellow, Green, Blue);
Station = (WHAI, WHMP, WKVT, WPOE, WRSI, WTTT);
AxleCount = Integer;
ProjectStatus = (NotStarted, InProcess, Completed, Unknown);
Pet = (Dog, Cat, Bird, Fish, Snake, Other);
Presence = Boolean;
ShoeSize = 5..13;
```

Fill in the Blanks

1. Type declarations appear after _____ declarations and before _____ declarations.

2. A declaration for an enumerated type consists of an equal sign with an identifier on the left, and on the right a list of values separated by commas. The list is enclosed by _____.

3. A Boolean type variable can take on only two values; the two values are _____ and _____.

4. A variable which will take on any single letter can be declared as char or _____ or _____.

5. The operator in is followed by a set of values enclosed by _____ _____.

6. If no size attribute is given in a string type, it is assumed to be _____.

7. Subranges can be defined for integer, character, and_____ types.

● ● ●

Type declarations appear after **const** declarations and before **var** declarations.

A declaration for an enumerated type consists of an equal sign with an identifier on the left, and on the right a list of values separated by commas. The list is enclosed by PARENTHESES.

A Boolean type variable can take on only two values; the two values are TRUE and FALSE.

A variable which will take on any single letter can be declared as char or STRING[1] or A..Z. Actually, it could also be declared as string without a size attribute, but a lot of internal space would be wasted, since the default size for a string is 255.

The operator in is followed by a set of values enclosed by BRACKETS. Be sure of your intentions when using parentheses and brackets in type declarations. Parentheses are used for enumerated lists; brackets for sets and the size attribute of a string.

As mentioned above, if no size attribute is given in a string type, it is assumed to be 255.

Subranges can be defined for integer, character, and ENUMERATED types.

True or False

1. An assignment statement can contain an integer-type variable on the left and a real-type variable on the right.

2. The length of a string-type variable can be the same as the size of the variable.

3. A type identifier can be used as a variable.

4. Predefined types must be declared in the declarations part of a program.

5. Calling for the successor of the last value in an enumerated list causes the first value in the list to be returned.

6. A character value must be enclosed by single quotes.

7. In order for a subrange to be used, it must be given a type identifier and declared.

8. Character-type values can be compared with string-type values.

9. The values listed within the parentheses in an enumerated-type declaration are the only values allowed for a variable of that type.

An assignment statement cannot contain an integer-type variable on the left and a real-type variable on the right. The real-type value would have to be truncated or rounded before assignment. However, an integer-type variable can be assigned to a real-type variable; for instance,

        RealNum := IntNum   { IntNum = 3 }

causes RealNum to receive the value 3.0.

The size of a string variable is the highest number of characters that the string is allowed to contain. The length is the number of characters it contains at a particular point in the program. They can be the same, but need not be. The length, of course, must not exceed the size or an error results.

A type identifier absolutely cannot be used as a variable. Once a name has been reserved as a type identifier, it remains so throughout the program.

Predefined types do not need to be declared as types; their names can be used as type descriptions without a type declaration.

There is no successor to the last value in an enumerated list. Calling for the successor to the last value will result in an error.

Yes, a character value must, indeed, be enclosed by single quotes.

Although it is not a requirement that a subrange be given a type identifier, it is, nonetheless, a good practice. For instance, instead of the variable declaration

        Counter1 : 1..35;

we can declare a type Range1 as follows:

        type
            Range1 = 1..35;

and a variable Index, as in

var
    Index : Range1;

Numbers 8 and 9 are true.

9.7 ○

9.1   Page Numbering
The numbers on the pages of a book of course go in ascending order. The first page is 1, the second 2, and so forth.

If you are a typesetter in a printing shop, you need to have enough digits to print the page number for each page. For example, in a book with only 51 pages, you need

5 ZEROS	7 FIVES
16 ONES	5 SIXES
15 TWOS	5 SEVENS
15 THREES	5 EIGHTS
15 FOURS	5 NINES

Assuming you never have to print a book with more than 1000 pages, write a program to input the number of pages in a book and to output the number of each digit required.

9.2   Expressing Calendar Dates in Readable Form
On many computer systems, a calendar date is expressed as a six-digit integer. For example,

022243

means the month 02, day 22, year 1943, or in more familiar terms:

FEBRUARY 22, 1943

Write a program to read in a six-digit integer and output the corresponding date in day-to-day notation. If the six-digit integer does not represent a valid date, the integer and an appropriate message should be printed.

For example, with

132243

the output could be

132243 IS NOT A VALID DATE, WHO ARE YOU KIDDING?

Note: Don't forget about leap years.

9.3   Secret Number: Version 5

An entry code that is used to access an Automatic Teller Machine does not necessarily have to consist of digits only. It could be made up of any series of characters. Write a program which gives the user three chances to correctly enter the code. The code is to consist of a three-digit number followed by a color. The allowable colors are to be listed in an enumerated type declaration.

9.4   Binary versus Octal Notation

The internals of a computer are such that it is very convenient to store all information in a form called *binary*, meaning "two states." The computer stores the information it receives from the outside in the form of 1's and 0's, and thus numbers notated in this manner can be used for calculation without a lot of manipulation inside the computer. However, binary numbers are difficult for humans to use because they need so many 1's and 0's to write out. Like the number 1024, for instance, requires 11 binary digits, 10000000000.

A somewhat better system for humans to use is the *octal* system, which uses the eight digits 0 through 7 to denote its numbers. There is another advantage in that conversion to octal from binary is very easy. We take the binary number and arrange it in groups of three starting from the right side. Then each group of three is translated into its corresponding octal number, from right to left. The resulting number is the same number that the binary digits represented, but in octal notation. For example the decimal number 1401 is

10	101	111	001	Binary
2	5	7	1	Octal

For your exercise, write a program that converts a given binary number to an octal number. For the more adventuresome, the reverse problem of converting an octal number to binary is interesting. Though the problem seems to be about the same, it has some interesting twists.

9.5   Binary versus Decimal Notation

As mentioned previously, in most computers numbers are represented in binary notation. For example, 10011 represents the decimal integer 19. This may be computed as follows:

10011

represents

$$1*2^4 + 0*2^3 + 0*2^2 + 1*2^1 + 1*2^0$$

i.e.,

$$1*16 + 0*8 + 0*4 + 1*2 + 1*1$$

which equals 19.

Write a program to read a binary number with up to 16 binary digits and print its decimal equivalent. Test your program with the following numbers.

Input	Output
1	Value is 1
001	Value is 1
100	Value is 4
111	Value is 7
1010101	Value is 85

9.6   Reading Month Abbreviations

Many problems can be solved in more than one way, using more than one approach. Some approaches are better than others in certain situations, but few are clearly superior in all cases.

Let us consider the problem of month abbreviations as they are entered as data to a program. There are many ways to convert the three-letter representations of the months into digits that can be sorted or compared, but the simplest involves using a direct comparison of characters.

Write a program that will accept as input three letters, check them, and give the correct ordinal number or return an error message if the letters entered are not a correct three-letter abbreviation of a month of the year. The abbreviations, in order, are:

JAN FEB MAR APR MAY JUN JUL AUG SEP OCT NOV DEC

Note: After the next chapter, you may want to try to accomplish the same task using arrays.

Prelude to Arrays

The Ciphered Message

THE intimate relations that had existed between Sherlock Holmes and myself were, to an extent, modified in those years following my marriage, during which my practice increased steadily. I was occasionally able to follow my old companion's activities in the daily papers, which reported on his service to the Royal Family of Scandinavia and a matter of great importance to the French government, the details of which may never fully reach the public. While these cases brought him fame and princely rewards, they, and the one that I am about to relate, gave him the opportunity of demonstrating a fresh idea in his use of the Analytical Engine.

I called upon him late one winter's evening. As we sat on either side of the fire, Holmes was telling me once again, with great exultation, how he had purchased at a broker's in Tottenham Court Road for only fifty-five shillings a Stradivarius that was valued at over five hundred guineas. He suddenly held up his hand in a gesture of silence.

"We have a visitor," he said softly. "A gentleman of some importance, a government official perhaps."

When Mrs. Hudson showed a fellow dressed more like a gardener than a statesman into his lodgings, I must confess I had a slight feeling of amusement in my heart and hoped that this would be a lesson against the somewhat dogmatic tone Holmes often exhibited.

"Tell me, sir," said Holmes, before any introductions had been exchanged, "do you always tend your flower beds in patent-leather boots, or is this the manner of attire appropriate to Whitehall these days?"

"Mr. Holmes," he replied solemnly, "I come on a matter of the utmost delicacy concerning the security of our nation." As he spoke he handed Holmes his card, which identified him as an undersecretary in the Home Office.

Holmes rubbed his hands and his eyes glistened. Once our visitor was seated, Holmes leaned forward eagerly in his chair.

"State your case," he said briskly.

Uncomfortable, I rose to excuse myself.

"Please stay, Watson," asked Holmes. Then, turning to our visitor, he said, "this is Dr. Watson. You may say before this gentleman anything which you choose to say to me."

"It is known that you have assisted other heads of state on matters of the utmost confidence," said the man. "I am here, disguised so as not to draw attention to myself, on behalf of the Secretary to ask your help on a delicate matter concerning the transmission of diplomatic messages."

"Surely you are aware," answered Holmes, "that this is the special province of my brother, Mycroft. Though a government accountant, he also serves as an advisor in such matters."

"True, very true indeed, sir. However, as you yourself know very well, work of this nature neither begins nor ends in an armchair. While your brother's services remain indispensable, he lacks a certain energy."

Holmes merely nodded. "Pray continue," he said.

"He endeavoured to read them."

"Diplomatic ciphered messages are being regularly intercepted, deciphered, and acted upon. Acted upon with great damage," the Undersecretary stated in a clear and determined manner. With that, he produced a small packet of papers, unfolded them, and disclosed to us some of their contents. Holmes retrieved a small pince-nez and endeavoured to read them.

"I thought that diplomatic ciphers were extremely difficult to break and that their keys were changed regularly. I understand also that the material they contain is often urgent, so that by the time someone could reasonably be expected to decode it, the information would no longer be important," Holmes said.

"This is true for the most part," replied the Undersecretary. "But some of our clerks are—how shall I say it—incapable of handling a cipher of great complexity or of remembering the scheme required to decipher it, and certainly incapable of relearning a new one as often as necessary. Indeed, the same code, a simple one, is used for months, so that confusion is kept to a minimum."

I am not at liberty to reveal the content of the next hour's discussion. Suffice it to say that the matters discussed were grave indeed.

As our visitor was restoring his papers to an inner pocket, Holmes said, "How may I be of assistance to you, sir?"

"Mr. Holmes, we need a more secure cipher. Will you devise one for us?"

"I shall do my best," said Holmes steadily.

"Very good," replied the Undersecretary, and he then withdrew.

"Well, Watson, what do you make of it?" asked Holmes, once we were again alone.

"A nasty business, I should say, by the sound of things. But I am afraid I cannot help you much, for I am quite unfamiliar with ciphers and codes."

"Perhaps," said Holmes. "But this cipher is one of the simplest imaginable. It is so transparent that even a Scotland Yard official could see through it. The foreign agents who intercepted the messages probably believed the cipher was so elementary that it was a blind for a deeper and more complex cipher, embedded within. Each letter of the alphabet is simply replaced by some other letter. Allow me to show you."

Holmes wrote a sequence of letters on a sheet of paper:

A B C D E F G H I J K L M N O P Q R S T U V W X Y Z

"Assume now that our cipher letters are given in the following sequence.

H I J K L M N O P Q R S T U V W X Y Z A B C D E F G

Now we write the message on top, and below it the ciphered message.

TWELVE SHIPS   WILL LEAVE ...
ADLSCL ZOPWZ DPSS SLHCL ...

Thus we get a letter for each letter of the message; and as long as we have a standard table to use, enciphering the message is an easy task."

"Well, all this seems childishly simple to me," I said.

"Too simple; and therein lies our problem, Watson."

"But surely, Holmes, you must know of some other cipher the Home Office could substitute for this one."

"I am fairly familiar with all forms of secret writings; and am myself the author of a trifling monograph upon the subject, in which I analyze one hundred and sixty separate ciphers. This one, however, as I have already stated, is by far the simplest—and I need not remind you with whom we are dealing."

After a considerable pause he returned to his sample ciphering sequence. "Here again is the sequence I have just written:

HIJKLMNOPQRSTUVWXYZABCDEFG

We can shift this sequence by one letter and get

IJKLMNOPQRSTUVWXYZABCDEFGH

We can do likewise for a shift by two letters or three letters or even 25 letters. Each of these permutations is displayed in this table."

Holmes then showed me the table that I have duplicated here as Fig. 10.1.

"Now for the key, Watson. From time to time passwords, or keywords, if you will, can be provided to the clerks. For demonstration, suppose the keyword is WATSON."

"I am flattered, Holmes," I remarked quite involuntarily.

"Now," Holmes continued, "we write the password over the message, like this:

WATSON WATSO NWAT SONWA ...
TWELVE SHIPS   WILL   LEAVE   ...

For the first letter (T) of the message, we look at the W row of the cipher table under the column T. We get a W. For the next message letter (W), look at the A row under column W. We get a D. Simply continuing as prescribed, the message is coded as

WDEKQY VOION QLSL KZUYL...

Elementary, is it not?"

MESSAGE LETTER

	A B C D E F G H I J K L M N O P Q R S T U V W X Y Z
A	H I J K L M N O P Q R S T U V W X Y Z A B C D E F G
B	I J K L M N O P Q R S T U V W X Y Z A B C D E F G H
C	J K L M N O P Q R S T U V W X Y Z A B C D E F G H I
D	K L M N O P Q R S T U V W X Y Z A B C D E F G H I J
E	L M N O P Q R S T U V W X Y Z A B C D E F G H I J K
F	M N O P Q R S T U V W X Y Z A B C D E F G H I J K L
G	N O P Q R S T U V W X Y Z A B C D E F G H I J K L M
H	O P Q R S T U V W X Y Z A B C D E F G H I J K L M N
I	P Q R S T U V W X Y Z A B C D E F G H I J K L M N O
J	Q R S T U V W X Y Z A B C D E F G H I J K L M N O P
K	R S T U V W X Y Z A B C D E F G H I J K L M N O P Q
L	S T U V W X Y Z A B C D E F G H I J K L M N O P Q R
M	T U V W X Y Z A B C D E F G H I J K L M N O P Q R S
N	U V W X Y Z A B C D E F G H I J K L M N O P Q R S T
O	V W X Y Z A B C D E F G H I J K L M N O P Q R S T U
P	W X Y Z A B C D E F G H I J K L M N O P Q R S T U V
Q	X Y Z A B C D E F G H I J K L M N O P Q R S T U V W
R	Y Z A B C D E F G H I J K L M N O P Q R S T U V W X
S	Z A B C D E F G H I J K L M N O P Q R S T U V W X Y
T	A B C D E F G H I J K L M N O P Q R S T U V W X Y Z
U	B C D E F G H I J K L M N O P Q R S T U V W X Y Z A
V	C D E F G H I J K L M N O P Q R S T U V W X Y Z A B
W	D E F G H I J K L M N O P Q R S T U V W X Y Z A B C
X	E F G H I J K L M N O P Q R S T U V W X Y Z A B C D
Y	F G H I J K L M N O P Q R S T U V W X Y Z A B C D E
Z	G H I J K L M N O P Q R S T U V W X Y Z A B C D E F

"Quite," I replied. "And I suppose that you intend to hand this material over to the Analytical Engine?"

"Precisely. Think of it, Watson, a device made of wood and metal that will actually print the results of its most complicated calculations as soon as they are obtained, without any intervention of human intelligence, or lack of it, as this case would suggest. Our Engine will guarantee the mathematical accuracy of its work, so ciphering the message will be flawless."

One of the most remarkable characteristics of Sherlock Holmes was his ability to put his brain out of action, switching his thoughts to lighter things whenever he had satisfied himself that he could no longer work to advantage. With a casual remark that this was indeed one of the most unimaginative tasks he had been called upon to deliver, he lapsed into our earlier discussion of violins. This led him to Paganini; and before I departed we sat for another hour over a bottle of claret, while he told me anecdote after anecdote of that extraordinary man.

I promised to return the next evening, and did so promptly at eight. Upon entering, I found Holmes peering into the internals of the device on the centre-table, which had been cleared of everything else. From where I stood I could see a very closely packed collection of meshing gears and cams. There appeared to be a cover that was swung upwards, forwards, and out of the way. Holmes studied the box for a moment and then beckoned to me.

"An amazing machine, Watson. The way Babbage uses the gears and cams to store his data is truly ingenious. We are now faced with the problem of how we are to proceed with the enciphering programme. I have been giving the matter some consideration and have written down my thoughts in the order that the machine should perform them to accomplish the task. What do you think, Watson?"

On a piece of paper Holmes had written the following:

Read in the cipher table

Repeat the following:
   read message character
   if message character is a letter then
     select cipher character using keyword and message letter
     write cipher character
   else
     write message character
until no characters are left

"Holmes, although this sketch is simple, it will actually be very cumbersome to implement, will it not?"

"How would you do it, Watson?"

I started to write almost without thinking:

If key letter is A and message letter is A then cipher is H
If key letter is A and message letter is B then cipher is I
  . . .   .
If key letter is A and message letter is Z then cipher is G
If key letter is B and message letter is A then cipher is I
If key letter is B and message letter is B then cipher is J
  . . .   .

and so on.

"My goodness, Holmes, this would take hundreds, if not thousands, of instructions. I do not see how they could possibly fit into the Engine."

"Six hundred and seventy-six, to be precise, Watson. Your method is indeed cumbersome. Perhaps a table—or as our mathematician friends call it, an *array*—would help to reduce the size of the programme. It would also eliminate the element of redundancy that your scheme requires."

"Exactly what is an array?" I enquired.

"An array is much like a chessboard," explained Holmes. "For our problem the cipher table is a 26-by-26 array, a chessboard is an 8-by-8 array.

"Each position in the cipher table or chessboard can be identified by naming the particular array and the specific element or position with which we are concerned. In the message, the first cipher letter is the letter residing at the crossing of the W row and the T column. Thus the cipher for the letter T can be obtained with the description:

CipherTable ['W', 'T']

Equivalently, if Row is set to 'W' and Column to 'T', we can write,

CipherTable [Row, Column]

Indeed, the description can be assumed to be the same as the actual element.

"It is a powerful concept for describing data, as it compresses the information into a form that is entirely suitable for a machine such as Babbage's, and is much more economical with the amount of space used. It also removes the need for all the words describing the choices to be made in the cipher. Rather, it uses the position in the array to convey all of this. However, I am still faced with the problem of the keyword. If it is not made to reside in the Engine, anyone could steal it and use it. The keyword will reside in the programme, so that we shall have no problems with the operator."

Holmes paced anxiously about the room for a moment and then constructed a sort of Eastern divan in one corner. He perched himself upon it, cross-legged, with a quantity of shag tobacco and a box of matches laid out before him. In the dim light of the lamp I watched him sitting there, an old briar pipe between his lips, his eyes fixed vacantly upon the corner of the the ceiling, the blue smoke curling up from him, silent, motionless, with the light shining upon his strong-set aquiline features.

I knew that seclusion and solitude were necessary for Holmes in those hours of intense mental concentration, and it was noon the next day when I again found myself in his sitting room. My first impression was that a fire had broken out, for the room was thick with smoke and I could barely see Holmes in his dressing-gown, coiled up in his armchair by the fireplace.

"So you've been up all the night and all the morning poisoning yourself," I said.

"Actually, Watson, I have just returned from the Home Office," he answered.

"You have been there in spirit, perhaps?"

"Exactly. The body of Sherlock Holmes has remained here in this armchair and has, I regret to report, consumed in my absence two large pots of coffee and an incredible amount of tobacco."

"And what have you brought back with you to Baker Street?"

He then unrolled a large document upon his knee. On it were the final algorithm and the final programme, which I have duplicated as Figs. 10.2 and 10.3, respectively.

As I examined the material he exclaimed, "Well, Watson, let us escape from this weary workaday world by the side door of music. Carina sings tonight at the Albert Hall, and we still have time to dress, drop these off at Whitehall, dine, and enjoy an evening of supreme inspiration."

Figure 10.2 ● Holmes's algorithm for enciphering a message

```
Definitions:
Row, Column :   a letter for a row or column of the cipher table
MessageChar :   a character
CipherChar   :   a character
CipherTable :   an array giving the cipher letter for each
                keyword letter and message letter
KeyWord      :   the characters used for ciphering messages

Algorithm:
  Read cipher letters for each Row and Column of CipherTable
  Repeat the following:
    read MessageChar
    if MessageChar is a letter then
      set Row to next letter of Keyword
      set Column to MessageChar
      set CipherChar to CipherTable [Row, Column]
      write CipherChar
    else
      write MessageChar
  until no characters are left
```

```
program Encipher;
{ -- This program reads in the characters of a message and }
{ -- enciphers each letter. Based on the letter and the next }
{ -- letter of the keyword, the enciphered letter is obtained }
{ -- from a cipher table initially read into the program. }
{ -- The message is terminated with a slash. }
  const
    NumKeyLetters = 6;
    Slash = '/';
  type
    Letter = 'A' .. 'Z';
  var
    Row, Column : Letter;
    MessageChar, CipherChar : Char;
    CipherTable : array[Letter, Letter] of Char;
    KeyWord : packed array[1..NumKeyLetters] of Char;
    KeyIndex : Integer;
begin
  KeyWord := 'Watson';
  for Row := 'A' to 'Z' do
    begin
      for Column := 'A' to 'Z' do
        Read(CipherTable[Row, Column]);
      ReadLn;
    end;
  KeyIndex := 1;
  repeat
    Read(MessageChar);
    if MessageChar in ['A' .. 'Z'] then
      begin
        Row := KeyWord[KeyIndex];
        Column := MessageChar;
        CipherChar := CipherTable[Row, Column];
        Write(CipherChar);
        if KeyIndex = NumKeyLetters then
          KeyIndex := 1
        else
          KeyIndex := KeyIndex + 1
      end
    else
      Write(MessageChar)
  until MessageChar = Slash
end.
```

Figure 10.3 ● Program Encipher

Chapter 10

Arrays and Strings

Until now we have been dealing with items like a room number, a hair color, a type of cigar, and the time of day. All of these items have a common characteristic: they denote a single piece of data in the real world. With the introduction of Holmes's enciphering table, we come to an entirely different kind of entity, that of a composite object. A composite object has components that bear some relation to one another. In Holmes's enciphering program, the cipher table is a composite object consisting of the cipher characters corresponding to each possible pair of letters.

The enciphering table raises a very general issue. In many instances we have collections of related data. To turn such data into a usable tool, we need some means of organizing the data to reflect the way they are used.

We turn here to one of the most important schemes for organizing data, the *array;* in later chapters we will examine how data may be organized into a file or a record structure. But the various methods for structuring data have the same objective: the ability to describe organized patterns of information.

You can think of an array as an ordinary table of entries. A table expresses a correspondence; that is, for each one of several items, we have a corresponding item.

For example, each of the following correspondences can be expressed in a table:

$\quad$ *city* $\qquad \rightarrow \quad$ arrival time

10.1 ● Array Types

month   →   corresponding number of days
coin   →   corresponding value

In the first case, we have several cities, each having a corresponding arrival time. In the second case, the correspondence is between the name of a month and the number of days in the month. In the third case, taken from our problem to count change, we have six coins, each with a corresponding value in cents. A simple table describing the correspondence between coins and values is shown in Fig. 10.4.

An array has two fundamental properties. The first is its set of indexes, and the second is the set of components that may be stored within it. For example, the table of coin values may be described in Pascal as follows:

array[1..6] **of** Integer

This array contains six values, indexed by the numbers 1 through 6. The components of the array, the coin values, are integers. The integers give corresponding values for each of the six coins. Notice that the number of components in the array is implicitly specified when the range of index values is given in the array definition.

The indexes of an array need not be limited to integer values. In Pascal, the indexes of an array may be specified in the following ways:

1. by giving an explicit *range* of integer, character, or enumerated values.

2. by giving the *name* of a previously declared integer, character, or enumerated type, or the *name* of a subrange.

For instance, with the type definitions

type
    CoinNum = 1..6;
    Coin   = (Penny, Nickel, Dime, Quarter, HalfDollar, Dollar);

we can give the array definitions:

array[1..6]   **of** Integer
array[Penny..Dollar] **of** Integer

array[CoinNum]   **of** Integer
array[Coin]   **of** Integer

Each of these array definitions describes the simple arrangement shown in Fig. 10.4. In the first and third definitions, the indexes are the numbers 1 through 6; in the other two definitions, the indexes are the values Penny through Dollar.

Naturally we want to do something with arrays, and this means we want to give them names and refer to their components. Just as we can write,

Counter : Integer;

to declare a variable Counter of type Integer, we can write,

CoinValue : **array**[1..6] **of** Integer;

to declare a variable of an array type.

To refer to array components, we give the name of the array followed by the component index enclosed in square brackets. Accordingly, just as we can write,

Counter := 1

to assign a value to a simple variable, we can write,

CoinValue[2] := 5

to assign a value to an array component. Similarly, just as we can refer to the value of a simple variable in an expression like

Counter + 1

we can also refer to the value of an array component in an expression like

CoinValue[2] * NumCoins

The general rule here is that we can treat a reference to an array component just the same as a simple variable.

Many of these ideas are illustrated in Fig. 10.5, yet another program for counting change. Here the values of the individual coins are stored in the array named CoinValue. The first six assignment statements simply set the values of each coin to their respective value in pennies. In the computation of the total change, the value of each individual coin is obtained from the array CoinValue. The rest of the program remains as it was in previous versions.

Coin	Value
Penny	1
Nickel	5
Dime	10
Quarter	25
Half Dollar	50
Dollar	100

Figure 10.4 ● Table of coin values

Figure 10.5 ● Program
CountChange using an
array of coin values

```
program CountChange;
{ -- This program reads in six integer values, respectively }
{ -- representing the number of pennies, nickels, dimes, quarters, }
{ -- half-dollars, and silver dollars in coinage. }
{ -- This program outputs the total value of the coins }
{ -- in dollars and cents. }
  var
    NextCoin, CoinCount, TotalChange, Cents, Dollars : Integer;
    CoinValue : array[1..6] of Integer;
begin
  CoinValue[1] := 1;
  CoinValue[2] := 5;
  CoinValue[3] := 10;
  CoinValue[4] := 25;
  CoinValue[5] := 50;
  CoinValue[6] := 100;

  TotalChange := 0;
  for NextCoin := 1 to 6 do
    begin
      Read(CoinCount);
      TotalChange := TotalChange + (CoinValue[NextCoin] * CoinCount)
    end;

  if (TotalChange = 0) then
    Write('NO COINS')
  else
    begin
      Dollars := TotalChange div 100;
      Cents := TotalChange mod 100;
      Write('CHANGE IS ', Dollars : 2, 'DOLLARS AND ', Cents : 2, 'CENTS.')
    end;
end.
```

Next consider Fig. 10.6. Here we see an even greater improvement when the individual coins are represented with an enumerated type. Notice here the clarity in referring to each coin by a name rather than by a number. This clarity is especially evident in the assignments, such as

```
CoinValue[Nickel] := 5
```

or in the following loop:

```
for NextCoin := Penny to Dollar do begin
  Read(CoinCount);
  TotalChange := TotalChange + (CoinValue[NextCoin] * CoinCount)
end
```

```
program CountChange;
{ -- This program reads in six integer values, respectively }
{ -- representing the number of pennies, nickels, dimes, quarters, }
{ -- half-dollars, and silver dollars in coinage. }
{ -- This program outputs the total value of the coins }
{ -- in dollars and cents. }
   type
      Coin = (Penny, Nickel, Dime, Quarter, HalfDollar, Dollar);
   var
      CoinCount, TotalChange, Cents, Dollars : Integer;
      NextCoin : Coin;
      CoinValue : array[Penny..Dollar] of Integer;
begin
   CoinValue[Penny] := 1;
   CoinValue[Nickel] := 5;
   CoinValue[Dime] := 10;
   CoinValue[Quarter] := 25;
   CoinValue[HalfDollar] := 50;
   CoinValue[Dollar] := 100;

   TotalChange := 0;
   for NextCoin := Penny to Dollar do
      begin
         Read(CoinCount);
         TotalChange := TotalChange + (CoinValue[NextCoin] * CoinCount)
      end;

   if (TotalChange = 0) then
      Write('NO COINS')
   else
      begin
         Dollars := TotalChange div 100;
         Cents := TotalChange mod 100;
         Write('CHANGE IS ', Dollars : 2, 'DOLLARS AND ', Cents : 2, ' CENTS.')
      end;
end.
```

Figure 10.6 ● Program CountChange using the type coin

Finally, notice that array types can be named in a type declaration just as for any of the other types in Pascal. For example, consider the following type declarations:

```
type
   Letter      = 'A'..'Z';
   Vector      = array[1..100] of Real;
   GolfScore   = array[1..18] of Integer;
```

```
CoinTable      = array[Penny..Dollar] of Integer;
CipherTable    = array[Letter, Letter] of Letter;
```

These types may be used just as any other types in Pascal, for example, to name the type of variables in

```
var
  YCoordinate    : Vector;
  ParForCourse   : GolfScore;

  CoinValue      : CoinTable;
  CipherCode     : CipherTable;
```

10.2 • Strings as Arrays

Whenever we use a string type in Pascal, the computer treats it as an array of characters. The array is assumed to be "packed," which means that the computer should be very careful about economizing storage for the characters in a string. Do not worry about this "packed" business, simply use it as we explain in this section.

Consider the string

'Birmingham'

This string has 10 characters and is treated as a value of the type

packed array[1..10] **of** Char

Once a variable has been declared as a packed array of 10 characters, any string 10 characters in length can be assigned to that variable, as in

```
var
  City : packed array[1..10] of character;
begin
  City := 'Birmingham'
```

When using strings as arrays, a problem arises when the length of the string changes. Arrays have a fixed number of components. If we wished to assign the city of London to the variable City, we would be required to add four spaces to the string.

City := 'London

This leads us to an important fact about packed strings.

  • Packed strings are assignment compatible only if they have the same number of components.

This, of course, creates difficulties for the programmer. In most cases it is preferable to declare a variable of string type with a size that can accommodate the largest value that will be assigned to that variable, such as

City : **string**[10];

Since string types are treated internally in a way similar to arrays, the individual characters that make up the string can be accessed just as if they were components in an array. This is done by enclosing the character index in square brackets following the variable name. Consider our MultipleChoice program, Fig. 7.4. We declared a variable

Dummy : **string**[10];

and then used Dummy to store the correct answer for each question. The Choice was tested by using

CorrectAnswer := Dummy[QuestionNum];
if Choice = CorrectAnswer **then**
    —*what to do if answer is correct*

The first statement indicates that a particular character from the string Dummy is to be assigned to CorrectAnswer. If the current question is number 4, then the fourth character in the string Dummy indicates the correct answer.

The ability to access an individual character in a string as if it were an array is an extremely useful feature. However, there are situations where it is preferable to declare the variable as an array. In the example given a problem arises if we wish to add questions to the test. In the constants declarations section there is a constant named LastQuestionNum. The constant can easily be changed to any number we wish. However the string Dummy is restricted to 10 characters. Changing the number of questions would require us to change the size attribute of the string. A packed array of characters allows the range of the array to be declared by the use of a variable name, as in

Dummy : **packed array**[1..LastQuestionNum] **of** Char;

The same kind of situation arises in program Encipher. The constant NumKeyLetters would be likely to change whenever the keyword is changed. It is preferable, therefore, to use the variable declaration

KeyWord : **packed array**[1..NumKeyLetters] **of** Char;

rather than

KeyWord : **string**[6];

Another instance where the packed array of character would be needed is in the case of a very long string. Strings are limited to 255 characters in length.

A few more points must be mentioned here concerning the compatibility of string types, character types, and packed strings.

- Packed strings can be assigned to string-type variables provided the number of characters in the packed string does not exceed the size of the string-type variable.

- String-type values can be assigned to packed string variables if the length of the string-type value is equal to the number of components in the packed string variable.
- String-type values can be assigned to string-type variables provided the length of the new value does not exceed the size of the variable.
- String-type values of length 1 can be assigned to character-type variables.
- Character-type values can be assigned to string-type variables.

10.3 ○ Practice

Arrays

Figure 10.7 lists a fairly straightforward program using arrays. If the declaration

Score : **array**[1..18] **of** Integer;

is changed to

Score : **array**[1..19] **of** Integer;

what effect does this have on the program?

● ● ●

The first declaration allows for 18 values in the array of scores; the second allows for 19 values. The two for loops which make use of these values are each performed 18 times, with a new value each time. In the first loop, 18 values are read in and assigned to locations in the array. No value is read for the 19th position. In the second loop, each of the 18 values is used. Since the 19th value is never called, the results of the program are unchanged from when it is run in its original form.

However, what happens to the program if the declaration is changed to

Score : **array**[1..9] **of** Integer;

● ● ●

In this case the program runs into trouble when it reaches the Read statement and starts to read values for the scores. By declaration, only 9 scores can be stored in the array. Therefore, when the 10th execution of the loop is attempted, and Score[10] is encountered, an error results. This is exactly as it should be, since the declaration has set a limit of 9 on the number of scores possible.

```
program Golf;
{ -- This program reads in a sequence of scores for each of 18 }
{ -- golf holes on a par 4 course. The program prints the total }
{ -- score, the amount over (or under) par, and makes note of }
{ -- any birdies (holes under par). }
  const
    ParForHole = 4;
    ParForCourse = 72;
  var
    HoleNum, TotalScore : Integer;
    Score : array[1..18] of Integer;
begin
  WriteLn('ENTER SCORES FOR EACH HOLE: ');
  for HoleNum := 1 to 18 do
    Read(Score[HoleNum]);
  TotalScore := 0;
  for HoleNum := 1 to 18 do
    begin
      TotalScore := TotalScore + Score[HoleNum];
      if Score[HoleNum] < ParForHole then
        WriteLn('BIRDIE ON HOLE ', HoleNum : 3)
    end;
  WriteLn('TOTAL SCORE IS ', TotalScore : 3);
  WriteLn((TotalScore - ParForCourse) : 3, ' OVER PAR')
end.
```

Figure 10.7 ● Program Golf

The for loop that causes the values to be read is to be performed 18 times. What happens if the user enters only 5 input values?

● ● ●

Whenever the computer is waiting for information from the keyboard, the cursor flashes on the text window. The for statement instructs the computer to read 18 integers; until those 18 integers have been entered, the cursor continues to flash, indicating that data is expected. Execution cannot pass to the next statement until the current statement is finished.

What happens if the line

    Read(Score[HoleNum]);

is changed to

    Read(Score);

● ● ●

In the declarations part of this program, Score is declared as a variable. It is further declared to be of type **array**. Therefore, Score is not associated with an individual value, but with a group of values. Without the index, the identifier is incomplete. Therefore, when the Read statement is attempted, an error results.

The following may be confusing to you. But if you ever have to read or update someone else's program, you may be shocked to find the same kind of mysterious code. Consider the following three arrays containing the real values shown,

array R :   0.0   0.0
array S :   3.14   2.718
array Q :   1.0   2.0   3.0   2.0   1.0   3.0   3.0   2.0   2.0   2.0

and the program segment shown in Fig. 10.8.

What does each of the loops do? What values are printed by the Write statement?

● ● ●

Let's take this step by step. The first loop is performed 10 times. The first five times, I is not greater than 5, so the else part of the loop is performed giving the following values.

R[2] := 0.0 + 2.0   { R[2] =   2.0 }
R[2] := 2.0 + 2.0   { R[2] =   4.0 }
R[2] := 4.0 + 2.0   { R[2] =   6.0 }

Figure 10.8   **for** I := **to** 10 **do**
              begin
                if (I > 5) **then**
                  R[1] := R[1] + Q[1]
                else
                  R[2] := R[2] + Q[2]
              end;
              for J := **to** 2 **do**
                S[J] := 0.0;
              N := 1;
              for K := **to** 3 **do**
              begin
                S[N] := S[N] + Q[K];
                S[N + 1] := S[N + 1] + Q[K + 3]
              end;
              Write(R[1] : 4 : 1, R[2] : 4 : 1, S[1] : 4 : 1, S[2] : 4 : 1)

R[2] := 6.0 + 2.0   { R[2] =   8.0 }
R[2] := 8.0 + 2.0   { R[2] = 10.0 }

The next 5 times that the loop is executed, I is equal to 6 through 10, therefore, the if part is performed, giving the following values:

R[1] := 0.0 + 1.0   { R[1] = 1.0 }
R[1] := 1.0 + 1.0   { R[1] = 2.0 }
R[1] := 2.0 + 1.0   { R[1] = 3.0 }
R[1] := 3.0 + 1.0   { R[1] = 4.0 }
R[1] := 4.0 + 1.0   { R[1] = 5.0 }

When the first loop ends, the values of $R[1]$ and $R[2]$ have been set to 5.0 and 10.0, respectively.

The second loop is performed twice, setting the first and second components of array S to 0.0.

The third loop is performed three times, each time adding one of the components of array Q to one of the components of array S. Which component of Q is added depends on the variable K, which is also the control variable for the for loop. The three executions of the loop produce the following results.

S[1] := S[1] + Q[1] or S[1] := 0.0 + 1.0   { S[1] = 1.0 }
S[2] := S[2] + Q[4] or S[2] := 0.0 + 2.0   { S[2] = 2.0 }

S[1] := S[1] + Q[2] or S[1] := 1.0 + 2.0   { S[1] = 3.0 }
S[2] := S[2] + Q[5] or S[2] := 2.0 + 1.0   { S[2] = 3.0 }

S[1] := S[1] + Q[3] or S[1] := 3.0 + 3.0   { S[1] = 6.0 }
S[2] := S[2] + Q[6] or S[2] := 3.0 + 3.0   { S[2] = 6.0 }

You are probably thinking at this point that there must be a better way to write this program, and you may be right. However, reading someone else's program requires this kind of careful step-by-step procedure. The Write statement gives the following output.

5.0   10.0   6.0   6.0

If you have followed through these exercises, you have a fair understanding of how a one-dimensional array works. The enciphering program is a good example of a two-dimensional array with rows and columns. If you had any difficulty with Encipher the first time through, now is a good time to review it.

10.4 ○

10.1   Not Using Arrays
It isn't as rare as you think that someone will go through extra trouble when a simple solution exists. Rewrite the program in Fig. 10.7 without using arrays.

10.2   Reading Month Abbreviations

Solve Exercise 9.6, this time using arrays; that is, storing the month numbers in an array of strings.

10.3   Cryptic Encoding of Messages

The encoding of messages is a very complex area, certainly of use in military applications as well as other applications where information needs to be camouflaged. Here we treat a very simple encoding (and decoding) method.

Write a program to input a message and then output a decoded version of the message. Each letter of the input message is to be encoded as a letter, three characters higher in alphabetic sequence. In particular, we have the following substitution table:

letter   : A B C D E F G H I J K L MN O P Q R S T U V WX Y Z
substitute : A B C D E F G H I J K L MN O P Q R S T U V WX Y Z

For example, the input message

THE TROOPS ARE ADVANCING

should be encoded as

WKH WURRSV DUH DGYDQFLQJ

Note: In "The Case of the Ciphered Message," Holmes rejected this scheme because it was too easy to decipher. Can you think of an application where this method will be sufficient?

10.4   Deciphering a Message

Now make the preceding program into one that deciphers messages, that is, one that reads in a coded message and prints the original message. Test your program using the output for the previous program as input.

10.5   Legal Area Codes

There are over a hundred legal area codes in the continental United States. When you dial a long-distance telephone number, you can be sure there are many computer circuits analyzing the number you dialed. Of course one of these circuits checks to see if the area code is correct.

When a program to read in a three-digit number (e.g., 413) and to print a message indicating whether the area code is correct or not.

Note: You may have to get a phone book to solve this problem.

10.6   Sorting Items into an Order

The process of arranging a list of items (for example, the names of suspects or a table of area codes) into some given order is called "sorting."

One simple but slow method of sorting is called a "bubble" sort. It goes like this:

Examine pairs of items to produce a partial ordering (i.e., compare item 1 to item 2, compare item 2 to item 3, and so forth). If item j is greater than item $j + 1$, interchange the two items; then compare item $j + 1$ with $j + 2$; continue this procedure through the entire list. After going through the list once, the largest item will be the last item of the list.

Now go through the list again. This time, however, omit the comparison of the item in the last place. Thus on each pass through the list, one fewer item is examined. The last time through the list will be when item 1 is compared with item 2 or when a pass is made through the list and no interchange takes place.

For example, if your list has the numbers

  3 −16 0 9 1

after the first interchange you will have

  −16 3 0 9 1

and when you complete your first pass, you will have

  −16 0 3 1 9

The second pass gives

  −16 0 1 3 9

The third pass results in no interchange and we are done. Clever? Yes.

Your problem is as follows: Write a program to read in ten integer values and print the values in numerical order, as well as the number of passes needed to sort the list. Test your program with the lists

  1 2 3 4 5 6 7 8 9 10

and

  10 9 8 7 6 5 4 3 2 1

Prelude to Subprograms

A Study in Chemistry

IT was a singular combination of events in the spring of '91 that found Mr. Sherlock Holmes and myself again sharing his quarters at 221B Baker Street. I need not detail the circumstances attendant upon my temporary return; suffice it to say that with the aid of a noted Harley Street specialist, I was able to persuade Holmes not to undertake a single investigation at that time. It was absolutely imperative that the great detective lay aside all his work and surrender himself to complete rest, should he wish to avoid a complete breakdown.

The morning of the present narrative began abruptly. Holmes was at my bedside, shaking me from a deep and peaceful sleep and attempting to drag me from under my sheets.

"Quick, Watson!" he exclaimed. "On your feet, man, and to the window!" His face was tinged with colour and his brows drawn into two hard black lines with the steely glitter of his eyes shining out from under them. Only in times of great crisis have I observed these battle signals flying, and I scarcely needed to rely on my companion's great muscular strength to get me standing.

I immediately became aware of a loathsome, suffocating odour as I staggered with his aid to the windows. A thick, black cloud was filtering in from the sitting room where Holmes had been experimenting with chemicals, apparently throughout the night. He tossed aside the curtains and threw open the lead-paned windows, and in a moment we were leaning out, side by side, conscious only of the glorious sunshine and the fresh, early-morning air.

Some while later we sat near my bedside wiping our clammy foreheads and surveying each other with some apprehension. "I take it there is some justifiable reason for all of this?" I queried, letting the tone of my voice carry the full weight of my irritation.

"I have, with some success," replied Holmes, his eyes twinkling, "duplicated the poisonous gas employed in the Hyde Park case."

"Indeed you have, and nearly done away with us in the bargain!"

"Well, yes, I suppose I do owe you a word of apology, as I have almost added another chapter to what the papers are calling the Hyde Park Horrors. It was, I admit, an unjustifiable experiment to carry out on oneself and doubly so considering the presence of an unsuspecting friend."

It was difficult to remain angered at Sherlock Holmes for any great length of time. His apology had been put forth with such sincerity that I was considerably touched. My anger at a rude awakening no longer seemed worth pursuing.

"The vapours have diffused by now," he said presently. "It should be safe to return."

"I am greatly disappointed with you, Holmes. You promised to engage your energies in more scholarly pursuits. The first sensational headline to come along and you've broken your word. There you are, off like a racing engine, ready to tear yourself to pieces, with a hospital bed your destination for certain!" I cried.

"On the contrary, my dear Watson," he retorted. "It was just those scholarly pursuits that have led me here, and once you have performed your morning ablutions and breakfasted I shall be pleased to elaborate on how the Analytical Engine may be most helpful in my chemical dabblings. With the Engine at my disposal our predawn discomforts could have been totally avoided. I suggest for now, however, that we take our rashers and eggs at one of London's finer eating establishments, as arsenic vapours are not pleasing to the discriminating palate."

After a pleasing breakfast in Mrs. Woolwich's Tea Rooms, we returned to Baker Street. Holmes continued his discourse at a small card table on which he had set up a makeshift laboratory.

"Do you recollect anything of my friend Dimitri Ivanovich Mendeleeff?" he asked. "A man ahead of his time in many ways."

"A chemist, as I recall."

"Quite so," he replied. "A scientific mind of the first order. Mendeleeff was the first to bring both system and structure to the family of elements: gold, most highly praised of metals, which never tarnishes or rusts; base lead, common and despised; quicksilver, a metal in liquid form; sulphur and carbon, usually powders, sometimes crystals—why, a diamond is merely carbon! Or consider the very air, a mixture of many gases. And these elements combine chemically with one another to produce the amazing variety of materials that sustain us—or that can destroy us, as was nearly the case this morning.

"It has been Mendeleeff's great insight to categorize the various elements in the form of a table for handy reference. In his table, he arranges the elements, with each assigned a specific atomic weight, vertically in groups. The elements within each group bear chemical properties similar to one another. Dimitri Ivanovich has shown that the properties of elements recur periodically, much as the sounds of musical

"A chemist, as I recall."

notes recurs throughout the octaves—an idea much scorned by the Royal Society when the unfortunate Newlands first suggested it years ago."

Holmes then produced a chart from the great bundle of papers that littered his desk. It showed the elements arranged vertically in groups. Naturally I had come across this table, which I have reproduced as Fig. 11.1, during my medical studies at the University of London.

"This is all very interesting," I said, after looking over the chart. "But of what use is it to you? Surely it is of no importance to a criminal investigator?"

"Ah, but the value of the table to me is practical. Since it lists the atomic weights of the elements, I can use the information to calculate the weight of any compound I choose. Consider, for example, the poisonous arsenic vapors

$$As_4O_6$$

Figure 11.1 ●
Mendeleeff's periodic
table of the chemical
elements

Series	Group I	Group II	Group III	Group IV	Group V	Group VI	Group VII	Group VIII
1	H=1							
2	Li=7	Be=9.4	B=11	C=12	N=14	O=16	F=19	
3	Na=23	Mg=24	Al=27.3	Si=28	P=31	S=32	Cl=35.5	
4	K=39	Ca=40	—=44	Ti=48	V=51	Cr=52	Mn=55	Fe=56, Co=59, Ni=59
5	Cu=63	Zn=65	—=68	—=72	As=75	Se=78	Br=80	
6	Rb=85	Sr=87	?Yt=88	Zr=90	Nb=94	Mo=96	—=100	Ru=104, Rh=104, Rd=106
7	Ag=108	Cd=112	In=113	Sn=118	Sb=122	Te=125	I=127	
8	Cs=133	Ba=137	?Di=138	?Ce=140	—	—	—	
9	—	—	—	—	—	—	—	
10	—	—	?Er=178	?La=180	Ta=182	W=184	—	Os=195, Ir=197, Pt=198
11	Au=199	Hg=200	Tl=204	Pb=207	Bi=208	—	—	
12	—	—	—	Th=231	—	U=240	—	

that I produced this morning. According to Mendeleeff's table, arsenic weighs 75 units and oxygen weighs 16 units. The weight of a molecule of the gas is then

$$(75 * 4) + (16 * 6) = 396$$

"As you can see, Watson, the calculation is trivial. But there are many elements, all of differing weights. Obtaining correct results can be tedious and subject to error when there are many such calculations to make. I would like to develop a tool for use on the Analytical Engine to assist me in calculating molecular weights. Thus I wish to enter formulae of this sort and receive as output the molecular weight."

"Yes, Holmes," I remarked. "But the problem is not so simple as you make it appear. You must instruct the Engine to make sense of the formulae, and you must store Mendeleeff's table in the Engine's memory."

"Excellent, Watson! Compound of the Busy Bee and Excelsior!" cried Holmes. "That is precisely what must be done. You see, storing Mendeleeff's table in the Engine is of great value, and having the Engine recognise the atomic abbreviations will save my brain for more important matters. This is exactly where the method of instructing the Engine is of particular interest."

In an instant Holmes was at the Engine, continuing with his lecture.

"Now, Watson, pay close attention. Here is a general algorithm that will allow the Engine to solve the problem of molecular weights."

He showed me the following:

```
Set up atomic weights table
Set TotalWeight to 0.0

Repeat the following:
    Obtain NextElement and NumAtoms
    Add AtomicWeight[NextElement]*NumAtoms to TotalWeight
until no more elements

Write TotalWeight
```

"As you remarked earlier, there are two interesting lines. First,

```
Set up atomic weights table
```

This requires the Engine to fill a table with Mendeleeff's atomic weights. Second,

```
Obtain NextElement and NumAtoms
```

This requires that the programme ask what the next element is—for example H means hydrogen and AS means arsenic—and how many atoms there are of that element.

"The point is, Watson, that by expressing the algorithm in this way, we have reduced the larger problem to two smaller subproblems, each of which is easier and simpler to develop than the original problem.

"We can now face the two subproblems precisely. Just as for any problem, there are the

input — the "givens"

output — the "finds"

For the first subproblem, there is no input; and the output is to be the completed table of atomic weights. For the second subproblem the input is the molecular formula; the output is the next element and the number of times it occurs in the molecular formula."

Holmes then produced the sketch that I have duplicated as Fig. 11.2. His illustration shows the main algorithm, giving first the definitions of the variables used and then the algorithm itself. The main algorithm refers to the two subproblems. These are called algorithms SetUpTable and GetElement.

Holmes noted the ease with which I could follow the algorithm, and then produced two more sketches, which I have reproduced as Figs. 11.3 and 11.4. These contained the solutions to the two subproblems.

"Notice, Watson," he continued, "that the algorithm for each subproblem is separate and self-contained. Each contains, for example, definitions of data that are meaningful only within the local context of the subproblem.

"Every problem becomes elementary when once it is explained to you," said Holmes. "See how childishly simple this all is when you break

Figure 11.2 • Holmes's algorithm to determine molecular weight

Definitions:
    NextElement : an element
    NumAtoms   : an integer number
    TotalWeight : the weight of a molecule
    AtomicWeight: a representation of the periodic table,
                   giving the atomic weight of each element

Algorithm:
    Perform algorithm SetUpTable giving the AtomicWeight table
    Set TotalWeight to 0.0

    Repeat the following:
        perform algorithm GetElement giving NextElement, NumAtoms
        add AtomicWeight[NextElement]*NumAtoms to TotalWeight
    until no more elements

    Write TotalWeight

Algorithm SetUpTable—giving values for AtomicWeight table:
  — Note: only the elements in the first five series of
  — Mendeleeff's table are used
Set AtomicWeight[Hydrogen] to 1
Set AtomicWeight[Lithium]   to 7
Set AtomicWeight[Beryllium] to 9.4
. . .   . . .
Set AtomicWeight[Bromine]   to 80

Figure 11.3 ● Algorithm for subprogram SetUpTable

Algorithm GetElement—giving NextElement, NumAtoms
  Local definitions:
    Char1, Char2: characters of a formula
  repeat the following:
    read Char1 of element abbreviation
    if incomplete then
      read Char2
    else
      set Char2 to blank
    get full name of NextElement using Char1 and Char2
    if NextElement is unknown then
      write 'ELEMENT NOT RECOGNIZED.'
    else
      obtain NumAtoms
  until valid entry is made

Figure 11.4 ● Algorithm for subprogram GetElement

the problem down into smaller components? You see, Watson, a man possessing special knowledge and powers such as my own is encouraged often to seek a simpler approach to a seemingly complex problem. Here we need only break the problem down into smaller parts and solve them separately. One might say, divide and conquer."

"Or divide and calculate!" I rejoined.

"You are developing a certain vein of pawky humour, Watson, against which you must learn to guard yourself."

"So now we turn to the programme itself, I presume."

"Yes, Watson, we may nicely express this fundamental concept directly in Pascal with a 'sub-programme.' One method of writing sub-programmes is called a *procedure*. A procedure has two parts:

1. A *heading:* A summary of the sub-programme, giving its name, the inputs, and the outputs.
2. A *body:* The algorithm used, along with any local definitions.

"Consider the sub-programme to get the next element. The procedure to do this will have the form

```
procedure GetElement (parameters);
    — local declarations
begin
    — statements
end;
```

The parameters itemize the inputs and outputs. Each parameter must be given a name and a designation of its type.

"In addition," Holmes continued, "any output parameter must be preceded by the keyword **var**, which tells the Engine that the output will be assigned to a variable. So we have

```
procedure GetElement (var NewElement: Element;
                      var NumAtoms: Integer);
    — local declarations
begin
    — statements
end;
```

The statements, of course, describe the algorithm."

It all sounded simple, but I was still a bit puzzled. I did not at all like some of the strange notation, and did not quite understand how the so-called "procedures" would be used.

"To invoke a procedure in a programme," Holmes continued, "we give the name of the procedure followed by a list of values or *arguments*, one for each parameter, as in

```
GetElement (NextElement, NumAtoms)
```

This is called a *procedure call*; and means, quite simply, 'do it.' That is, the Engine is commanded to perform the algorithm as spelled out in the procedure. When the procedure is completed, NextElement will have the value computed for the first parameter, NumAtoms for the second parameter.

"The essential idea is that the effect of solving the subproblem is summarized by values calculated for each parameter."

To appreciate this sudden bounty of instruction I found it necessary to see the actual programme. It is here duplicated as Fig. 11.5. On some reflection, it was readily apparent that the wisest approach was breaking such complex programmes into smaller, more manageable parts.

Holmes forged on. "Notice, incidentally, that in procedure GetElement, we refer to another procedure GetName. This simply matches the abbreviated element name to the full element name and is an example of a sub-programme within a sub-programme."

"Enough, Holmes!" I moaned. "I can absorb no more. Are you absolutely certain that all of these complexities involve less work than simply calculating the molecular weights yourself?"

Sherlock Holmes merely smiled.

```
program MolecularWeight;
{ -- This programme reads in a chemical formula. Each element }
{ -- and its quantity are requested by the programme. Entering }
{ -- ZZ indicates the end of the formula. }
{ -- The programme determines the atomic components of the formula }
{ -- and prints out the total molecular weight. Only elements from }
{ -- the first five series of Mendeleeff's table are considered. }
  const
    Blank = ' ';

  type
    Element = (Hydrogen, Lithium, Beryllium, Boron, Carbon, Nitrogen,
              Oxygen, Fluorine, Sodium, Magnesium, Aluminum,
              Silicon, Phosphorus, Sulphur, Chlorine, Potassium,
              Calcium, Titanium, Vanadium, Chromium, Manganese,
              Iron, Cobalt, Nickel, Copper, Zinc, Arsenic, Selenium,
              Bromine, Done, Unknown);
    ElementName = Hydrogen..Bromine;
    PeriodicTable = array[ElementName] of Real;

  var
    NextElement : Element;
    NumAtoms : Integer;
    TotalWeight : Real;
    AtomicWeight : PeriodicTable;

procedure SetUpTable (var AtomicWeight : PeriodicTable);
begin
  AtomicWeight[Hydrogen] := 1.0;
  AtomicWeight[Lithium] := 7.0;
  AtomicWeight[Beryllium] := 9.4;
  AtomicWeight[Boron] := 11.0;
  AtomicWeight[Carbon] := 12.0;

  AtomicWeight[Nitrogen] := 14.0;
  AtomicWeight[Oxygen] := 16.0;
  AtomicWeight[Fluorine] := 19.0;
  AtomicWeight[Sodium] := 23.0;
  AtomicWeight[Magnesium] := 24.0;

  AtomicWeight[Aluminum] := 27.3;
  AtomicWeight[Silicon] := 28.0;
  AtomicWeight[Phosphorus] := 31.0;
  AtomicWeight[Sulphur] := 32.0;
  AtomicWeight[Chlorine] := 35.5;
```

Figure 11.5 ● Program MolecularWeight

Figure 11.5 continued

```
         AtomicWeight[Potassium] := 39.0;
         AtomicWeight[Calcium] := 40.0;
         AtomicWeight[Titanium] := 48.0;
         AtomicWeight[Vanadium] := 51.0;
         AtomicWeight[Chromium] := 52.0;

         AtomicWeight[Manganese] := 55.0;
         AtomicWeight[Iron] := 56.0;
         AtomicWeight[Cobalt] := 59.0;
         AtomicWeight[Nickel] := 59.0;
         AtomicWeight[Copper] := 63.0;

         AtomicWeight[Zinc] := 65.0;
         AtomicWeight[Arsenic] := 75.0;
         AtomicWeight[Selenium] := 78.0;
         AtomicWeight[Bromine] := 80.0;
     end;
     procedure GetName (Char1, Char2 :Char;
                     var Name : Element);

         var
             Abbreviation : packed array[1..2] of Char;

     begin
         Abbreviation[1] := Char1;
         Abbreviation[2] := Char2;

         if Abbreviation = 'H' then
             Name := Hydrogen
         else if Abbreviation = 'LI' then
             Name := Lithium
         else if Abbreviation = 'BE' then
             Name := Beryllium
         else if Abbreviation = 'B ' then
             Name := Boron
         else if Abbreviation = 'C ' then
             Name := Carbon
         else if Abbreviation = 'N ' then
             Name := Nitrogen
         else if Abbreviation = 'O ' then
             Name := Oxygen
         else if Abbreviation = 'F ' then
             Name := Fluorine
         else if Abbreviation = 'NA' then
             Name := Sodium
         else if Abbreviation = 'MG' then
             Name := Magnesium
         else if Abbreviation = 'AL' then
             Name := Aluminum
```

Figure 11.5 continued

```
        else if Abbreviation = 'SI' then
            Name := Silicon
        else if Abbreviation = 'P ' then
            Name := Phosphorus
        else if Abbreviation = 'S ' then
            Name := Sulphur
        else if Abbreviation = 'CL' then
            Name := Chlorine
        else if Abbreviation = 'K ' then
            Name := Potassium
        else if Abbreviation = 'CA' then
            Name := Calcium
        else if Abbreviation = 'TI' then
            Name := Titanium
        else if Abbreviation = 'V ' then
            Name := Vanadium
        else if Abbreviation = 'CR' then
            Name := Chromium
        else if Abbreviation = 'MN' then
            Name := Manganese
        else if Abbreviation = 'FE' then
            Name := Iron
        else if Abbreviation = 'CO' then
            Name := Cobalt
        else if Abbreviation = 'NI' then
            Name := Nickel
        else if Abbreviation = 'CU' then
            Name := Copper
        else if Abbreviation = 'ZN' then
            Name := Zinc
        else if Abbreviation = 'AS' then
            Name := Arsenic
        else if Abbreviation = 'SE' then
            Name := Selenium
        else if Abbreviation = 'BR' then
            Name := Bromine
        else if Abbreviation = 'ZZ' then
            Name := Done
        else
            Name := Unknown
    end;
    procedure GetElement (var NewElement : Element;
                   var NumAtoms : Integer);

      var
        Char1,Char2 : Char;
        ValidEntry : Boolean;
```

Figure 11.5 continued

```pascal
begin
  Validentry := False;
  repeat
    Write('ENTER ELEMENT ABBREVIATION;');
    Read(Char1);
    if not EOLn then
      Read(Char2)
    else
      Char2 := Blank;
    ReadLn;
    GetName(Char1, Char2, NewElement);
    if NewElement = Done then
      ValidEntry := True
    else if NewElement = Unknown then
      WriteLn('ELEMENT NOT RECOGNIZED.')
    else
      begin
        WRITE('ENTER QUANTITY OF ELEMENT :');
        ReadLn(NumAtoms);
        ValidEntry := True
      end
  until ValidEntry
end;

begin { -- MAIN ALGORITHM }
  SetUpTable(AtomicWeight);
  TotalWeight := 0.0;

  WriteLn('ENTER EACH ELEMENT: WHEN DONE,ENTER 22.');
  GetElement(NextElement,NumAtoms);
  while NextElement <> Done do
    begin
      TotalWeight := TotalWeight + AtomicWeight[NextElement] *
              NumAtoms;
      GetElement(NextElement,NumAtoms)
    end;

  WriteLn('THE MOLECULAR WEIGHT IS ', TotalWeight : 6 : 1)
end.
```

Chapter 11

Functions and Procedures

We now encounter the idea of breaking a problem into parts and packaging each part as a *subprogram*. In its essence, a subprogram is a language unit that embodies the solution to a subproblem. As we attempt to scale up our programming skills to solve larger and more complex problems, the use of subprograms becomes almost indispensable. The solution to a subproblem, with all of its details and internal calculations, can be summarized into its givens and finds.

All subprograms have two general characteristics:

- A *heading* summarizes the relationship of the subproblem to the rest of the program. It includes the name of the subprogram and an itemized list of its parameters.

- A *body* specifies the method by which the subproblem is solved. It includes the definitions of any relevant internal data and the statements for carrying out the algorithm needed to solve the subproblem.

Let us now turn to the particulars for writing subprograms in Pascal.

A *procedure* is a subprogram that causes some desired effect. Consider, for instance, the simple procedure of Fig. 11.6. When executed, the three lines of text:

11.1 ● Packaging and Subprograms

THE LOST PASCAL PROGRAMS
OF
SHERLOCK HOLMES

are printed, centered within each line. This is the so-called effect of the procedure.

The procedure in Fig. 11.6 has the form

> **procedure** WriteTitle;
>   *—local declarations*
> **begin**
>   *—statements*
> **end**

This procedure, like all procedures, has a name, in this case WriteTitle. The procedure also contains local declarations, which specify any entities needed. The statements within the procedure specify the algorithm to be carried out.

A procedure is considered a "subprogram" because, as you will note, it has a form as well as an effect similar to that of a program. Like a program, a procedure can have both declarations and executable statements.

In order to cause the actions of a procedure to be carried out, we use a *procedure call* statement. For example, the procedure of Fig. 11.6 can be invoked with the call:

> WriteTitle

When this statement is executed, the algorithm specified by the procedure will be carried out.

Figure 11.6 ● A simple procedure

```
program WriteTitle;
  const
    Space = ' ';
  var
    Column : Integer;
begin
  for Column = 1 to 24 do
    Write(Space);
  WriteLn('THE LOST PASCAL PROGRAMS');

  for Column = 1 to 35 do
    Write(Space);
  WriteLn('OF');

  for Column = 1 to 29 do
    Write(Space);
  WriteLn('SHERLOCK HOLMES');
end;
```

Notice that in the procedure WriteTitle, the body itself calls other procedures. In particular, consider

```
for Column := 1 to 35 do
    Write(Space);       { -- one procedure call }
    WriteLn('OF')       { -- another procedure call }
```

Here the called procedures, Write and WriteLn, are predefined in Pascal.

In Pascal, all procedures defined by the programmer must be stated in the declarative part of a program. For example, in Holmes's program we have the following general structure.

```
program MolecularWeight;
    —constant declarations
    —type declarations
    —variable declarations
    —subprogram declarations
begin
    —statements
end.
```

All procedures are declared after the constant, type, and variable declarations are given. Notice also that the statement part of the program may contain calls not only to the declared procedures but to the procedures that are predefined in Pascal.

This now allows us to state two precepts, elementary yet hard-and-fast to the fundamentals of problem solving:

- The solution to a subproblem may be written as a procedure, which must be given in the form of a procedure declaration.

- The actions specified by the procedure are carried out when the procedure is invoked by a procedure call statement.

11.2 ● Parameters

One important feature for writing subprograms is the ability to parameterize their behavior. The parameters allow you to characterize the net effect of the subprogram.

Consider Holmes's procedure to determine the element corresponding to its one-or two-character abbreviation:

```
procedure GetName
    Char1, Char2 : Char; { given }
    var Name : Element; { result }
    —local declarations
begin
    —statements
end;
```

This procedure uses the values of Char1 and Char2 and from these two characters deduces the element corresponding to that two-letter symbol. The importance of the parameters is that we can characterize the entire effect of the procedure. That is, given input values for Char1 and Char2, we can determine the Name of the element.

All procedures can be summarized in this simple form. A procedure takes certain inputs and produces certain outputs. We can view the procedure as a "black box" of the form

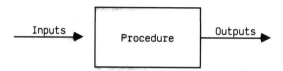

Thus we can summarize the behavior of GetName as

From an outsider's point of view the parameters characterize the entire effect of the named procedure.

To invoke a procedure with parameters, we simply give the name of the procedure followed by a parenthesized list of arguments, one for each parameter. For example, in Holmes's program we may have the procedure call

GetName (Char1, Char2, NewElement)

Before the procedure GetName is called, values will have been assigned to Char1 and Char2. After the call, the name of the next element will be assigned to the variable NewElement.

Now there are several tricky points that we must take up in order to describe the use of parameters. For one, the names of the parameters given in the procedure declaration are an entirely internal matter as far as the rest of the program is concerned. These names have no significance outside the procedure.

For example, if we wanted, we could have written the procedure GetName as

procedure GetName (Ch1, Ch2 : Char;   { given }

```
    var
      Result: Element);       { result }
    —local declarations
  begin
    —statements with parameters names changed
  end;
```

That is, we could have changed all occurrences of the name Char1 to Ch1, Char2 to Ch2, and Name to Result. These changes would have to be made uniformly throughout the procedure. It is in this sense that we say the names of the parameters are "dummy." We are free to choose these names as we wish without regard to any other names outside the procedure.

The ability to coin the names of parameters freely is an extremely useful feature. When you are writing a procedure to solve a subproblem, you can really think of the procedure as an entirely new program with its own inputs and outputs and its own local declarations of variables.

In describing the parameters of a procedure, you must be a bit cautious. First of all, the parameters must be given in some particular order. For the procedure GetName, there are three parameters given in the order Char1, Char2, and Name. Second, a type must be specified for each parameter in the procedure header. For input parameters, the type of one or more parameters can be specified in the form

parameter-list : type-name

In Holmes's case, we have

Char1, Char2 : Char

This specification has the same meaning as

Char1: Char;   Char2 : Char

Notice here, however, that each definition in a list of parameters must be followed by a semicolon if more parameter definitions follow.

The specification of output parameters is almost identical to that of input parameters, except that each list of parameters must be preceded by the keyword **var**, indicating that the corresponding argument must be a variable. In the procedure GetName we have one output parameter, specified by

var Name : Element

Thus the full list of parameters is given as

(Char1, Char2 : Char; **var** Name : Element)

where the parentheses enclose the entire list.

The output parameters for procedures must be either predefined simple types, type identifiers, or indefinite string types. To use a structured type it is necessary to declare a type name in the declarations part of the program and then use the type name in the procedure parameter. An indefinite string type is declared simply as string and is compatible with all string types.

Occasionally you will have a need for parameters whose values both serve as input from the caller and are updated as a result of the procedure call. Consider the procedure PlusOne, defined as follows:

```
procedure PlusOne (var X : Integer);
begin
  X := X + 1
end;
```

This somewhat trivial procedure adds one to its argument. Thus X serves as both input and output for the procedure. Such a parameter must also be specified with the keyword **var**, indicating that the corresponding argument must again be a variable.

From the caller's side, we also have to be concerned with a few special rules. If a procedure has one parameter, you must call it with only one argument; if the procedure has two parameters, you must call it with exactly two arguments, and so forth.

The argument corresponding to an input parameter can be any expression in Pascal as long as the type of the expression is identical to the type of the corresponding parameter. Thus, with the procedure GetName, we could have the call:

```
GetName ('N', 'A', Value)
```

Similarly for the predefined procedure Write, which takes any number of arguments of integer, real, or string type, we may have the calls:

```
Write(0.0)
Write(NumAtoms + 1)
Write('THE SQUARE ROOT OF X IS ', SqRt(X))
```

For arguments corresponding to output parameters, the case is different. Such an argument must always be the name of a variable whose type is the same as that of the corresponding parameter. Thus in the call

```
GetName ('N', 'A', Value)
```

the third argument must be the name of a variable of type Element.

11.3 ● Functions versus Procedures

Consider Fig. 11.7(a). Here we see a simple procedure named GetArea, which when given a value for a radius computes the area of a circle having that radius. If, say, the value of R is 3.0, the procedure call

GetArea (R, Area)

results in assigning to Area the area of a circle of radius 3.0, or 28.2743.

Next consider the "function" of Fig. 11.7(b). This example defines a function named Area which has a single argument, a real value. It computes the area of a circle having this argument as a radius. Like the predefined functions in Pascal, this function can be called within an expression. If the value of R is 3.0, evaluation of the expression

1.0 + Area(R)

yields 1 plus the area of the circle, or 29.2743.

A *function* is a subprogram that returns a value. Generally speaking, functions are used in place of expressions to return values, whereas procedures are used in place of statements to perform assignments to variables. The ability to define functions in Pascal is thus an important counterpart to the ability to define procedures.

Conceptually a function behaves just like a function in ordinary mathematics. That is, given one or more values, we can compute some result. For example, consider the following informally described functions.

- Given two numbers, the result is the greater of the two.
- Given three points, the result is the area of a triangle connecting the three points.
- Given a molecular formula, the result is the molecular weight of the formula.
- Given the initial velocity of a projectile, its angle, and a duration of time, the result is the distance traveled.

In each of these cases we have one or more givens and a single result.

The rules for declaring functions are quite similar to the rules for declaring procedures. In particular, a function declaration has the form

function Area *(parameters) : result-type;*
   —local declarations
begin
   —statements
end;

Here we see that, like a procedure, a function may have parameters as well as local declarations describing any internal data. As with a procedure, the algorithm performed by the function is specified in the statements. Furthermore, a function returns a single result, and the type of the result must be specified in the program heading.

Figure 11.7 ● Functions versus procedures

(a) A Simple Procedure

```
procedure GetArea (Radius : Real;        { given }
     var Area : Real);          { result }
   const
      PI = 3.14159;
begin
   Area := PI * (Radius*Radius)
end;
```

(b) A Simple Function

```
function Area (Radius : Real) : Real;
   const
      PI = 3.14159;
begin
   Area := PI * (Radius*Radius)
end;
```

To establish the actual result returned by a function in Pascal, you must use an assignment statement that gives a value to the name of the function. For example, in the function of Fig. 11.7(b) we have the statement,

```
Area := PI * (Radius*Radius)
```

This statement assigns a value to the name Area, which is, in fact, the name of the function itself. When the statements in the body of the function are completed, whatever value has been assigned to this name will be returned as the result of the function.

The facility for defining functions in Pascal is quite general. For instance, the parameters may be of any type defined in your program. Thus you may have parameters that are arrays, strings, or values of an enumerated type. Watch out though; the type must be either a predefined simple type or a type identifier or string. Thus, for arrays a type identifier must be used.

Furthermore, the statements describing the algorithm performed by the subprogram may be as complex as you like, and of course, may even contain calls to other procedures or other functions. Thus the facility for defining subprograms in Pascal is extremely powerful.

11.4 ● Global Information

Consider the following simple procedure:

```
procedure SkipSpaces (NumSpaces : Integer);
```

```
const
    Space = ' ';
var
    Count : Integer;
begin
  for Count := 1 to NumSpaces do
    Write(Space)
end;
```

This procedure has only one parameter, an input parameter named NumSpaces. When this procedure is executed, it prints the number of spaces given as input to NumSpaces.

Let us next consider a revised version of the procedure WriteTitle given earlier in Fig. 11.6.

```
procedure WriteTitle;
begin
    SkipSpaces(24);
    WriteLn('THE LOST PASCAL PROGRAMS');
    SkipSpaces(35);
    WriteLn('OF');
    SkipSpaces(29);
    WriteLn('SHERLOCK HOLMES')
end;
```

This procedure has the same effect as Fig. 11.6. Here, however, the procedure WriteTitle explicitly invokes another procedure, SkipSpaces, defined in the previous procedure.

The use of the procedure SkipSpaces within WriteTitle demonstrates an important general point. A procedure may refer to the entities (constants, types, variables, and subprograms) declared outside the procedure in the main program. These entities are said to be *global* to the procedure.

The use of several procedures in one program is commonplace as programs solve larger and more intricate problems. Furthermore, doing this in Pascal is quite easy. You simply declare the procedures one after another.

For example, consider the general structure of Holmes's program for calculating molecular weights.

```
program MolecularWeight;
    —constant declarations
    —type declarations
    —variable declarations
    —declaration of SetUpTable
    —declaration of GetName
    —declaration of GetElement
begin
    —statements
end
```

This program uses the three procedures SetUpTable, GetName, and GetElement. Notice, however, in program MolecularWeight, the procedure GetName is invoked *within* the procedure GetElement. This brings us to the following rule in Pascal:

- A procedure or function must be declared before it can be called.

Thus the declaration of GetName must precede the declaration of GetElement. Otherwise, the order of subprogram declarations is immaterial.

11.5 ● Side Effects

At this point we have to talk about one of the most subtle but dangerous problem in programming. In computer parlance this problem is called the use of *side effects*. A subprogram can produce a side effect in two ways: by altering its arguments or by altering a variable that is global to the procedure.

Programmers who write subprograms with side effects often get unpleasant surprises. Consider the two programs in Fig. 11.8. These two programs are identical except for the replacement of the expression

F(B) + F(B)

in Fig. 11.8(a) by the expression

2 * F(B)

in Fig. 11.8(b). These two programs are not equivalent because

$$F(B) + F(B) = (11)^*(3) + (12)^*(3)$$
$$= 69$$
$$2 * F(B) = (2)^*(11)^*(3)$$
$$= 66$$

Hence we lose a fundamental property of addition. The problem is caused by the side effect in the function F with the assignment

A := A + 1

where A is global to the function.

Certainly most people *would* be surprised to discover that evaluation of

F(B) + F(B)

is not equivalent to

2 * F(B)

despite the familiar notation for such expressions.

(a) One Program

Figure 11.8 ● Side effects in functions

```
program SideEffect;
   var
      A, B, C : Integer;
function F (X : Integer) : Integer;
begin
   A := A + 1;
   F := A * X
end;
begin
   A := 10;
   B := 3;
   C := F(B) + F(B);      { -- Watch out }
   WriteLn(C)
end.
```

(b) An Equivalent Program?

```
program SideEffect;
   var
      A, B, C : Integer;
function F (X : Integer) : Integer;
begin
   A := A + 1;
   F := A * X
end;
begin
   A := 10;
   B := 3;
   C := 2 * F(B);         { -- Watch out }
   WriteLn(C)
end.
```

The difficulties with side effects become even greater when we need to change a program. Change is a daily occurrence in programming. Someone may find a more efficient algorithm, more output may be needed, a bug may be detected, or specifications may be revised.

If a piece of a program to be changed has side effects, we may need to delve deeply into the entire program for a clear understanding of any effects on other parts of the program. Adding a few extra lines of program for that desirable change may render another piece of the program incorrect. To set matters right again, another change may be needed, and so on. Even if this process succeeds, it is not likely to add to the clarity or flexibility of the program. Had the original program been written without side effects, the subprogram could be changed *without* studying the rest of the program.

The purpose of a procedure is to produce some effect external to itself, not to return a value. Essentially, a procedure consists of a group of statements isolated from the main algorithm for convenience or clarity. The problems encountered with side effects in procedures are quite similar to those encountered in functions. There is one important exception: when a procedure is designed to update a specific set of variables, each of the changed variables should be included in the list of parameters.

Consider Fig. 11.9. In this program, the procedure P causes a side effect on the global variable B. Thus the call

P (A)

gives no clue that the variable B will be changed.

There are, of course, cases where global information may indeed be useful. For example, there may be types, constants, and arrays whose (often used) values remain constant within the program. Making these quantities global to the entire program certainly causes no problems, as they do not change as the program progresses. The real culprit remains the *global variable*.

In brief, global variables and side effects can cause very serious problems. If they are used, they should be used sparingly. We close with the following rules of thumb.

Figure 11.9 ● Side effects in procedures

```
program Globals;
  var
     A, B : Integer;
procedure P (var X : Integer);
begin
   X :=2 * (X + 1);
   B := 5 * X
end;
begin
   A := 2;
   B := 3;
   WriteLn(A, B);        { Prints A as 2, B as 3 }
   P(A);                 { Changes B as well! }
   WriteLn(A, B)         { Prints A as 6, B as 30 }
end.
```

- *Functions*
  Use a function only for its returned value.
  Do not use a function when you need a procedure.
  Do not alter the parameters.
  Do not alter global variables.
- *Procedures*
  Do not use a procedure when you need a function.
  Do not alter global variables.
- *Both*
  Be very, very careful when you use global variables.

Loosely speaking, *recursion* is a method of definition in which the object being defined is used within the definition. For example, consider the following definition of the word "descendant:"

11.6 ● Recursion

> A descendant of a person is a son or daughter of the person, or a descendant of a son or daughter.

In this definition *all* the descendants of the person are simply and precisely accounted for. A nonrecursive definition of descendant that takes all possibilities into consideration would be the following:

> A descendant of a person is a son or daughter of the person, or a grandson or granddaughter of the person, or a great-grandson or great-granddaughter of the person, and so forth.

This definition is lengthier and less succinct than the recursive definition. It is interesting to note how dictionaries attempt to skirt recursion in the definition of descendant. "Descendant" is often defined in terms of "ancestor," whereas "ancestor" is defined in terms of "descendant." The two definitions are, in fact, mutually recursive.

In programming, recursive definitions apply to function and procedure declarations. A recursive subprogram is one that has the potential to invoke itself. In other words, it is defined partially in terms of itself.

In many instances recursive definitions are clearer, more succinct, or more natural than their nonrecursive counterparts, even if they are less efficient. A clear understanding of the nature and power of recursive definitions can be a valuable aid to a Pascal programmer.

Suppose we wish to sum the elements of an integer array. Simple arithmetic gives us the following equality.

$$\text{Sum}(a_1, a_2, \dots, a_n) = a_1 \quad n = 1$$
$$\text{Sum}(a_1, a_2, \dots, a_n) = a_n = \text{Sum}(a_1, \dots, a_{n-1}) \ n > 1$$

Stated in English, the sum of the elements of an array is the last element plus the sum of the first n−1 elements. If the array has only one element, the sum is the single element.

With these facts in mind, it is possible to write the function Sum recursively, as follows:

```
function Sum (A : IntArray;  N : Integer) : Integer;
begin
  if N = 1 then
    Sum := A[1]
  else
    Sum := A[N] + Sum(A, N–1)
end;
```

Its nonrecursive counterpart is also given as follows:

```
function Sum (A : IntArray;  N : Integer) : Integer;
  var
    Index : Integer;
begin
  Sum := 0;
  for Index := 1 to N do
    Sum := Sum +A[Index]
end;
```

Here the type IntArray is defined as

array[1..10] **of** Integer

To understand the recursive definition of Sum, observe the following analysis of the subprogram when applied to a four-component array containing the numbers 3, 6, 8 and 2.

Depth of Recursive Calls	Value of Sum
1	Sum(A,4)
2	2 + Sum(A,3)
3	2 + (8 + Sum(A,2))
4	2 + (8 + (6 + Sum(A,1)))
4	2 + (8 + 6 + 3))
3	2 + (8 + 9)
2	2 + 17
1	19

11.7 ○ Practice

Using Subprograms

There once was a frog named Mr. Croak who was beset with three daughters of marriageable age, Ribbit1, Ribbit2, and Ribbit3. Now the only eligible male frog, Horatio, fell for Ribbit2 and proceeded to ask for her leg in marriage. However, Mr. Croak, concerned with the marriage prospects for Ribbit1 and Ribbit3, proposed that whichever one of his daughters leaped the farthest would be Horatio's wife.

Now Horatio knew, but Mr. Croak didn't, that Ribbit2 could jump twice as far as Ribbit1, and that Ribbit3 could jump only one third as far as Ribbit 2. Thus Horatio readily agreed and persuaded Mr. Croak that the computer program shown in Fig. 11.10 should determine who would wed him. What is the moral of this story?

● ● ●

If you think Horatio is a wise frog, we suggest that you run the program listed in Fig. 11.10 using the Observe window to follow the values of JumpRib1, JumpRib2, JumpRib3, and X. This problem asks you to think about what you have learned about side effects. A variable that is used as a parameter in the heading of a subroutine, and is then given a new value within the subroutine has the side effect of changing the original variable. In the case of Horatio's proposal, when X is multiplied by 2 in function F,

```
program Ribbits;
   var
      JumpRib1, JumpRib2, JumpRib3 : Real;

   function F (var X : Real) : Real;
   begin
      X := 2 * X;
      F := X
   end;
   function G (var X : Real) : Real;
   begin
      X := (1/3) * X;
      G := X
   end;
   begin
      JumpRib1 := 3.0;
      JumpRib2 := F(JumpRib1);
      JumpRib3 := G(JumpRib2);
      if (JumpRib1 > JumpRib2) and (JumpRib1 > JumpRib3) then
         WriteLn('MARRY RIBBIT1')
      else if (JumpRib2 > JumpRib1) and (JumpRib2 > JumpRib3) then
         WriteLn('MARRY RIBBIT2')
      else
         WriteLn('MARRY RABBIT3')
   end.
```

Figure 11.10 ● Program Ribbits

JumpRib1 also takes on the new value of 6.0. Then in function G, the problem is compounded when dividing X by 3, causes JumpRib2 to also be divided by 3. Poor Horatio becomes a victim of the side effect of using a global variable.

The controversy over local versus global variables is not a trivial one; it has a very basic effect on the way people write programs. The problem in Fig. 11.10 could have been avoided by making X a local rather than global variable, as shown in the following:

```
function F (var JumpRib1 : Real) : Real;
  var X : Real;
begin
  X := JumpRib1;
  X := 2 * X;
  F := X
end;
```

The result then would be as Horatio desired:

MARRY RIBBIT2

The following is a simple procedure to be used to exercise your understanding of procedures.

```
procedure Swap (var X, Y : Integer);
var
  Temp : Integer;
begin
  Temp := X;
  X := Y;
  Y := Temp
end;
```

Consider the following changes and their effects.

1. What happens if the header is changed to:
   procedure Swap (**var** X : Integer; **var** Y : Integer);
2. What happens if the header is changed to:
   procedure Swap (**var** Y, X : Integer);
3. What happens if the header is changed to:
   procedure Swap (**var** A, B : Integer);
4. What happens if the name of the local variable Temp is changed to **Nil**?
5. What happens if the name of the local variable Temp is changed to X?

● ● ●

Parameter definitions must be carefully written. Variables of the same type can be defined individually, or as a list followed by a colon and the type name. Number 1 will have no effect on the procedure.

If the order of the variables is changed in the parameter definition, then the actual values given by the statement calling the procedure must also be reversed. The values given in the procedure call (the actual parameters) are assigned to the variables listed in the parameter definition (the formal parameters) in the order in which they are given. In the procedure Swap, if X is given to Y and Y is given to X, and then they are swapped, both variables will end up with the value they started out with.

If the variables given as formal parameters are A and B, the variables within the procedure must be changed to A and B also, if the procedure is to be effective in swapping the two values. Additional statements may be needed in the program, perhaps assigning the values of A and B to X and Y.

Nil is a reserved word. It cannot be used as a variable identifier.

The procedure already has an X; if you change Temp to X, you will be in big trouble.

True or False

1. A procedure can have no parameters.
2. If a procedure with three integer parameters is called with two integer arguments, the third parameter is taken as zero.
3. A Real parameter can correspond to an Integer argument.
4. Two parameters can have the same name.
5. A function can have **var** parameters.
6. New types can be declared within a procedure.
7. Both functions and procedures can be called recursively.
8. The procedure declaration

    procedure DoThis(**var** X : 1..50);

    is a legal declaration.
9. A function can be declared within a procedure.
10. All of the parameters of a function must be of the same type.
11. A procedure can be used to assign a value to a variable.
12. Write is a Macintosh Pascal keyword.

● ● ●

A procedure may have parameters, but it is not a requirement.

If a parameter list is present, then the procedure call must provide a number of arguments equal to the number of parameters in the procedure declaration. If the procedure declaration lists three parameters and only two arguments are given, an error results.

When an Integer argument is given corresponding to a Real parameter, the number is accepted and stored as an Extended number.

Trying to use two parameters with the same name raises havoc with a program.

Numbers 5, 6, and 7 are true.

A subrange cannot be used as a type in a procedure declaration. A type must be declared as in

type
  NumRange = 1..50;

and the type identifier, in this case NumRange, used in the procedure declaration.

Yes, a function can be declared within a procedure.

Various types of parameters can be used in a function, provided they are all properly listed.

A procedure can be used to assign a value to a variable.

Write is not a keyword, it is a predefined procedure.

11.8 ○

11.1 Programming Tools

The important part of a program is the answer it gives back to the operator. Making this answer pleasant and informative is an important part of programming. This means we must have some means of handling character data. A single number or set of numbers printed in the middle of a screen means little, but a well-formatted, neatly labeled output fulfills the purpose of the program, to give a clear and concise answer to the person who entered the data, and presumably, needs it. To this end, your task is to build two simple procedures to handle character strings.

The first such tool is a function called NumChars. This function has one argument, a string containing 20 characters. It returns the length of the string, defined as the number of characters in the string excluding any trailing blanks. For example, the length of the string

'MYCROFT HOLMES

is 14. Using this function you can proceed to more useful (although you will use this one alone many times) character-handling procedures.

The second tool is a character-handling procedure called Position. This procedure has two arguments, a 20-character string and the column (tab) position on an output line. The procedure prints the string starting at the given column position, removing any trailing blanks. For example,

```
HisName     := 'MYCROFT HOLMES        ';
CurrentTab  := 10;
Position (HisName, { at } CurrentTab)
```

prints the name MYCROFT HOLMES in positions 10 through 23 on a line. The procedure Position can make use of the function Length.

Finally, incorporate these two simple tools in a program to test that they behave correctly.

11.2   Random Numbers

Everyone understands intuitively what a random number is. When you roll one of a pair of dice, you get a random number between 1 and 6. If the die is loaded, the numbers are not so random.

In many computer applications, random numbers are very important. Suppose you are testing some pattern for directing traffic flow, and want to see how your idea works. Given some model for the arrival of vehicles at each period of the day, you will want to simulate "random" arrivals into your traffic area. To do this, you need a subprogram for generating sequences of random numbers.

Returning to our dice, suppose we wish to simulate 50 fair throws of a die. We need to generate 50 random integers between 1 and 6. Now many programming languages have a subprogram that generates random numbers for you. Most often the numbers generated lie between 0 and 1, for example 0.22 or 0.67, and you have to scale these numbers up to get a random number between 1 and 6. This is easy, for you just multiply the numbers by 6, take the integer part of the result, and add 1. Thus

.22 times 6 is 1.32
.67 times 6 is 4.02

and your random die throws are 2 and 5.

There are many ways of generating random numbers. Let us look at one that is particularly simple (although it doesn't always produce the most random random numbers).

We start by picking three numbers:

the "seed", say .56
the "multiplier", say 21
the "adder", say .33

To get our first number, we multiply the seed by the multiplier, add the adder, and take the fractional part of the result; that is,

$$(.56)*(21) + (.33) = 12.09$$

Keeping only the fractional part of 12.09, we have .09, our first random number.

To get the second random number, we do the same thing again, only this time replacing the seed by the first random number. Thus

$$(.09)^*(21) + (.33) = 2.22$$

and, we have .22, our next random number. And so it goes. Now for the problem:

a) Write a procedure named Random to generate random numbers between 0.0 and 1.0. The procedure has one output parameter, giving the next random number.

b) Use this procedure to generate 50 throws of one of a fair pair of dice. The program must print these 50 random integers.

c) Keep a count of each 1, 2, 3, 4, 5, and 6 generated, and print the count of each digit generated. This will give you an idea of the "randomness" of your procedure.

Note: You may have noticed that .10 is not such a good multiplier, and .02 is not such a good adder. If your multiplier is 1 plus a multiple of 10, and your adder is not divisible by 2 or by 5, you should be safe.

11.4 Ordering
Write a program to read in 10 integer values and print the values in reverse order. You may not use loops in your program. Instead, of course, you will have to define a recursive procedure.

11.5 Drawing an Icon
The icons used on the Macintosh are drawn in a box 16 pixels wide by 16 pixels high. Write a procedure to create an icon. Since you will want to be able to create the icon anywhere on the screen, you may not use MoveTo or LineTo.

11.6 Recursion versus Iteration
Just about everyone has heard of Fibonacci, who invented the famous sequence 1, 1, 2, 3, 5, 8, 13, 21, . . .

Assume it takes a rabbit about one month to reach reproductive maturity, and a pair of rabbits can give birth to one litter every month. Even further, suppose each litter consists of exactly two rabbits, one of each sex. And finally, suppose the rabbits live a very long time, responding to nature's call.

If you started with one pair of baby rabbits, how many pairs of rabbits would you have in a year? In two years? In three years? Ask Fibonacci. To start you have 1 pair, and in one month, you still have 1 pair.

But in two months you have 2 pairs, in three months 3 pairs, in four months 5 pairs, then 8, and away you go.

You see, at the end of each month, every pair that was around two months ago has had babies. Thus we have

```
Month        : 0   1   2   3   4   5   6    7 . . .
Rabbit Pairs : 1   1   2   3   5   8   13   21 . . .
```

exactly Fibonacci's sequence. Notice that each number in the sequence is the sum of the previous two numbers. So we have the following recursive definition of the function Fibb:

$$Fibb(0) = 1$$
$$Fibb(1) = 1$$
$$Fibb(n) = Fibb(n-1) + Fibb(n-2) \quad \text{for } n > 2$$

Now for your problem. You are to find out how many rabbits there are at the end of 1 year, 3 years, and 5 years (by computer, of course). Further, you are to write two programs to do this. One of your programs will define the function Fibb using recursion, the other will define it without using recursion. Your main program in both cases will simply contain calls to the function Fibb.

Note: The idea for this exercise is taken from the *Fortran Coloring* by Roger Kaufman (MIT Press).

The Coroner's Report

THE murder of the Honourable Colin Wiggs, with its curious, if not to say extraordinary circumstances, had long ceased to be a subject of interest in Fleet Street, where for months the front pages of London's many daily papers had trumpeted the disturbing details as they unfolded. Thus I was surprised to find that, more than a year after this tragedy was laid to rest, it had again become a subject of interest in Baker Street. Early one October evening I called upon my friend Sherlock Holmes, who had had a considerable share in clearing up the Wiggs case. I found him deeply engrossed in reviewing the details attendant upon the matter.

I was apprehensive of what Holmes's humour might be that evening, for his eccentricities became more pronounced when he was engaged on a case and at times his curious habit and mood, which some would call reticent, succeeded in alarming even such an old companion as myself.

To my surprise and pleasure, however, Holmes ushered me into his quarters with an exuberant gesture of welcome and propelled me into the only chair that was not cluttered with books, papers, and scientific specimens.

"You will remember, Watson," he said, "how the dreadful business in which Colin Wiggs was engaged ultimately led to his tragic end, and how the matter was first brought to my notice by a small scar on his left shoulder. A trifling point at first overlooked by the coroner."

"Indeed," said I, "and I well recall your indignation at Scotland Yard's handling of that affair. The case might have dragged on indefinitely had you not chosen to inspect the body yourself."

"Exactly, Watson, why I have now undertaken to reconstruct the material circumstances of that case. I wish to design a systematic, yet simple, means of organizing notes, documented observations, and other data that are used in compiling special presentations, such as a coroner's report."

I listened intently to this explanation, which Holmes delivered between puffs on his cigar. It was evident by a pile of manuscripts within my sight that he had contrived just such a plan for use by the Analytical Engine.

"You have devised some new programme, I take it," I ventured, "though I fear it may lie beyond my comprehension."

"I assure you, my dear Watson, that the algorithm is elementary. If you have understood our other exercises with the Engine, I believe you will find little difficulty with this one."

Holmes thereupon removed a few slips of paper from one of several notebooks that lay open nearby.

"Observe, if you will, the total disarray of these papers, which contain crucial information pertaining to the Wiggs autopsy," he said, handing them to me. "Would it not be more practical to store this data in the Engine's memory, where it would be infinitely more secure and from which a concise report could be called upon whenever necessary?"

Holmes then displayed a summary of the data usually given in a medical examiner's report, as follows:

General Information: 1. Coroner's name, 2. Subject's name, 3. Subject's stated age.

"Observe the total disarray of these papers."

Data and Test Results: 4. Subject's height in inches, 5. Subject's hair colour, 6. Subject's eye colour, 7. Subject's sex, 8. Results of alcohol test, 9. Test for salicylates, 10. Bile morphine indication, 11. Gastric content, 12. Presence of bruises, 13. Presence of lacerations, 14. Presence of lesions, 15. Detected haemorrhages, 16. Fractures.

Remarks: 17. Coroner's observations.

"Now, Watson, in designing a programme to store and recall this information, I dealt with several important points. In the first place, you will observe that the data in each section of the report are of variable length and appearance. Thus when we enter the data into the machine, we do not wish to be confined to a *fixed format*, consisting of rigid columns and predetermined schemes of punctuation, letters, and numbers. Rather, we wish to use a so-called *free format*, which will allow us to separate data items as we please, with blanks and ends of lines. In fact, often a character, for instance a comma, is used to separate items. I decided to use a colon for this purpose, as commas and blanks will likely occur in the data.

"Notice also that it is always a good idea to prepare a sample of the input before coding the programme, as I have also done here. This helps clarify the task at hand. Do you follow me this far, Watson?"

Holmes's conventions are summarized in the table that I have replicated here:

FORMAT CONVENTIONS

a) Each item is treated as a sequence of characters.

b) Items 1 through 3 (general information) contain at most 20 characters.

c) Items 4 through 16 (data and test results) contain at most 40 characters.

d) Except for item 17 (coroner's observations), spaces and ends of lines preceding an item are ignored.

e) Item 17 (coroner's observations) contains an arbitrary number of lines of characters. The first character must appear at the beginning of a line.

SAMPLE INPUT VALUES

General Information: 1. Dr. Harrison, 2. Colin Wiggs, 3. 42,

Data and Test Results: 4. 68, 5. Black, 6. Grey, 7. Male, 8. Negative, 9. Negative, 10. +, 11. Negative for organic bases, 12. Face, neck, 13. None, 14. Neck, 15. None, 16. Upper windpipe

Remarks: 17. Subject was apparently struck on the left side of the neck. Double fracture of the upper windpipe, just below the larynx, suggesting strangulation. A small scar was detected on the left shoulder.

I nodded that his explanation was extremely clear to me and begged him to continue.

"Very good," said Holmes, resuming his manner of a patient lecturer. "Now, so far as the output is concerned, our main objective is to provide a report that is at once complete, orderly, and readily intelligible to the clerks and investigators who are likely to use it. This principle is what I call the *consideration of human factors*. One must remember at all times that one is devising a programme for the benefit of other persons, not only for the Engine—though I cannot refrain from observing that our artificial brain has more aptitude for deduction than many of the natural ones employed by Scotland Yard."

Holmes paused a moment to take another cigar and then continued, as I sat attentively beside him.

"There are two simple concepts involved in the creation of output," he said as he blew a thin stream of smoke into the room.

"First, note that each item of data is viewed as a string of characters. Upon output, each is printed in a specific place.

"Second, the data are grouped into lines, and there must be some predetermined design for the appearance of the report. Thus, when the programme has printed the desired item, advancement to a new line may be called for."

"Really Holmes," I interrupted. "I fear this is all a bit much for my mind to digest at one time."

"No, no, Watson, there are unexplored possibilities about you to which you have given small attention amid your exaggerated estimates of my own performances. If you will bear with me for another moment, I am sure this will all become quite clear to you."

As he spoke he tore two more sheets from his notebook which I have reproduced as Tables 12.1 and 12.2.

"Here are my specimens," he remarked as I examined them, "which should shed some light on these concepts. Tell me, Watson, if they are sufficiently clear, as I intend to offer them to Scotland Yard for their own instruction."

I studied Holmes's diagrams, paying special attention to the appearance of his sample output. The specimens looked perfectly clear and readable, and once again I was astonished at the practical use that resulted from a few simple principles applied by an eminently logical mind.

"Why, Holmes," I said, "if the Engine can be programmed to fulfill a wide variety of similar purposes, the entire profession of clerking may well be undermined within a few years!"

"Nonsense, Watson!" snapped Holmes. "The Engine will surely never replace the need for human intelligence. Rather, it will free mankind from mundane tasks, those that shackle the mind and keep it from more challenging and rewarding exercises.

Table 12.1 ● Output layout of the Coroner's Report

```
                       CORONER'S REPORT
                       -------------------------

        CORONER: ...               SUBJECT'S NAME : ...
                                   STATED AGE      : ...

   BASIC DATA
   ----------------

           HEIGHT IN INCHES : ...
           HAIR COLOUR      : ...
           EYE COLOUR       : ...
           SEX              : ...

   TOXICOLOGY DATA
   ---------------------------

           ALCOHOL TEST     : ...
           SALICYLATES      : ...
           BILE MORPHINE    : ...
           GASTRIC CONTENT : ...

   ANATOMIC DATA
   ------------------------

           BRUISES          : ...
           LACERATIONS      : ...
           LESIONS          : ...
           HAEMORRHAGES     : ...
           FRACTURES        : ...

   GENERAL REMARKS
   ------------------------

           ...
```

"Moreover," he continued, "once the Engine has been programmed correctly, it will always perform correctly, or at least with negligible chance of a random error. Time invested in programmes is cumulative, always adding to the precision of the process."

I have included Holmes's entire algorithm as Fig. 12.1, so that the diligent reader can follow the exact steps taken by Holmes to accomplish the task described herein. You may notice that, while the algorithm is certainly straightforward, accounting for all the details is painstaking. It is especially tedious to ensure that the output is spaced properly.

The program is given in Fig. 12.2. It follows the stated algorithm almost exactly.

"You see, Watson," Holmes remarked, "the programme is a simple collection of procedures that extract each stored piece of information

Table 12.2 ● Sample output from the Coroner's Report Program

```
                        CORONER'S REPORT
                        --------------------------

    CORONER:     Dr. Harrison           SUBJECT'S NAME : Colin Wiggs
                                        STATED AGE      : 42

    BASIC DATA
    ----------------
         HEIGHT IN INCHES  : 68
         HAIR COLOUR       : Black
         EYE COLOUR        : Grey
         SEX               : Male

    TOXICOLOGY DATA
    ---------------------------
         ALCOHOL TEST     : Negative
         SALICYLATES      : Negative
         BILE MORPHINE    : +
         GASTRIC CONTENT : Negative for organic bases

    ANATOMIC DATA
    -----------------------
         BRUISES          : Face, neck
         LACERATIONS      : None
         LESIONS          : Neck
         HAEMORRHAGES     : None
         FRACTURES        : Upper windpipe

    GENERAL REMARKS
    -------------------------
         Subject was apparently struck on the left side of the
         neck. Double fracture of the upper windpipe, just below
         the larynx, suggesting strangulation. A small scar was
         detected on the left shoulder.
```

that is given to it. The important point is that the programme makes the information pleasing for the enquirer to read. If it were printed in a haphazard fashion, the Engine would not be used to its full potential to assist a human undertaking."

"A truly useful concept, Holmes, with great possibilities, assuming the Engine always works without mechanical error!"

To this he made no reply, but it was plainly evident that he was pondering the shortcomings of the Engine. Like all great artists, he was easily impressed by his surroundings; and I fear my comment had thrown him into the blackest depression. How I had learned, long ago, to dread periods of inaction for Holmes. His gaze was now fixed on the mantelpiece, where lay scattered a collection of syringes and bottles; and I knew that the sleeping friend was very near waking in times of such idleness.

Main Algorithm:
  Skip 7 lines
  Perform algorithm PrintTitle
  Skip 2 lines
  Perform algorithm PrintGeneralInfo
  Skip 2 lines
  Perform algorithm PrintBasicData
  Skip 2 lines
  Perform algorithm PrintToxicologyData
  Skip 2 lines
  Perform algorithm PrintAnatomicData
  Skip 2 lines
  Perform algorithm PrintRemarks

Algorithm PrintTitle:
  Write 25 spaces, 'CORONER'S REPORT' header
  Advance to next line

Algorithm PrintGeneralInfo:
  Write 'CORONER:'
  Perform algorithm ProcessNextItem using 20 characters
  Write 6 spaces, 'SUBJECT'S NAME:'
  Perform algorithm ProcessNextItem using 20 characters
  Advance to next line
  Write 35 spaces, 'STATED AGE   :'
  Perform algorithm ProcessNextItem using 20 characters
  Advance to next line

Algorithm PrintBasicData:
  Write 'BASIC DATA' header
  Skip one line
  Perform algorithm ProcessField using 'HEIGHT IN INCHES :'
  Perform algorithm ProcessField using 'HAIR COLOUR   :'
  Perform algorithm ProcessField using 'EYE COLOUR   :'
  Perform algorithm ProcessField using 'SEX   :'

Algorithm PrintToxicologyData:
  Write 'TOXICOLOGY DATA' header
  Skip 1 line
  Perform algorithm ProcessField using 'ALCOHOL TEST   :'
  Perform algorithm ProcessField using 'SALICYLATES   :'
  Perform algorithm ProcessField using 'BILE MORPHINE   :'
  Perform algorithm ProcessField using 'GASTRIC CONTENT :'

Figure 12.1 ● Algorithm for the Coroner's Report Program

Figure 12.1 continued

```
Algorithm PrintAnatomicData:
    Write 'ANATOMIC DATA' header
    Skip 1 line
    Perform algorithm ProcessField using 'BRUISES          :'
    Perform algorithm ProcessField using 'LACERATIONS       :'
    Perform algorithm ProcessField using 'LESIONS           :'
    Perform algorithm ProcessField using 'HAEMORRHAGES      :'
    Perform algorithm ProcessField using 'FRACTURES         :'

Algorithm PrintRemarks:
    Write 'GENERAL REMARKS' header
    Skip 1 line
    As long as more lines remain, do the following:
        write 5 spaces
        copy next line

Algorithm ProcessField using Header:
    Write 5 spaces, Header, spaces to fill header width, ':'
    Perform algorithm ProcessNextItem using 40 characters
    Advance to new line

Algorithm ProcessNextItem using NumChars:
    Read and print item
    Pad with spaces to fill the item to NumChars
```

Figure 12.2 ● Program
CoronersReport

```pascal
program CoronersReport;
{ -- This program reads in data corresponding to the items in }
{ -- a coroner's report. The items are separated by colons(:). }
{ -- The program prints a summary report of the coroner's data. }
    const
        Space = ' ';
    type
        HeaderStr = string[17];
    var
        ReportFile : Text;
        TextLine : string;
    procedure SkipLines(NumLines : Integer);
        var
            I : Integer;
        begin
            for I := 1 to NumLines do
                WriteLn(ReportFile)
        end;
```

Figure 12.2 continued

```
procedure ProcessNextItem ({using}
            Item   Width : Integer);
  var
    DataString : string[40];
    I : Integer;
begin
  ReadLn(DataString);
  Write(ReportFile, DataString);
  for I := 1 to (ItemWidth – Length(DataString)) do
    Write(ReportFile, Space)
end;
procedure ProcessField ({using}
            Header : HeaderStr);
  var
    I : Integer;
begin
  for I := 1 to 5 do
    Write(ReportFile, Space);
  Write(ReportFile, Header);
  Write(Header,':');
  for I := 1 to (17 – Length(Header)) do
    Write(ReportFile, Space);
  Write(ReportFile, ':');
  ProcessNextItem(40);
  WriteLn(ReportFile)
end;
procedure PrintTitle;
begin
  WriteLn(ReportFile,'               CORONER''S REPORT');
  WriteLn(ReportFile,'               ---------- ------');
end;
procedure PrintGeneralInfo;
begin
  Write('CORONER: ');
  Write(ReportFile, 'CORONER: ');
  ProcessNextItem(20);
  Write('SUBJECT''S NAME: ');
  Write(ReportFile,'       SUBJECT''S NAME: ');
  ProcessNextItem(20);
  WriteLn(ReportFile);
  Write('STATED AGE: ');
  Write(ReportFile,'                    STATED AGE: ');
  ProcessNextItem(20);
  WriteLn(ReportFile)
end;
```

Figure 12.2 continued

```
    procedure PrintBasicData;
    begin
      WriteLn(ReportFile, 'BASIC DATA');
      WriteLn(ReportFile, '----- ----');
      SkipLines(1);
      ProcessField('HEIGHT IN INCHES');
      ProcessField('HAIR COLOUR');
      ProcessField('EYE COLOUR');
      ProcessField('SEX')
    end;
    procedure PrintToxicologyData;
    begin
      WriteLn(ReportFile, 'TOXICOLOGY DATA:');
      WriteLn(ReportFile, '---------- ----');
      SkipLines(1);
      ProcessField('ALCOHOL TEST');
      ProcessField('SALICYLATES');
      ProcessField('BILE MORPHINE');
      ProcessField('GASTRIC CONTENT')
    end;
    procedure PrintAnatomicData;
    begin
      WriteLn(ReportFile, 'ANATOMIC DATA');
      WriteLn(ReportFile, '--------- ----');
      SkipLines(1);
      ProcessField('BRUISES');
      ProcessField('LACERATIONS');
      ProcessField('LESIONS');
      ProcessField('HAEMORRHAGES');
      ProcessField('FRACTURES')
    end;
```

Figure 12.2 continued

```pascal
    procedure PrintRemarks;
      var
        I : Integer;
        NextChar : Char;
    begin
      WriteLn(ReportFile, 'GENERAL REMARKS');
      WriteLn(ReportFile, '-------- --------');
      SkipLines(1);
      Write('GENERAL REMARKS:');
      Read(NextChar);
      repeat
        Write(ReportFile,NextChar);
        Read(NextChar)
      until NextChar = '/';
      WriteLn(ReportFile)
    end;
  begin { -- Main Algorithm}
    Open(ReportFile, 'CORONER''S REPORT ');
    SkipLines(7);
    PrintTitle;
    SkipLines(2);
    PrintGeneralInfo;
    SkipLines(2);
    PrintBasicData;
    SkipLines(2);
    PrintToxicologyData;
    SkipLines(2);
    PrintAnatomicData;
    SkipLines(2);
    PrintRemarks;
    Close(Output);
    Rewrite(Output, 'PRINTER:');
    Reset(ReportFile);
    while not EOF(ReportFile) do
      begin
        ReadLn(ReportFile, TextLine);
        WriteLn(TextLine)
      end;
  end.
```

Chapter 12

Input and Output

We have been treating the reading of data and printing of results quite casually up to this point; but, as we are well aware, these matters are essential components of any computer program.

The initial concern in reading data should be that the data are there and in the correct form; otherwise the program will stop and the computer will issue some strange sort of cease and desist order. What is needed when actually using the computer is to second-guess it and check for possible errors in input. For simplicity's sake, we've been loose about this point in the text; but in programs to be used routinely, you should be very careful to check for input mistakes.

As for output, your major concern should be its presentation. Anyone using the program should be able to understand the results easily. Granted, producing quality output can be a tedious task, but your efforts will be amply rewarded even if you are the only person who will use the program.

In Pascal, the basic how-to's of carrying this out are actually quite simple, though sometimes inconvenient.

There are two basic procedures that can accomplish most of what is needed for reading and writing data. These are the procedures Read and Write, along with their variants ReadLn and WriteLn, as described in Table 12.3. Unless other instructions are given, these procedures operate on the standard input file named Input and the standard output file named Output.

Table 12.3 ● Basic Procedures for Reading and Writing Data

Read (v)	Reads the next value from the input file and assigns the value to the variable v. The variable v must be of type Integer, Real, or Char. For integers and reals, leading spaces and line boundaries are skipped; for characters, a line boundary is treated as a blank space.
ReadLn	Causes a skip to the beginning of the next line, that is skips to the character after the next end of line marker.
Read(v_1, ... , v_n)	Same as n individual calls to Read.
ReadLn(v_1, ... , v_n)	Same as n individual called to Read followed by the call ReadLn.
Write(e)	Prints the value of the expression e on the output file. The value must be an integer number, real number, Boolean, character, or character string. If the printed value is too large to fit on the current output line, the value is printed on the following line.
WriteLn	Causes printing to continue on the following line, that is puts an end-of-line marker on the current line.
Write(e_1, ... , e_n)	Same as n individual calls to Write.
WriteLn(e_1, ... , e_n)	Same as n individual called to Write followed by the call WriteLn.
Page	Causes a skip to the beginning of the next page.

Note: v denotes a variable, e an expression.

12.1 ● Input

For reading data, the variables that will hold the data are specified. Furthermore, the type of each input value must be compatible with the type of the corresponding variable, just as usual.

For example, if you are reading some value into an integer variable named NumWeapons, the value must be an integer. Thus, if you input

6

the Read statement will assign 6 to NumWeapons. On the other hand, if you input the real value

14.33

the computer will take the value as 14, and use .33 for the next value. Even worse, if you input

Q1A%

then the computer will probably complain, as the whole thing makes no sense. Notice that if you input the value

–6

into NumWeapons, the computer will not complain, even though from a conceptual viewpoint –6 weapons just doesn't make any sense.

When reading numeric data, leading blanks and line boundaries are ignored. Thus, if you are reading the values of two integer variables, say NumWeapons and NumSuspects, then you may input the data as

6 8

or

6   8

or even

6
8

As far as the computer is concerned, these cases are the same and they're handled in the same manner.

When reading string-type values, the computer will read every character (including spaces) up to the first end-of-line character. If more characters than the declared string width appear before the end-of-line mark is encountered, an error is reported.

The conventions for input of data are summarized in Table 12.4.

12.2 ● Output

The printing of data is just like the reading of data, with one important exception: you get to tell the computer how to display the data. If you don't tell it how to display the data, the computer has its own ideas about how the data should appear and that may not be what you had in mind.

The conventions for displaying data are given in Table 12.5. Notice here that if the space provided for a value is larger than needed, the value is justified to the right: that is, the value is preceded by blanks so as to fill the given field, or the area set aside for it.

Some examples

Recall our program for counting change, given in the previous chapters. This program contains the procedure call

Table 12.4 ● Input Conventions

Integer-Type Values
Blanks preceding the first digit or sign are skipped. End-of-line characters are considered blanks. Reading continues until a noninteger character is encountered.

Real-Type Values
Blanks preceding the first digit or sign are skipped. End-of-line characters are considered blanks. Reading continues until a nonreal character is encountered. One decimal point will be read, but reading will stop if a second is encountered.

Character-Type Values
One character, even if it is a space, is read. An end-of-line character is considered a space.

String-Type Value
Reads until an end-of-line character is encountered. The end-of-line character is noted but not read; it remains in the file buffer. If a second string call is given, the end-of-line character will be immediately encountered. To avoid this situation, use ReadLn.

Enumerated-Type Values
Blanks preceding the first letter are skipped. End-of-line characters are considered blanks. Reading continues as long as the characters read are consistent with an enumerated identifier.

Table 12.5 ● Output Conventions

Width of Values
The width of each value in a layout is controlled by giving arguments of the form $e{:}w$ where e is the expression whose value is to be printed, and w specifies the minimum width of the field on the printed page.

Integer-Type and Real-Type Values
1. If e can be written with w or fewer characters, the value is preceded with an appropriate number of blank spaces (that is, right justified).
2. Otherwise, the number of characters needed to write the full value is used.
3. If no field width is given for integer-type value, it is assumed to be 8.

Table 12.5 continued

4. If no field width is given for real-type values, the number is printed with a scale factor (for example 2.1000E–5) with a field width of 10.

Enumerated-Type Values
1. If the value can be written with w or fewer characters, the value is preceded with an appropriate number of blanks.
2. Otherwise the entire string is written.

Character-Type Values
1. The character is preceded by $(w-1)$ blank spaces.
2. If no field width is given, a default width of 1 is used; thus just the character is printed.

String-Type Values
1. If the string has w or fewer characters, the value is preceded by an appropriate number of blank spaces.
2. Otherwise, only the first w characters are printed.
3. If no field width is given, a default width equal to the length of the string is used.

Decimal Point Representation of Real-Type Values
1. For real-type values, an additional field width parameter can be provided in the form $e{:}w{:}d$. The presence of this parameter causes the real value to be printed in decimal form (for example 22.3 or 0.0002).
2. The parameter causes the value to be printed with d digits to the right of the decimal point.

Write('CHANGE IS ', Dollars : 2. ' DOLLARS AND ', Cents : 2, ' CENTS.')

This statement will print something like

CHANGE IS   3 DOLLARS AND 41 CENTS.

If we omitted the field widths for Dollars and Cents and wrote

Write('CHANGE IS ', Dollars, ' DOLLARS AND ', Cents, ' CENTS.')

the statement would print

CHANGE IS   3 DOLLARS AND   41 CENTS.

The output doesn't look quite right, since the length of each of the four output fields is fixed by the computer. In particular, for strings, the number of characters printed is exactly the number of characters in the string; but for integers, a default of 8 is assumed.

Now for the step up. Suppose we wish to get fancy and print something like

CHANGE IS $3.41

A good and seemingly logical approach would be something like

Write('CHANGE IS $', Dollars : 2, '.', Cents : 2)

This will result in printing the following:

CHANGE IS $ 3.41

Notice here that a space appears after the dollar sign. This is because the printed number of dollars only needs to occupy one digit. If the number of dollars were 13, we would get

CHANGE IS $13.41

and if the number of dollars were 113, we would then get

CHANGE IS $113.41

Notice in this last case that, although the field width of Dollars is given as 2, an additional digit is used, since the number 113 requires more than two digits to be printed. This is typical of the kind of detail that you need to be concerned about when you want to produce readable output.

But wait a minute. Suppose the change were $3.05, that is, the value of Dollars would be 3 and Cents would be 5. The above Write statement would give

CHANGE IS $ 3. 5

This odd result occurs because the number of cents is printed as 5 not 05. The remedy here is an explicit test for this case, as in

if Cents < 10 **then**
    Write('CHANGE IS $', Dollars : 1, '.', '.0', Cents : 1)
else
    Write('CHANGE IS $', Dollars : 1, '.', Cents : 2)

Here the 1 in

Dollars : 1

will even eliminate the space after the dollar sign.

12.3 ● File Types

The data on the standard input and output files Input and Output are recorded as a sequence of characters. Of course, when you read in an integer it is expected that the characters will form a meaningful number, but the basic Read and Write operations are performed over characters. This sequence of characters is said to form a *text file*.

In Pascal, a file of data can be explicitly declared in a program. For example, we may have

```
type
    SuspectName = string[20]
    SuspectData = file of SuspectName;
var
    SuspectFile : SuspectData;
```

Here the type SuspectData represents a file of the names of possible suspects.

All files have certain properties. For one, a file may have an arbitrary number of items. In the above case, SuspectFile may contain 2, 10, or even 500 suspect names. Second, the last item in the file is always followed by a special marker called an "end-of-file." Obviously this marker is put there so your program can know when it has read all of the data.

Third, recall the files Input and Output. These are, in fact, the names of two predefined files whose declarations would be

```
var
    Input, Output : Text;
```

where Text is a predefined type given as

```
type Text = file of Char;
```

That is, Input and Output are the names of text files through which your program can read and transmit information.

Now let us revisit the basic procedures Read and Write. When we use these procedures, input and output take place on a file. The relevant file may be explicitly named in the procedure call by giving the name of the file as the first argument. For example, if we have

```
var
    YardFile, MasterFile : SuspectData;
    NewName : SuspectName;
```

we may have the procedure call

```
Read(YardFile, NewName)
```

which reads a suspect name from YardFile and assigns it to NewName, or

```
Write(MasterFile, NewName)
```

which appends the value assigned to NewName to the file MasterFile. Notice that for files other than Input or Output, arbitrary types of data may be stored and read in.

And now for the final blessing. If it happens, as has been the case throughout this text, that no file name is given with a Read or Write statement, the standard files Input and Output are assumed. So when you say,

    Read(NumWeapons);
    Write(NumWeapons + 1)

this really means

    Read(Input, NumWeapons);
    Write(Output, NumWeapons + 1)

A file can have an unspecified number of items. However, at some point you will have finished reading all of the data and there will be nothing else left in the file. You can test for this condition with the Boolean-valued end-of-file function EOF. You can apply this function to any file, for example, you may write,

if EOF(SuspectFile) **then**
   —*what to do if no more suspects on file*
else
   —*what to do otherwise*

The function EOF will return the value True if there are no more data items in the file, and False otherwise. As indicated by our example, this function is useful whenever you want to test if you are at the end of your data. Just as for the basic procedure Read, you may omit the name of a file to be tested. In this case, the standard text file Input will be used, as in

if EOF **then**
   —*what to do if no more Input data*

Thus the function call EOF is the same as EOF(Input).

Similarly, when you are reading data from Input, you may test for an end-of-line by saying

if EOLn(Input) **then**
   —*what to do if at the end of a line*

or equivalently

if EOLn **then**
   —*what to do if at the end of a line*

Watch out, though, for one tiny detail: the ends of lines are considered as blanks, so normally when you're reading data you can pass right over them. If you need to be careful about what's on a line, you must call EOLn.

The function EOLn raises another point for consideration. The function EOLn may be applied to any file declared with type

file of Char

of with the predefined type

text

Every once in a while you may want to "peek" at a file, for example, to see if some item you are looking for is there before you actually read it. To do this you simply place the symbol ˆ immediately after the name of the input file. For example, you may wish to say something like

if SuspectFileˆ = KnownCriminal **then**
   —what to do if the next suspect is a known criminal

You must be a bit careful here. Assuming that the value of KnownCriminal is the 20-character name of some suspect, the Boolean test compares the next name in the SuspectFile with the value of KnownCriminal. Importantly, the name given on the SuspectFile is not read in during this comparison but is used only for the comparison.

Before an external file can be used in any way, it must be opened. There are three procedures which can be used for opening files.

Reset(NewData)

opens the NewData as a read-only file. The information in the file can be examined and even used for comparison and assignment, but it cannot be changed, and new information cannot be added.

Rewrite(ResultFile)

erases ResultFile and opens it as a write-only file. New data can then be stored in it. With both the Reset and Rewrite procedures a title, or file name, is sometimes used, as in

Reset(NewData, 'CORONER''S REPORT')

With Reset the title is used if there is already an existing external file with that name, and if the file has not already been opened. With Rewrite using a title creates a new external file with that name. If a file with that name already exists, it is deleted and rewritten.

There certainly are times when you need to both read from and write to a file. The procedure

Open(DataFile, 'Census Record')

opens DataFile as a read/write file with the title 'Census Record'. This file accepts both Read and Write procedures.

To close any file simply use the Close procedure, as in

Close(DataFile)

At the bottom of Pascal's facility for input and output lies a pleasant conceptual model. Consider the declarations

type
  Item = *definition of type Item;*
  DataFile : **file of** Item;
var
  F : DataFile;
  NextItem : Item;

We can picture a file as a sequence of items, the length of which is initially unspecified. At a given time one, and only one, of the items is accessible to a program; and this item is denoted by F^. F^ is the *buffer variable* for the file F. Within a program, F^ can be used just as any other variable.

When a file is reset, the first item is assigned to the buffer variable. To assign the value of this item to NextItem simply say,

  NextItem := F^

and to move the second item into the buffer say,

  Get(F)

When you say,

  Read(F, NextItem)   { Read one item from the file F and assign the value to NextItem. }

this is exactly the same as saying,

  NextItem := F^;   { Read the item presently assigned to the buffer variable of file F, assign the item to NextItem. }
  Get(F)   { Replace the item presently assigned to the buffer variable with the next item in the file. }

When a file has been opened using Rewrite, the file buffer is empty and EOF is true. To assign a value to F^ simply say something like

  F^ := NextItem

and then add the item to the file by saying,

  Put(F)

In a write-only file, when an item is moved from the buffer to the file, it becomes the last item of the file and EOF becomes true.

  Write(F, NextItem)   { Assign the item NextItem to the end of file F. }

is exactly the same as saying,

  F^ := NextItem;   { Assign NextItem to the file buffer. }
  Put(F)   { Add the item in the file buffer to the end of file F. }

Since a file is a sequence of items, each component has a position in the sequence. The items are numbered starting with zero. When a file has been opened using the Open procedure, it is possible to request a particular item by using

Seek(*filename, item number*)

To find the number of the current item, use

FilePos(*filename*)

The procedures for manipulating files are summarized in Table 12.6.

Table 12.6 ● Procedures for Manipulating Files

FileName is the file-variable used during the execution of the program.

Title is the name under which the file is stored on the disk.

PosNumber is the sequential position of the item in the file. The first item in the file is numbered zero.

Reset (FileName, 'Title')
Opens an existing file as a read-only file or rewinds an open file. If the file was opened with Rewrite, it becomes read-only. Title is optional. It is used only if there is an existing external file with the name Title and if the file has not already been opened.

Rewrite (FileName, 'Title')
Creates a new write-only file or rewinds and erases an open file. If the file was opened with Reset, it becomes write-only. Title is optional. If it is used and there is no existing file with that name, a new external file with the name Title is created and associated with FileName. If there is an existing file with the name Title, it is deleted and a new one created.

Open (FileName, 'Title')
Creates a new read/write file with the name Title or opens the existing file with the name Title.

Close (FileName)
Closes the file. The file must be reopened in order to refer to it again.

EOF (FileName)
Checks for end-of-file. Returns True if the current position is beyond the last item. Otherwise returns False.

EOLn (FileName)
Applicable to text files only. Checks for end-of-line. Returns True if the current position is the end of a line. Otherwise returns False.

Table 12.6 continued

Get (FileName)
Assigns the next item in the file to the file buffer.

Put (FileName)
Writes the item in the file buffer to the current position of the file and moves the current file position to the next file component.

Seek (FileName, PosNumber)
Causes the file position Number to become the current position. Assigns the item in that position to the file buffer unless Number is greater than the component number of the last item in the file. To use this procedure the file must have been opened using Open.

FilePos (FileName)
Returns the component number of the current item.

12.4 ○ Practice

The program in Fig. 12.3 is supposed to count the number of blanks and nonblanks in a document. There are two errors; what are they?

The Reset procedure can be used without a title only if the file has been previously opened. In the program shown in Fig. 12.3 a title is required for the document file, for instance,

Reset(Document,'Letter 308');

The Rewrite procedure, however, can be used without a title to open an anonymous file associated with a file variable.

The other error is in the declaration of the variable Document. The difference between a file of Char and Text is that a text file is organized into lines. In this program, Text must be used.

In preparing reports or correspondence with a pleasing appearance, it is often nice to center a heading. Consider the program in Fig. 12.4, which centers a single line of text.

If the text for this program is to be read from a file, what statement must be modified?

```
program CountBlanks;
   const
     Blank = ' ';
   var
     NumBlanks, NumNonBlanks : Integer;
     Document : file of Char;
     NextChar : Char;
begin
   Reset(Document);
   NumBlanks :=0;
   NumNonBlanks := 0;
   while not EOF(Document) do
     begin
       while not EOLn(Document) do
         begin
           Read(NextChar);
           if NextChar = Blank then
             NumBlanks := NumBlanks + 1
           else
             NumNonBlanks = NumNonBlanks + 1
         end;
       ReadLn(Document)
     end;
   WriteLn('NUMBER OF BLANKS IS: ', NumBlanks);
   WriteLn('NUMBER OF NON BLANKS IS: ', NumNonBlanks);
end.
```

Figure 12.3 ● Program CountBlanks

```
program CenterText;
   const
     ColumnsPerPage = 72;
     Blank = ' ';
   var
     TextLine : string;
     LeadingSpaces : Integer;
     I : Integer;
begin
   ReadLn(TextLine);
   LeadingSpaces := (72 – Length(TextLine)) div 2;
   for I := 1 to LeadingSpaces do
     Write(Blank);
   WriteLn(TextLine)
end.
```

Figure 12.4 ● Program CenterText

If no file variable is listed in a Read or Write statement, the standard files Input and Output are assumed. Whenever data is to be read from some other file, the file identifier must be included as the first identifier within the parentheses following the Read, as in

ReadLn(CorrespondenceFile, TextLine)

In the statement assigning a value to LeadingSpaces, **div** is used rather than a slash. What does this accomplish?

When an odd number is divided by 2, a fraction results. The line of text may very well contain an odd number of characters. In such a case, TextLine subtracted from 72 leaves an odd number of blanks. Therefore, the counter *I* is declared as an integer, and **div** is used to keep the division result in the integer category. What happens, effectively, is that the half space is moved to the far end of the text.

Actually, the program CenterText would be much more useful as a procedure. What changes would be required to use it as a procedure instead of a program?

● ● ●

The variable TextLine would be given by the original program and must be listed as a parameter of the procedure instead of as a local variable. Probably, the constants would be global variables, since blanks and the number of columns per page would likely be used throughout the program. The ReadLn statement would not be needed in the procedure, since the text line would be given. The following short procedure would suffice.

```
procedure CenterText (TextLine : string);
  var
    LeadingSpaces, I : Integer;
begin
  LeadingSpaces := (72 – Length(TextLine)) div 2;
  for I :=1 to LeadingSpaces do
    Write(Blank);
  Write(TextLine)
end;
```

12.5 ○

12.1 Printing a Calendar
January 1 was a Tuesday. The objective of this exercise is to write a

program that reads in the number of a month from 1 to 12 and prints as output a calendar for the month.

For example, the calendar for a January might look like

```
           JANUARY
           ------------

    S   M   T   W   T   F   S
    -----------------------------------

            1   2   3   4   5
    6   7   8   9  10  11  12
   13  14  15  16  17  18  19
   20  21  22  23  24  25  26
   27  28  29  30  31
```

12.2   Plotting Data

In many computer applications we need to plot data. In displaying the data we need to plot the horizontal and vertical axes, as well as provide labels or titles indicating what the values on the horizontal and vertical axes mean.

Write a program to display the following:

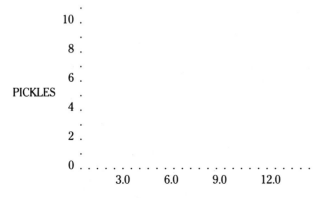

Note: You may wish to plot something as well.

12.3   Printing a Report

The report shown below is typical of the thousands generated every day by computer. Unfortunately, most computer-generated reports are not as simple (perhaps they should be) and are often quite unreadable. This is a problem originating from humans, not machines.

Putting this aside, write a program to generate the report exactly as shown. No input is needed, just print the values shown.

```
Item Code : 1234
Item       : Easy Applicator
Unit Price : $4.36
```

Quantity	Price
1	$ 4.36
2	$ 8.72
3	$13.08
4	$17.44
5	$21.80
6	$26.16
7	$30.52
8	$34.88
9	$39.24
10	$43.60
11	$47.96
12	$52.32
13	$56.68
14	$61.04
15	$65.40
16	$69.76
17	$74.12
18	$78.48
19	$82.84
20	$87.20

12.4 Pascal's Triangle

Have you ever heard of Pascal's triangle? The first six lines look like this:

```
                 1
              1     1
           1     2     1
           1  3     3  1
        1  4     6     4  1
     1  5  10    10  5     1
```

Notice that each of the numbers (for example, 4 in the fifth row) is the sum of the two numbers above it (1 and 3). Write a program to read in a number N and print N rows of Pascal's Triangle. The triangle must be centered of course, and you may assume that N is less than 15.

Note: This exercise is a bit trickier than it first appears. If you want to try something even more tricky, try printing the triangle on its side.

12.5 Putting Line Numbers on Programs

It is common practice on many computers to print programs with line numbers, for example,

```
00010   program CountBlanks(Document, Output);
00020     const
00030        Blank = ' ';
00040     var
00050        NumBlanks, NumNonBlanks : Integer
00060        Document : File of Char;
00070        NextChar : Char;
00080   begin
00090     Reset(Document);
00100     NumBlanks := 0;
```

and so forth. Normally, successive line numbers are incremented by 10. The line numbers allow for easy reference to a statement, and are especially useful for large programs.

Write a program to read in another program and print it with line numbers. Test your program using one of your favorite programs as input. What do you think of incrementing by 10 versus incrementing by 1?

Prelude to Records

The Adventure of the Gold Chip

I T is really very good of you to come along, Watson," said Sherlock Holmes, as he rummaged through a litter of newspapers. We had the carriage to ourselves and were sitting in the two corner seats opposite each other as our train moved rapidly along to Reading. We were responding to a summons from Lestrade which arrived as we were breakfasting.

"It does make a considerable difference, having someone with me on whom I can thoroughly rely. I am sure the aid we will find in Reading will be so terribly biased as to render it worthless. You are familiar with the particulars of this ghastly murder?"

"Not at all," I replied. "My practice has kept me quite busy and I have not seen a newspaper in days."

"The press have not had very full accounts," he replied. "But it has been reported that our unfortunate victim was something of a recluse and a miser, with over three thousand pounds to his name at the time of his death. It was also widely known that he had numerous acquaintances in the London blackmail industry, hence the interest of Scotland Yard in the affair. He was last seen walking away from the village of Eyford late yesterday morning with a man who witnesses say had a bald patch crowning his matted hair. While there is no strong evidence that this stranger was the murderer, the police are left with no other suspects."

It was fairly late in the afternoon when we arrived to find Inspector Lestrade of Scotland Yard waiting for us upon the platform.

"I have ordered a carriage," said Lestrade, as we disembarked. "I know your energetic nature and that you would not be happy until you had been on the scene of the crime.

"We certainly appreciate your help, Mr. Holmes," added the Inspector. "But let me forewarn you that I myself and my best men could find no clue out here. As you will soon see, there is nothing but a jumble of footprints where the final confrontation apparently took place."

293

"Judge not too hastily, Lestrade," Holmes replied nonchalantly. "If I had a shilling for every clue your best men have overlooked in the last ten years, I would retire at once to the country and never want for the rest of my days. Surely you know, Lestrade, that there is no branch of detective science so important and so much neglected as the art of tracing footsteps."

A short while later we arrived at the scene. Holmes sprang down from our carriage, his face flushed and dark; once on a hot scent like this, he was transformed.

Like a foxhound, with gleaming eyes and straining muscles, Holmes was down on his knees, and at one point lay flat on the ground. For a long time he remained there, carefully surveying the earth with his pocket lens. Eventually, he scooped something up into a small envelope, which he returned to his pocket.

"Are there any points to which you would draw my attention?" asked Lestrade, as Holmes returned to us.

"Beyond the obvious facts that there were three men present here at the time of the incident, that the man who led our victim down this path wears a size nine boot and is in good standing with the London financial community, and that the killer himself is a highly underpaid labourer and former officer in the Royal Marine Light Infantry, I can deduce nothing else. After all, Lestrade, one cannot make bricks without clay."

"For a long time he remained there."

The Inspector opened his mouth to speak, but Holmes quickly added, "And do take the trouble of extinguishing your pipe before examining evidence. That left foot of yours with its inward twist and the ash from your Arcadia mixture are all over the place. A mole could trace your movements. Oh, how much simpler it would be if I could only get a look at things before you and your men come in here like a herd of buffalos, trampling over everything!"

Convinced that there was no further need for his services, Holmes called for the carriage, and we were soon heading for Baker Street again. In the privacy of our carriage he shed some light on our abrupt departure.

"As a rule, when I have observed some slight indication of the course of events, I am able to guide myself by the thousands of other similar cases which occur to my memory," he began. "As you are aware, over the course of my career I have amassed data on well over a thousand criminals. In recent years I have stored these data in files suitable for the memory of the Analytical Engine. Furthermore, I have designed a programme that will read the description of each criminal and then print out the names of all those fitting a given description."

I have reproduced here a small section of my companion's curious assortment of criminal data, which he showed me upon our return to Baker Street.

Name	:	The name of a person
Height	:	Height in inches, ranging from 48 to 84
Hair colour	:	One of the colours brown, black, red, or grey
Eye colour	:	One of the colours brown, blue, or hazel
Hat size	:	A number from 4 to 10
Shoe size	:	A number from 5 to 15
Teeth marks	:	One of the characteristics normal, crooked, gold-filled, partially missing, or (totally) missing
Cigar type	:	One of the cigar types Lunkah, Trichinopoly, Espanada, Heritage, Londoner, MacDuffy, Top Hat, or West Country
Facial scar	:	Yes or no
Hand scar	:	Yes or no
Eye patch	:	Yes or no
Bald patch	:	Yes or no
Leg limp	:	Yes or no
Tattoo	:	Yes or no

"I must confess Watson, as I look over these possibilities, that this case does have its points of interest. We know that the suspect has a slight bald patch and wears a size-nine boot. The most singular clue in this mystery, however, is this gold chip I found in amongst the gravel." He showed me the object. "It is a gold dental filling and surely narrows down our list of candidates. Just as you can tell an old master by the sweep of his brush, I can tell a Moriarty when I see one."

"A Moriarty?" I queried.

"The power behind half that is evil and nearly all that is undetected in this great city, Watson. I have been at great pains to work out all my programmes for the Analytical Engine before he becomes aware of its utility, for Moriarty is a mathematical mind of the highest order; and I shudder to think what he could carry out with the Engine at his command."

"What are the ingredients of this particular programme?" I asked, after a considerable pause.

"The most important feature of this programme is, aptly enough, called a *record*," replied Holmes. "A record is a collection of data on some item of interest. In this instance, of course, the record is a collection of facts about a known criminal. Each record consists of one or more *components*, with each component bearing a *name* and a *value*. Here is a sample of my record structures," he continued, handing me a sheet from his portfolio.

What he showed me is duplicated here:

Name	:	a 30-character string
Height	:	0 if unknown; 48 to 84 if known
Hair colour	:	0 if unknown; 1 if brown; 2 if black; 3 if red; 4 if grey
Eye colour	:	0 if unknown; 1 if brown; 2 if blue; 3 if hazel
Hat size	:	0 if unknown; 4 to 10 if known
Shoe size	:	0 if unknown; 5 to 15 if known
Teeth marks	:	0 if unknown; 1 if normal; 2 if crooked; 3 if gold-filled; 4 if partial; 5 if missing
Cigar type	:	0 if unknown; 1 if Lunkah; 2 if Trichinopoly; 3 if Espanada; 4 if Heritage; 5 if Londoner; 6 if MacDuffy; 7 if Top Hat; 8 if West Country
Facial scar	:	0 if unknown; 1 if yes; 2 if no
Hand scar	:	0 if unknown; 1 if yes; 2 if no
Eye patch	:	0 if unknown; 1 if yes; 2 if no
Bald patch	:	0 if unknown; 1 if yes; 2 if no
Leg limp	:	0 if unknown; 1 if yes; 2 if no
Tattoo	:	0 if unknown; 1 if yes; 2 if no

"For simplicity, such data as colour values and shoe sizes are entered as integers," said Holmes, jotting illustrations of his ideas on a scrap of paper, as follows:

Hair colour: 1 brown   2 black   3 red   4 grey

Moreover, truth values are also stored as integer numbers, as follows:

1 for yes,   2 for no

In all cases, if a value is unknown, its place is held by the number 0."

"How can you possibly use these records to find the name of a suspect?" I asked, for I still had no idea how he could use such data to advantage.

"Easily," remarked Holmes. "In Pascal, variables that stand for records can be declared as such, just like variables that stand for arrays or integers. Here is an example:

```
var
    Criminal : record
                Name    :   string[30];
                ShoeSize:   0..15
            end;
```

"An even better method of describing this information would be as follows:

```
type
    NameString = string[30];
    DataRecord =
        record
            Name    :   NameString;
            ShoeSize:   0..15
        end;
var
        Criminal : DataRecord;
```

"Moreover," continued Holmes, "one can refer to a component of a record by specifying the name of the record variable and the name of the component, as follows:

```
Criminal.ShoeSize
```

This reference can be used in Pascal statements like any other variable, such as

```
if Criminal.ShoeSize = 9 then
    — print criminal's name
```

or

```
Criminal.ShoeSize := 9
```

"What our programme will do, Watson, is read in the characteristics of a suspect, such as a bald patch or a size nine boot, and then print out the names of all those criminals in its files that fit the description. Let us give it a try, shall we? I can tell you well in advance, however, whose signature we shall find on this latest criminal masterpiece."

Holmes then carefully entered the data according to the programme, which I have duplicated here as Fig. 13.1, paying special attention to enter the codes for a size nine boot, gold-filled teeth, and the presence of a bald patch. We watched for several minutes before the names of three criminals within the file had been printed.

"Moriarty," Holmes whispered. "These other two, Watson, are certainly capable of carrying out such a crime. However, I happen to know one of them is in Newgate; and if I am not mistaken, this other is awaiting trial here in London."

"Surely you haven't enough evidence to convict Moriarty," I protested.

"Oh, hardly, Watson," replied Holmes. "But count on it, this crime fits into something much larger which we fail to see presently, for there are certain subtleties that even our Engine cannot detect. True, it has removed a lot of the painstaking drudgery from our work; but it is up to us to find where and how this piece fits into the larger scheme of things.

"For now, Watson, there is a cold partridge on the sideboard and a bottle of Montrachet here. Let us renew our energies before we make fresh calls upon them."

Figure 13.1 ● Program Search

```
program Search;
{ -- This program reads in values corresponding to data saved }
{ -- in a file of records kept on known criminals. }
{ -- For each item, a prompt indicates which item is to be input. }
{ -- A value of zero indicates that the item is unknown. }
{ -- The program outputs the name of each criminal for which }
{ -- the input values match those on the criminal's record. }
  const
    Unknown = 0;
  type
    YesNoCode = 0..2;
    NameString = string[30];
    DataRecord = record
      Name : NameString;
      Height : 0..84;
      HairColour : 0..4;
      Eye Colour : 0..3;
      HatSize : 0..10;
      ShoeSize : 0..15;
      TeethMarks : 0..5;
      CigarType : 0..8;
      FacialScar : YesNoCode;
      HandScar : YesNoCode;
      EyePatch : YesNoCode;
      BaldPatch : YesNoCode;
      LegLimp : YesNoCode;
      Tattoo : YesNoCode
    end;
```

Figure 13.1 continued

```
var
    Suspect, Criminal : DataRecord;
    MasterFile : file of DataRecord;
procedure GetSuspectInfo (var Suspect : DataRecord);
begin
  WriteLn('IN ENTERING DATA, USE 0 IF ITEM IS UNKNOWN.');
  WriteLn('ENTER HEIGHT IN INCHES:');
  ReadLn(Suspect.Height);
  WriteLn('ENTER HAIR COLOUR CODE:');
  WriteLn('1 BROWN,    2 BLACK,  3 RED,  4 GREY');
  ReadLn(Suspect.HairColour);
  WriteLn('ENTER EYE COLOUR CODE:');
  WriteLn('1 BROWN,  2 BLUE  3 HAZEL');
  ReadLn(Suspect.EyeColour);
  WriteLn('ENTER HAT SIZE:');
  ReadLn(Suspect.HatSize);
  WriteLn('ENTER SHOE SIZE:');
  ReadLn(Suspect.ShoeSize);
  WriteLn('ENTER TEETH MARKS CODE:');
  WriteLn('1 NORMAL,    2 CROOKED,   3 GOLD FILLED,');
  WriteLn('4 PARTIAL,    5 MISSING');
  ReadLn(Suspect.Teethmarks);
  WriteLn('ENTER CIGAR TYPE CODE');
  WriteLn('1 LUNKAH,       2 TRICHINOPOLY, 3 ESPANADA,');
  WriteLn('4 HERITAGE,    5 LONDONER,    6 MACDUFFY,');
  WriteLn('7 TOP HAT,   8 WEST COUNTRY');
  ReadLn(Suspect.CigarType);
  WriteLn('NOW USE 1 FOR YES, 2 FOR NO, 0 FOR UNKNOWN:');
  WriteLn('FACIAL SCAR?     HAND SCAR?  EYEPATCH?');
  ReadLn(Suspect.FacialScar, Suspect.HandScar, Suspect.EyePatch);
  WriteLn('BALD PATCH?     LEG LIMP?     TATTOO?');
  ReadLn(Suspect.BaldPatch, Suspect.LegLimp, Suspect.Tattoo)
end;
function ItemMatch (Item1, Item2 : Integer): Boolean;
begin
  if (Item1 = Unknown) or (Item2 = Unknown) or (Item1 = Item2)
  then
     ItemMatch := True
  else
     ItemMatch := False
end;
```

Figure 13.1 continued

```
function Match ({between}
                Suspect, Criminal : DataRecord) : Boolean;
begin
  Match := False;
  if ItemMatch(Suspect.Height, Criminal.Height) then
   if ItemMatch(Suspect.HairColour, Criminal.HairColour) then
    if ItemMatch(Suspect.EyeColour, Criminal.EyeColour) then
     if ItemMatch(Suspect.HatSize, Criminal.HatSize) then
      if ItemMatch(Suspect.ShoeSize, Criminal.ShoeSize) then
       if ItemMatch(Suspect.TeethMarks, Criminal.TeethMarks) then
        if ItemMatch(Suspect.CigarType, Criminal.CigarType) then
         if ItemMatch(Suspect.FacialScar, Criminal FacialScar) then
          if ItemMatch(Suspect.HandScar, Criminal.HandScar) then
           if ItemMatch(Suspect.EyePatch, Criminal.EyePatch) then
            if ItemMatch(Suspect.BaldPatch, Criminal.BaldPatch) then
             if ItemMatch(Suspect.LegLimp, Criminal.LegLimp) then
              if ItemMatch(Suspect.Tattoo, Criminal.Tattoo) then
               Match := True
end;
begin { -- Main Algorithm }
  GetSuspectInfo(Suspect);
  Reset(MasterFile, 'Criminal Data');
  while not EOF(MasterFile) do
    begin
      Read(MasterFile, Criminal);
      if Match(Suspect, Criminal) then
        WriteLn('POSSIBLE SUSPECT ', Criminal.Name)
    end;
  WriteLn('ALL ENTRIES HAVE BEEN CHECKED');
end.
```

Chapter 13

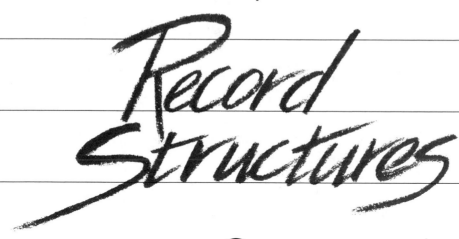

Record **S**tructures

Certainly one of the most useful features of Pascal is its capability for defining record structures. A *record* is a collection of information pertaining to some real-world entity. It can contain various types of information including other records.

Consider the following declarations:

13.1 ● **Record Types**

```
var
   Suspect : record
      Height : 0..84;
      HatSize : 0..10;
      ShoeSize : 0..15
   end;

   Cigar : record
      Brand : (Trichonopoly, Lunkah, OldWood, Londoner);
      Texture : (Flaky, Caked, Granular, Fluffy);
      Nicotine : (Plus1, Plus2, Plus3);
      Particles : Boolean;
      Data : record
         UnitVolume : Real;
         UnitWeight : Real;
         Density : Real
      end
   end;
```

The first declaration defines a variable named Suspect, whose type is a record. The record has three components, Height, HatSize, and ShoeSize. Each component is a subrange of integers.

The components of a record can be of any type, even other records. This is shown in the second declaration, which defines a record variable named Cigar. Here the components Brand, Texture, Nicotine, and Particles have values that are from enumerated types. The component Data is itself a record structure defining the physical characteristics of the cigar's ash. These declarations demonstrate two characteristics of record structures.

- Record types are composed of specified lists of *fields*, each of which has a declared identifier and type.
- The fields can be of differing types, including other record types.

Record structures can be defined in a type declaration, just as for any other type. Thus we may rewrite the definitions of cigar properties as follows:

```
type
    CigarBrand = (Trichonopoly, Lunkah, OldWood, Londoner);
    AshTexture = (Flaky, Caked, Granular, Fluffy);
    TestResult = (Plus1, Plus2, Plus3);

    DensityData = record
       UnitVolume : Real;
       UnitWeight : Real;
       Density : Real
    end;

    CigarInfo = record
       Brand : CigarBrand;
       Texture : AshTexture;
       Nicotine : TestResult;
       Particles : Boolean;
       Data : DensityData;
    end;
```

and then simply say

```
var
    Cigar : CigarInfo;
```

to declare the variable Cigar. We strongly recommend the second alternative. The habit of declaring types and then using their identifiers in variable declarations will stand you in good stead as your programming skills increase and the challenges become greater.

Just as for components of arrays, we can refer to the components of a record. For example, we may say,

```
Suspect.Height; = 71;
Suspect.HatSize: = 7;
Suspect.ShoeSize: = 9;
```

to establish values for each of the properties of Suspect. The general rule here is that if

> R is the name of a record variable
> C is the name of one of its components,

then

> R.C is the name of the record component.

Notice in the cigar example that

> Cigar.Data

is also a record. Thus it makes sense to say

> Cigar.Data.Density

to refer to the density of the cigar ash. For example, we may have

> Cigar.Data.Density := Cigar.Data.UnitWeight/Cigar.Data.UnitVolume

Again, just what you would expect.

Pascal provides a shortcut here, a with statement, such as

> **with** Cigar.Data **do**
>   Density := UnitWeight/UnitVolume

This accomplishes the same result as the longer statement. The names Density, UnitWeight, and UnitVolume are associated with the record Cigar.Data, and thus the operation is performed on these fields. By using a compound statement following the **do**, several operations can be performed on components of Cigar.Data within the single with statement.

In Pascal, one record can be assigned to another provided the types are compatible. Thus, with

> MyCigar, YourCigar : CigarInfo;

you can say:

> MyCigar := YourCigar   { ok }

But there is one little anomaly to watch out for here. You cannot say something like:

> **if** MyCigar = YourCigar **then**   { trouble }

To get the same effect, you must write

> **if** (MyCigar.Brand = YourCigar.Brand) **then**
> **if** (MyCigar.Texture = YourCigar.Texture) **then**
>   **if** (MyCigar.Nicotine = YourCigar.Nicotine) **then**
>   **if** (MyCigar.Particles = YourCigar.Particles) **then**

$$\text{if } (\text{MyCigar.UnitVolume} = \text{YourCigar.UnitVolume}) \textbf{ then}$$
$$\text{if } (\text{MyCigar.UnitWeight} = \text{YourCigar.UnitWeight}) \textbf{ then}$$
$$\text{if } (\text{MyCigar.Data.Density} = \text{YourCigar.Data.Density}) \textbf{ then}$$
—what to do if all components match

which certainly is tedious. In practice, it will probably not be necessary to compare all the components. For example, in the preceding case

if (MyCigar.Brand = YourCigar.Brand) **then**

may suffice.

The record fields that we have discussed so far have all been *fixed*, that is, each of the fields is accessible whenever that record is used. These fields are contained in the fixed-part of the record type. There is also available a variant part.

Consider our suspect information. Suppose that we want to add to our list of data information regarding employment. Specifically we want to know whether or not the suspect is presently employed; if so, the name and address of the employer; if not, the name of the last employer and the last date of employment. The following declaration shows this option.

```
type
  SuspectInfo = record
    Height : 0..84;
    HatSize : 0..10;
    ShoeSize : 0..15;
    case NowEmployed : Boolean of
      True : (EmployerName : string;
              EmployerAddress : string);
      False : (LastEmployerName : string;
              (LastDateEmployed : Integer)
  end;
```

In a variant field, only one of the field lists is available at a time. The line

case NowEmployed : Boolean **of**

indicates that NowEmployed can take on one of two values, True or False. When one of the fields is activated by assigning a value to its tag field or to any one of its components, the other field is deactivated. Either of the following assignments will activate the True field.

```
SuspectInfo.NowEmployed := True;
NowEmployed.EmployerName := 'Verigood Construction Co.'
```

The concept of pointers (or the more erudite phrase "dynamically varying structures") is one of the most difficult constructs in programming. Pointers offer the programmer a basic facility for creating rather rich and elaborate structures of data. On the other hand, the facility in Pascal for using pointers is quite simple and quite primitive. Let's have a look first at the basic primitives for pointers in Pascal.

Let us start by considering the following declaration.

13.2 ● Pointers and Dynamic Structures

type
   EntryData = **record**
      Name : **string**;
      IDNum : Integer;
      ArrivalTime : Integer;
   end;

Here we have a record structure with four fields, presumably representing (1) the name of a person, (2) the identification number of a person, and (3) the arrival time of a person upon entering a building. For argument's sake, let us suppose we are keeping this information for security purposes when each employee enters a building to report to work. Let us also assume that the arrival time is given as an integer which can be interpreted as representing the hours and minutes since the previous midnight, but let us not get involved in these details here. Let us just assume that an integer represents the time of day.

If we are to keep a record of employee arrivals and departures we will need a rather large and initially unspecified number of such records, one for each entry into the building. If we imagine a large building there may be hundreds or even thousands of such entries. We could keep each record in a file of records for a given day. That is, if there were several hundred arrivals, we would have several hundred records in the file, presumably put there in order of the time of arrival. But now let us suppose that we wished to print out a list of all the persons entering the building on a given day and print this file in order by identification number. This presents a problem. If we put each record into the file in order of arrival, we would have quite a bit of processing in order to print the file in order of increasing identification number. On the other hand, if we try to keep the file in order by identification number, we would have to do quite a bit of organization each time a new person entered the building in order to keep the file in its proper order. The point of all this is to suggest that we have a relationship that is not well embodied by a linear file. We could harken back to an array of records to keep this information, but then there is the question of how big to make the array and whether the array can represent the relationship that we want, records ordered by increasing identification number. This problem is suggestive of the wide range of problems to which pointers can be applied.

Consider the following additional type declaration

type
    EntryPtr = ^ EntryData;

This type declaration introduces a new named type called EntryPtr. We can think of EntryPtr as an address or a location where a record containing the entry data on a given person is stored. Such a type is called a *pointer type*. We can declare variables that have a pointer type just as we can variables that have an integer type or a string type. For example we can say

var
    Person, PrevPerson : EntryPtr;

So far we have not introduced anything particularly striking. But how do we deal with pointers?

The basic operation for using pointers is a predefined procedure called New. If we give the procedure call

New(Person)

two things happen.

1. Space for a record containing the three fields of type EntryData are allocated in the memory of the computer.
2. A pointer to this space is assigned as the value of the variable Person.

So we see that New both allocates space and returns a "pointer" to the space that was allocated. We don't have any values yet stored in the record structure for which space was allocated, but that is handled subsequently. For example, after the foregoing procedure call we can say,

    Person^.Name := "Cristie";
    Person^.IDNum := 5491707;
    Person^.ArrivalTime := 1130

Notice here that Person has a pointer type; Person^ (the item pointed to by Person) has a record type. We can name the components of this record type just as for ordinary records. In the above example, we refer to the Name, IDNum, and ArrivalTime fields of Person^. Now the space allocated for the record actually contains some values. After this we can say something like

    PrevPerson := Person

This is an assignment statement. Both the left side and the right side of the assignment statement are of the same type; both are pointers to records of type EntryData. This assignment simply takes the pointer value of Person and assigns it to PrevPerson. Now both PrevPerson and Person point to the same record structure. Now we can even say things like

```
I := PrevPerson^.IDNum;
WriteLn(PrevPerson^.ArrivalTime)
```

The first of these two assignments, assuming I is an integer variable, will give I the value 5491707. The second statement will print the value 1130. This shift from Person to PrevPerson should cause no problems.

We can allocate space for another record structure by now saying

```
New(Person)
```

When this statement is executed, the computer will allocate space for another record and assign a pointer to this new space to the variable Person. Note well here, that now PrevPerson and Person will point to different spaces in memory! The old values of Name, IDNum, and ArrivalTime are still associated with PrevPerson, but Person now is a pointer to a new record structure which has yet unspecified values. All of this brings us to a dead end where we meet the next major hurdle.

In our initial problem we assumed that we would have many, many arrivals into the building with many record structures needed to record all of this information. As we have declared only two pointer variables, Person and PrevPerson, there is no way to get any more data into our system. To do something about this, we add yet another field to the records of type EntryData. Consider a new rendering of this type.

```
type
  record
    Name : string;
    IDNum : Integer;
    ArrivalTime : Integer;
    Next : EntryPtr          { -- a pointer }
  end;
```

Here we have added one more field, itself a pointer. This pointer points to another record of type EntryData. These can be chained together to form a whole structure of records.

The procedure shown in Fig. 13.2 compares the IDNum of each NewArrival with the IDNum in other records of the chain and then adjusts the Next field to keep the chain in order. A variable, Start, of type EntryPtr is given in the procedure call. This variable points to the first record in the chain and will change whenever a new arrival has a lower ID number than that of the present start person. As each person arrives, the ID number is compared first with Start^.IDNum and then with the IDNum in each succeeding record, until the proper location for the record is found; the

Next fields are then changed to reflect the new conditions. Two variables of type EntryPtr are used during the comparisons. TestPerson is the record being checked for a higher ID number; PrevPerson is the record immediately preceding TestPerson, that is, PrevPerson^.Next points to TestPerson.

The following diagrams help to clarify this procedure. Assume that the start person has an ID number of 5491707 and that three people arrive in order with the following ID numbers.

    2473492
    6655532
    7810023

When the procedure is called, the Start record shown in Fig. 13.3 exists.

There may or may not be more records in the chain. For the moment we assume there are no other records; therefore, the value of Start^.Next is nil. **Nil** is one of Pascal's reserved words; it is used with pointers to indicate that the pointer, at the moment, points to nothing. It is similar to setting a counter to zero.

The three diagrams in Fig. 13.4 show the relationships as they exist after each new arrival.

Figure 13.2

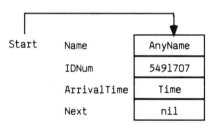

Start	Name	AnyName
	IDNum	5491707
	ArrivalTime	Time
	Next	nil

Figure 13.3 ● Procedure AddArrival

```
procedure AddArrival (var Start : EntryPtr);
    var
        NewArrival, TestPerson, PrevPerson : EntryPtr;
        Done : Boolean;
    begin
        New(NewArrival);
        ReadLn(NewArrival^.Name, NewArrival^.IDNum,
                    NewArrival^.ArrivalTime);
```

Figure 13.3 continued

```
    if NewArrival^.IDNum < Start^.IDNum then
      begin
        NewArrival^.Next := Start;
        Start := NewArrival;
        Done := True
      end
    else
      begin
        PrePerson := Start;
        TestPerson := Start^.Next;
        Done := False;
        while (not Done) do
          begin
            if TestPerson = nil then
              begin
                PrevPerson^.Next := NewArrival;
                NewArrival^.Next := nil;
                Done := True
              end
            else if TestPerson^.IDNum > NewArrival^.IDNum then
              begin
                PrePerson^.Next := NewArrival;
                NewArrival^.Next := TestPerson;
                Done := True
              end
            else
              begin
                PrevPerson := TestPerson;
                TestPerson := TestPerson^.Next
              end
          end
      end
end.
```

13.3 ○ Practice

A quick review of the concept of records is in order before we get into more discussion about pointers.

True or False

1. The components of a record are referenced by giving the record identifier and the field identifier separated by a period.

2. A field of a record can be any type except another record.

Figure 13.4

After first NewArrival

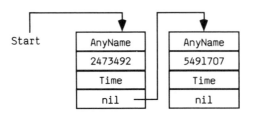

After second NewArrival

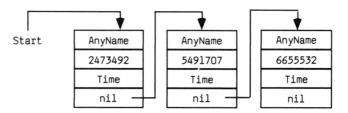

After third NewArrival

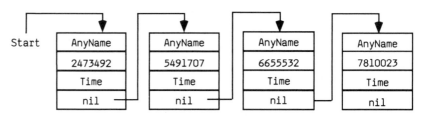

3. A record can be assigned to another record if they have the same type identifier.
4. An array can be used any place that a record can be used.
5. Pointers always point to records.
6. Record structures are only useful for very advanced programming.
7. All criminals have gold fillings.
8. Records can be compared with other records.
9. Program Search cannot be used unless information is available for each category.

Fill in the Blanks

1. Record types are composed of _____.
2. Record structures can be defined in a _____ declaration.
3. A record can have two parts, a fixed part and a _____ part.
4. A record field consists of an _____ and its _____.
5. In a list of statements containing record fields, repetition of the record identifier can be avoided by the use of a _____ statement.
6. YesNoCode in program Search is a _____ type.
7. A record declaration ends with the word _____.

● ● ●

In the True/False quiz, only numbers 1 and 3 are true. A field of a record can itself be a record.

The components of an array must all be of the same type; this is not true of a record.

A pointer can point to a variable of any type.

Record structures are useful at any level of programming and do not require an advanced level of knowledge.

Holmes's criminal did indeed have a gold filling.

Records cannot be compared with other records; the individual items which make up the record must be compared.

Function ItemMatch provides for missing information by assuming a match if the information is not available.

The blanks should be filled with the following: fields, type or variable, variant, identifier, type, **with**, subrange, **end**. In regard to number 2, although records can be defined in a variable declaration, it is much safer, in the long run, to declare them in a type declaration and then use the type identifier in the variable declaration.

Consider the program listed in Fig. 13.5.

1. Describe the variables Member and LastBorn.
2. What does the first statement accomplish?
3. What happens when Member is assigned to LastBorn?
4. In the statement

    LastBorn^.NextOfKin := Member

    what is actually assigned to the component NextOfKin ?

Figure 13.5 ● Program
Geneology

```
program Geneology;
    type
        Person = ^ Info;
        Info = record
            Name : string[10];
            SSNum : LongInt;
            NextOfKin : Person
        end;
    var
        Member, LastBorn : Person;
begin
{ -- initial state, no one on earth }
    LastBorn := nil;

{ -- birth of Adam }
    New(Member);
    Member^.Name := 'ADAM';
    Member^.SSNum := 1;
    Member^.NextOfKin := nil;
    LastBorn := Member;

{ -- birth of Adam's spouse }
    New(Member);
    Member ffl.Name := 'EVE';
    Member ffl.SSNum := 2;
    Member ffl.NextOfKin := LastBorn;
    LastBorn ffl.NextOfKin := Member;
    LastBorn := Member;

    Write(LastBorn ffl.SSNum, LastBorn ffl.NextOfKin ffl.SSNum)
end.
```

5. When the program ends, what is the value of Member?

The variables Member and LastBorn are pointer type variables, which point to record structure values of type.

The statement

LastBorn := **nil**

is Pascal's way of saying that LastBorn is "a pointer to nothing." This is similar to setting an integer variable to 0. The statement sets the value of LastBorn to **nil**, indicating that no person has yet been born.

The birth of the first member of our family is accomplished with the predefined procedure New, as in

```
New(Member);
Member^.Name := 'Adam     ';
Member^.SSNum := 000000001;
Member^.NextOfKin := nil
```

Here the call to New allocates space for a new record structure and set Member to point to it. The next three assignments establish values for the record components. Notice that the ^ in Member^ refers to the object pointed to. Thus we have

Member   —   denotes the pointer value of Member
Member^   —   denotes the object pointed to by Member

With this first birth, we can now give an explicit value for LastBorn with the assignment:

```
LastBorn := Member;
```

This statement assigns the pointer value of Member to LastBorn. So after this we have the structure shown in Fig. 13.6.

Next consider another birth, given in the statements

```
New (Member);
Member^.Name := 'Eve       ';
Member^.SSNum := 000000002;
Member^.NextOfKin := LastBorn
```

Here again a new record structure is allocated and its values are established for Eve. Furthermore consider the statements

```
LastBorn^.NextOfKin := Member;
LastBorn := Member
```

Figure 13.6

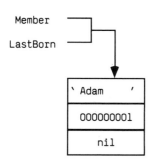

The first statement results in setting the NextOfKin component associated with Adam as a pointer to Eve. The second statement updates the value of LastBorn to point to Eve.

The situation now is as shown in Fig. 13.7.

Now that we have two people in our family, we can see the development of dynamic relationships during program execution. The NextOfKin components of Adam and Eve now refer to each other, and LastBorn has been maintained as a pointer to the person who was last born.

At the program's end, Member is a pointer to Eve.

13.4 ○

13.1   Duplicating a File

If you have a file of data and want to edit it, delete some of its parts, reformat it, or what have you, it is nice to have a spare copy in case something goes wrong.

Your problem is to write a program to duplicate a file. To test your program, make a copy of one of your programs into another file. The copy should be an exact replica, line by line.

13.2   Mailing Lists

You must be on at least one computerized mailing list, perhaps even too many. Your task here is to computerize one yourself. Typically, an entry in a mailing list has five components:

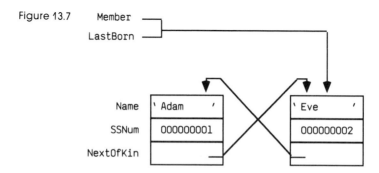

Figure 13.7

Name   : the name of the addressee
Address : a 1- or 2-line street address
City   : the name of a city
State   : the name of a state
Zip code: a 5-digit zip code

Write a program to read in a file of such entries and print out address labels for each entry. Prepare a short file of entries to test your program.

Note: In real life one must consider the following issues. How should extra long names be treated? What if the address takes more than two lines? What if the addressee resides in another country? What if the zip code is missing? Should the entries be ordered by zip codes? Or by names? You see, as for any real application, the full problem is never easy.

13.3   Investment Gains

Many investors prefer to put their money into "real goods" instead of paper. Your problem is to write a program that calculates the per cent of appreciation, or depreciation, in the value of the items in an art collection. The program is to read the following information about each item:

Item name
Artist
Date of purchase
Purchase price
Present appraised value

The output is to be a table showing:

Item name
Artist
Total appreciation or depreciation
Number of years since purchase

13.4   Inventory

Here you are to assume the existence of an external file. The external file is an inventory list containing the item number, item name, quantity in storage, and number on order.

The program first prints the item number and item name. The user then enters the count of the item on the shelf. The computer follows with the number in storage and the number on order.

The output must be carefully formatted to create a nice evenly spaced table.

13.5   Classification

Computers are very good at sorting and at keeping lists. This program is to select a category for each item and then add the item to the proper list for that category. Each list is an external file.

For this program, assume a pre-existing list containing the name, mailing address, and statistical profile for an undefined number of people. The program is to read the existing record, and then add it to the end of the list of homeowners or the list of renters.

Chapter 14

More on Graphics

We have covered a lot of ground in the past chapters. Unfortunately, what seems quite clear when read sometimes becomes complicated when an attempt is made to put it into practice.

14.1 ● Application: BarGraph Revisited

Figures 14.1 and 14.2 are example programs that show how some of the concepts discussed up to this point can be applied to the bar graph program presented in chapter 3.

Program CreateBreedFile (Fig. 14.1) creates a file of records containing information about various breeds of dogs. This file includes only the breed names and number of puppies; however, it could be revised to contain any number of other bits of information helpful to the user of the file, such as the total number of dogs registered, standards of the breed, and so forth. A different type declaration would be required to accommodate the changes.

The new file is opened as a write-only file and assigned the title BreedFile. A repeat loop is used to prompt the user to enter the items one at a time from the keyboard. After both items are read, they are written as a complete record to AnnualFile. When NO MORE is entered as a breed name, the loop ends and the file is closed.

The program as it is written requires that all items be entered at the same sitting and does not provide for changes to any of the records. In a real life situation, of course, a program that allows changes and additions is certainly more useful.

Figure 14.1 ● Program
CreateBreedFile

```
program CreateBreedFile;
  const
    LastName = 'NO MORE';
  type
    BreedInfo = record
        BreedName : string[20];
        NumOfPups : LongInt
      end;
    MasterFile = file of BreedInfo;
  var
    BreedData : BreedInfo;
    AnnualFile : MasterFile;
begin
  Rewrite(AnnualFile, 'Breed Statistics');
  repeat
    Write('Breed Name: ');
    ReadLn(BreedData.BreedName);
    if BreedData.BreedName <> LastName then
      begin
        Write('Number of Puppies: ');
        ReadLn(BreedData.NumOfPups);
        Write(AnnualFile, BreedData)
      end;
  until BreedData.BreedName = LastName;
  Close(AnnualFile)
end.
```

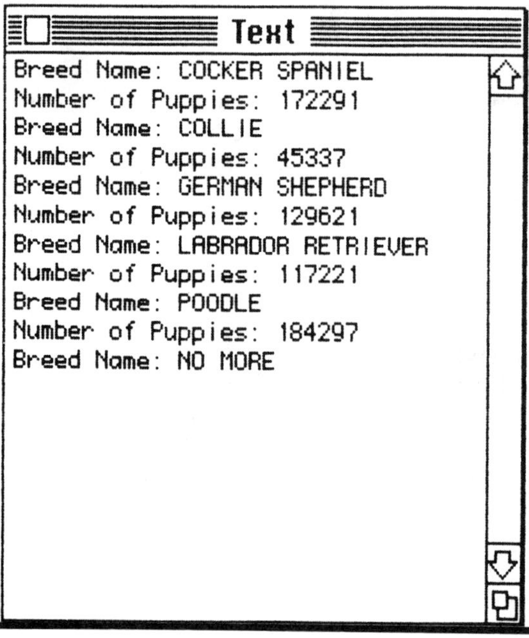

```
======= Text =======
Breed Name: COCKER SPANIEL
Number of Puppies: 172291
Breed Name: COLLIE
Number of Puppies: 45337
Breed Name: GERMAN SHEPHERD
Number of Puppies: 129621
Breed Name: LABRADOR RETRIEVER
Number of Puppies: 117221
Breed Name: POODLE
Number of Puppies: 184297
Breed Name: NO MORE
```

Figure 14.2 ● Program
BarGraph

```
program BarGraph;
   const
      MaxNumPups = 200;
      BarStart = 150;
      BarHeight = 12;
      BarSpace = 4;

      TypeSize = 9;
      TextHeight = 16;
      TextStart = 35;
      TitleLine = 30;

      MarkerLength = 3;
      ScaleUnit = 50;
      NumWidth = 5;
   type
      BreedInfo = record
            BreedName : string[20];
            NumPups : LongInt
         end;
      MasterFile = file of BreedInfo;

   var
      BreedDate : BreedInfo;
      InFile : MasterFile;
      ThousandPups : Integer;
      Top, Left, Bottom, Right, FrameTop : Integer;
      TextLine, StartScale, ScaleNum : Integer;

begin
   TextSize(TypeSize);

{ -- Write title and column heading }
   TextLine := TitleLine;
   MoveTo(BarStart, TextLine);
   WriteDraw('PUPPIES ENROLLED BY AKC IN 1983');
   TextLine := TextLine + TextHeight;
   MoveTo(TextStart, TextLine);
   WriteDraw('Breed');

{ -- Store frame top }
   FrameTop := TextLine;

{ -- Draw and label bars }
   Left := BarStart;
   Bottom := TextLine;
   Reset(InFile, 'Breed Statistics');
   if not EOF then
      begin
         Bottom := Bottom + BarHeight + BarSpace;
         Top := Bottom - BarHeight;
         MoveTo(TextStart, Bottom);
```

Figure 14.2 continued

```
            Read(InFile, BreedData);
            WriteDraw(BreedData.BreedName);
            ThousandPups := BreedData.NumPups div 1000;
            Right := BarStart + ThousandPups;
            PaintRec(Top, Left, Bottom, Right)
        end;
    { -- Draw frame }
      FrameRect(FrameTop, Left, Bottom, MxNumPups + BarStart);

    { -- Draw scale markers }
      MoveTo(BarStart, Bottom);
      ScaleNum := 0;
      repeat
        Line(0, MarkerLength);
        Move(ScaleUnit, –MarkerLength);
        ScaleNum := ScaleNum + ScaleUnit;
      until ScaleNum >= MaxNumPups;

    { -- Number bottom scale }
      TextLine := Bottom + TextHeight;
      StartScale := BarStart – NumWidth;
      ScaleNum := 0;
      repeat
        MoveTo(StartScale + ScaleNum, TextLine);
        WriteDraw(ScaleNum);
        ScaleNum := ScaleNum + ScaleUnit;
      until ScaleNum >= MaxNumPups;

    { -- Label bottom scale }
      TextLine := TextLine + TextHeight;
      MoveTo(BarStart, TextLine);
      WriteDraw('Thousand of Puppies Enrolled and AKC Registerable')
    end.
```

The external file from which to draw information and the availability of loops offer options for a more efficient bar graph program. The program BarGraphRevised (Fig. 14.2) uses a while loop terminated by EOF to read the information recorded in BreedFile and enter it into the variable InFile one record at a time. Notice that InFile is of type MasterFile, the same type used in the creation of the original file. This is an important point to recognize.

- One file record can be assigned to another file record only if the types are identical.

Once the record is assigned to BreedData, the record components BreedData.BreedName and BreedData.NumOfPups are used to write the name and draw the bar.

Another kind of loop, the repeat loop, is used to draw the scale markers and numbers. The repeat loops are terminated when the number of puppies exceeds MaxNumPups, which is declared in the constants section.

It is easy to see that this program has much more versatility than the original version, which required several statements for each breed.

14.2 ● PreDefined Quickdraw Types

Just as Integer and Real are predefined types that can be used to describe variables, there are predefined types pertaining to QuickDraw routines. For instance,

```
Rectangle = record case integer of
            0 : (Top : Integer;
                 Left : Integer;
                 Bottom : Integer;
                 Right : Integer);
            1 : (TopLeft : Point;
                 BotRight : Point);
```

is predefined in QuickDraw and can be used to define rectangles. For example, consider

```
var
    BoxA, BoxB : Rect;
```

Once values have been assigned to the corresponding components, any reference to BoxA or BoxB will use the rectangle described by those values. The assignment of four integer variables to the record components Top, Left, Bottom, and Right activates the case 0 record variant. The assignment of two values of type Point activates the case 1 variant.

Type Rectangle is used in the short program shown in Fig. 14.3 to produce a familiar figure.

There are two QuickDraw libraries that can be called from Macintosh Pascal. The procedures and functions included in QuickDraw1 are expected to be used frequently and therefore have been made automatically available. To use the more advanced routines in QuickDraw2, it is necessary to include a *uses clause* immediately after the program heading, as in

```
program DrawMore;
    uses QuickDraw2;
```

Figure 14.3 ● Program
Shape

```
program Shape;
    var
        BoxA : Rect;
begin
    BoxA.Top := 20;
    BoxA.Left := 20;
    BoxA.Bottom := 100;
    BoxA.Right := 100;
    Paint Oval(BoxA);
    EraseArc(BoxA, 75, 30)
end.
```

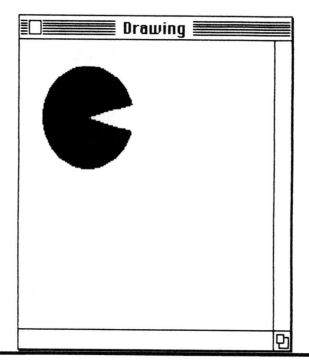

QuickDraw2 allows you to perform more complicated operations such as
defining separate drawing areas, drawing polygons and pictures, and
customizing the operations. Our discusssion here will be limited to
presenting a few of the features available in QuickDraw1.

In the earlier graphics chapter we covered several procedures for
operations on rectangles, ovals, round rectangles, and arcs. Now that we

have predefined types at our disposal, we can add to that list of operations a procedure for filling a shape with gray instead of black. Associated with the type Pattern is the following set of predefined variables shown below.

```
var
   White  : Pattern;
   Black  : Pattern;
   Gray   : Pattern;
   LtGray : Pattern;
   DkGray: Pattern;
```

These can be used in the predefined procedures

```
FillRect(Rectangle, ColorName)
FillOval(Rectangle, ColorName)
FillRoundRect(Rectangle, OvalWidth, OvalHeight, ColorName)
FillArc(Rectangle, StartAngle, ArcAngle, ColorName)
```

Fig. 14.4 gives a short program demonstrating the use of these procedures.

```
program Colors;
   var
      Rectangle : Rect;
begin
   Rectangle.Top := 20;
   Rectangle.Left := 20;
   Rectangle.Bottom := 200;
   Rectangle.Right := 200;
   PaintRect(Rectangle);

   Rectangle.Top := Rectangle.Top + 10;
   Rectangle.Left := Rectangle.Left + 10;
   Rectangle.Bottom := Rectangle.Bottom - 10;
   Rectangle.Right := Rectangle.Right - 10;
   FillOval(Rectangle, Gray);

   Rectangle.Top := Rectangle.Top + 30;
   Rectangle.Left := Rectangle.Left + 30;
   Rectangle.Bottom := Rectangle.Bottom - 30;
   Rectangle.Right := Rectangle.Right - 30;
   FillRect(Rectangle, White);

   MoveTo(95, 120);
   TextSize(24);
   WriteDraw('OK');
end.
```

Figure 14.4 ● Program Colors

Figure 14.4 continued

Another pair of predefined types

type
    StyleItem = (Bold, Italic, Underline, Outline,
                  Shadow, Condense, Extend);
    Style = set of StyleItem;

can be used in the procedure TextFace to change the face of the printing. For instance,

    TextFace([Italic])

causes all following text to appear in italics. Italic is a value in a set and therefore must be enclosed by brackets. The styles can be used in combination as shown in program TextFaces (Fig. 14.5).

```
program TextFaces;
begin
    TextSize(14);
    MoveTo(25,45);
    WriteDraw('Standard');

    TextFace([Italic]);
    MoveTo(25,65);
    WriteDraw('Italic')

    TextFace([Bold]);
    MoveTo(25,85);
    WriteDraw('Bold')

    TextFace([Underline]);
    MoveTo(25,105);
    WriteDraw('Underline')

    TextFace([Bold, Underline]);
    MoveTo(25,125);
    WriteDraw('Bold Underline')

    TextFace([Italic, Bold, Underline]);
    MoveTo(25,145);
    WriteDraw('Italic Bold Underline')
end.
```

Figure 14.5 ● Program TextFaces

14.3 ● Transfer Mode

When writing on the drawing screen, there are three text modes that copy the image in different ways. The normal text mode SrcOr draws with black regardless of the color of the pixels beneath. The mode SrcXOr inverts the pixels beneath, making the white ones black and the black ones white. The mode SrcBic draws in white. The procedure calls are

```
TextMode(SrcOr)
TextMode(SrcXor)
TextMode(SrcBic)
```

Fig. 14.6 shows the effect of each mode.

Routines are also available for changing the pen mode, affecting the way that any of the graphics shapes are drawn on the screen. The pen mode is set with the procedure call

```
PenMode(PatOr)
PenMode(PatXor)
PenMode(PatBic )
```

Figure 14.6 ● Program TextModes

```
program TextModes;
begin
    FrameOval(25, 50, 75, 250);
    MoveTo(80,59);
    TextSize(24);
    TextFont(5);
    TextMode(SrcOr);
    WriteDraw('GREETINGS');

    FrameRect(120, 50, 170, 250);
    PaintRec(145, 50, 170, 250);
    MoveTo(80,154);
    TextSize(24);
    TextFont(5);
    TextMode(SrcXOr);
    WriteDraw('GREETINGS');

    PaintOval(215, 50, 265, 250);
    MoveTo(80,249);
    TextSize(24);
    TextFont(5);
    TextMode(scrBic);
    WriteDraw('GREETINGS');
end.
```

Figure 14.6 continued

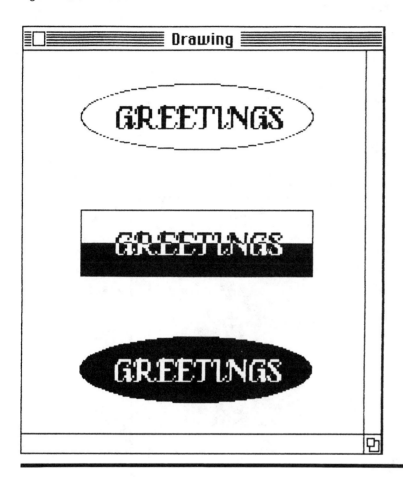

These three choices work in the same way as the ones discussed above for text drawing; PatOr draws in black, PatXor inverts whatever it covers, and PatBic draws in white. See Fig. 14.7 for an example.

What we have given here are the simple aspects of working with transfer modes. It is possible also to use these modes plus others to overlay one pattern on another. A single chapter is not enough to describe all of the complexities of QuickDraw. We suggest that if you want to delve more deeply into the possibilities, you will profit from a reference book devoted to the subject.

Table 14.1 summarizes some of the predefined types and variables, and some additional QuickDraw1 routines.

Figure 14.7 ● Program
PenModes

```
program PenModes;
begin
    PenMode(ParOr);
    PaintRect(10, 50, 75, 100);
    PaintRect(100, 100, 175, 200);
    PenMode(PatXor);
    PaintRect(60, 90, 120, 175);
    PaintMode(PatBic);
    PaintRec(155, 180, 165, 190)
end.
```

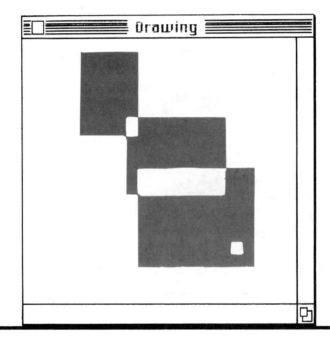

Table 14.1 • Some Predefined Variables, Types, and Procedures in
               QuickDraw1

Type

```
Str255 = string[255];
Pattern = packed array[0..7] of 0..255;
Bits16 = array[0..15] of Integer;
StyleItem = (Bold, Italic, Underline, Outline, Shadow, Condense, Extend);
Style = set of StyleItem;
Point = record case Integer of
            0 : (v : Integer;
            1 : (vh : array[VHSelect] of Integer);
            end;
Rect = record case Integer of
            0 : (Top : Integer;
                 Left : Integer;
                 Bottom : Integer;
                 Right : Integer);
            1 : (TopLeft : Point;
                 BotRight : Point);
            end;
```

Variables

```
White   : Pattern;
Black   : Pattern;
Gray    : Pattern;
LtGray  : Pattern;
DkGray  : Pattern;
```

Line Routines

PenSize(Width, Height);	{ Integer, Integer }
PenMode(Mode)	{ PatOr, PatXor, PatBic }
PenPat(Pattern)	{ White, Black, Gray, LtGray, DkGray }
PenNormal	

Text Routines

TextFont(Font)	{ Integer }
TextFace([StyleName])	{ Bold, Italic, Underline, Outline, Shadow, Condensed, Extend }
TextMode(Mode)	{ SrcOr, SrcXor, SrcBic }
TextSize(PointSize)	{ 9, 12, 14, 18, 24 }

Table 14.1 continued

Graphics Routines

In the following procedures, RectName can be replaced by either a value of type Rect, or by four integer values representing the Top, Left, Bottom and Right coordinates of the rectangle.

FrameRect(RectName, StartAngle, ArcAngle)
PaintRect(RectName, StartAngle, ArcAngle)
EraseRect(RectName, StartAngle, ArcAngle)
InvertRect(RectName, StartAngle,ArcAngle)
FillRect(RectName, Color)

FrameOval(RectName, StartAngle, ArcAngle)
PaintOval(RectName, StartAngle, ArcAngle)
EraseOval(RectName, StartAngle, ArcAngle)
InvertOval(RectName, StartAngle,ArcAngle)
FillOval(RectName, Color)

FrameRoundRect(RectName, StartAngle, ArcAngle)
PaintRoundRect(RectName, StartAngle, ArcAngle)
EraseRoundRect(RectName, StartAngle, ArcAngle)
InvertRoundRect(RectName, StartAngle,ArcAngle)
FillRoundRect(RectName, OvalDiameter, OvalHeight, Color)

FrameArc(RectName, StartAngle, ArcAngle)
PaintArc(RectName, StartAngle, ArcAngle)
EraseArc(RectName, StartAngle, ArcAngle)
InvertArc(RectName, StartAngle,ArcAngle)
FillArc(RectName, StartAngle, ArcAngle, Color)

Prelude to Planning

Holmes Delivers a Lecture

*N*O record of the doings of Mr. Sherlock Holmes and his contributions to the development and understanding of the Analytical Engine would be complete without a report on his brilliant address to the Royal Society in the late autumn of 1895. Shortly after the conclusion of the case involving Arthur H. Staunton, the rising young forger, came the publication of the great detective's much celebrated monograph, "Upon the Use of the Analytical Engine in the Work of the Criminal Investigator," which earned him an invitation to speak before the annual meeting of the Royal Society.

It may be remembered that I had sold my Kensington practise a year earlier and that I was again sharing lodgings with my old companion at 221B Baker Street. He insisted that I accompany him to the assembly, and it was my great privilege to do so. I offer here an account of his address, which I have reconstructed from my notes.

A special carriage was sent for us bearing two emissaries of the Royal Society. These gentlemen escorted us to a stately house situated off Pall Mall, to the rooms that were home to the learned group, where a reception was already in progress. Here Holmes and I had the opportunity to mingle with some of Britain's most renowned scientific figures.

At a certain point, Holmes was escorted to a podium and, following a brief introduction, commenced his lecture.

"Gentlemen and fellow scientific investigators," Holmes began. "It is without doubt an honour to appear before this assembly tonight in order to share a few of my ideas on the use of the Analytical Engine.

"Though all of you are doubtless already aware of the advantages that the Engine promises to bestow upon science, and although many of you may be considering applying this new device to your own areas of investigation, it is likely that you have as yet had little experience in designing programmes for the Engine. It is my hope that my lecture will furnish you with a general, logical method for organizing programming

"A special carriage was sent for us."

tasks and attacking scientific problems with the Analytical Engine. This method I have called "programming from the top-down." Although elementary in its fundamental concepts, it is invaluable as a technique for constructing all types of programmes, including the most complex ones you are likely to encounter.

"In my engagements as a criminal investigator I have always been careful to arrange all clues systematically and devise a complete hypothetical approach to a case before taking a single step out of my rooms in pursuit of a solution. This principle applies equally well to the use of the Analytical Engine. No matter how simple the task, it is necessary at the outset to formulate a *clear* and *complete* statement of the problem at hand, as well as a basic plan for solving it. The programmer should prepare sample input and output formats and design a general algorithm before writing any programme. This precaution ensures that a minimal amount of confusion and lost time will result during interactions with the Engine.

"Let me now enumerate the characteristics of the top-down approach.

"The first concept essential for a grasp of programming top-down is the idea of *design in levels*. The programmer should construct his programme according to a conceptual hierarchy. The upper levels of his hierarchy should indicate the more general features of the problem, with details and elaborations introduced at the lower levels.

"The highest level is thus the initial conception of the solution. The individual paths from each level represent the possible solutions at each conceptual stage. Each lower level thus elaborates the preceding level. Here is a chart," said Holmes, "that illustrates this idea."

I have reproduced this graphic representation as Fig. 15.1.

"Secondly, the language used to formulate this preliminary model need not be the special language of the Engine, and for this reason the top-down method is described as being *language independent*. At this early stage of programming, ordinary English will generally be sufficient. Later, of course, it should be possible to encode the programme in a form intelligible to the Engine.

"Thirdly, as in all forms of scientific reasoning, it is advisable to attain a firm grasp of the broad aspects of a problem before proceeding to the minute details of analysis. Accordingly, in the top-down approach, *details should be deferred* to lower levels. Typical of such detail is the internal representation of data.

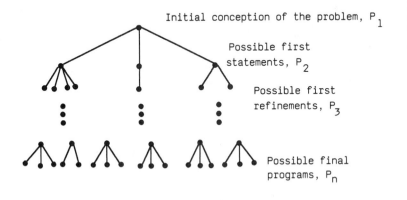

Figure 15.1 ● The top-down approach

Initial conception of the problem, P_1

Possible first statements, P_2

Possible first refinements, P_3

Possible final programs, P_n

"Fourthly, before advancing to a lower level, the programmer must ascertain that the solution is stated in *precise* terms. By this I mean that instead of using a very vague statement that has no immediate consequences, the programmer should seek a more meaningful statement that entails one or more submodules.

"Fifthly, as a new level unfolds in the programme's development, the programmer must take pains to *verify the solution.* You will conserve appreciable amounts of time and energy by detecting errors in style or content as early as possible, rather than after numerous sub-programmes have already been generated and the errors must be traced to their sources further up in the hierarchy.

"And finally, each step of the programme must be elaborated, improved, and meticulously examined until it is ready to be transformed into the Engine's special language.

"Although this lengthy process of refinement may seem tedious to the lofty theorists among you, I assure you that there is no other way to use the computing machine efficaciously. In fact, as you become more adept at designing programmes, this stage of the task will become less and less burdensome; and you may well discover that you enjoy the intellectual exercise it affords.

"I myself found no difficulty in adapting to the requirements of programme design, for my career as a detective has sharpened my faculties to such a degree that I routinely dissect cumbersome problems into manageable components with little effort.

"Now, gentlemen, if my explication is entirely clear to you thus far, I should like to offer some further observations concerning the art, or science, as you would perhaps prefer to designate it, of programming from the top down. I cannot emphasize too strongly that you must thoroughly understand the given task and its solution before attempting to write a programme.

"Therefore, you should initially be far less concerned with your notation—for example, ordinary English would suffice—than with your overall comprehension of the problem. This is especially important at the top levels of the hierarchy. Eventually, sub-programmes must be explicitly stated; and in particular all input and output arguments must be described.

"Again, allow me to emphasise the importance of scrupulous examination and refinement of each stage of a top-down model. One should always look for possible errors and provide against them.

"Here is an example at an intermediate level of refinement," continued Holmes, gesturing towards another illustration that I have duplicated as follows:

```
case DayOfWeek of
     Monday:       — generate last week's criminal summary
     Tuesday:      — do nothing
     Wednesday:  — update criminal records
     Thursday:     — process new reports
     Friday:        — generate lab item reports
     Saturday:     — generate weekly statistics
     Sunday:       — do nothing
end
```

"The language in this illustration is obviously informal, yet each statement can be transformed into instructions as required for the Engine. Of course, the programme must ultimately provide explicit instructions for performing each operation, such as the updating of criminal records, but this occurs at a later stage of the refinement process.

"Once again, gentlemen, may I direct your attention to our first illustration (Fig. 15.1). As I remarked previously, this is a graphic representation of the top-down concept. The highest level, P_1, constitutes the most general description of the problem; and the downward branchings represent the alternative methods of programme design available to the programmer at each step. As the programmer reaches each successive level, he must choose the branches that best fit the stated purposes. If all the branches at a certain level seem unsuitable, it may be necessary to return upward in the tree and select a different solution at a higher level. In advancing from P_1 to the bottom of the tree, the programmer thus moves from a general statement of the problem, through a series of decisions about the design, and finally to a working programme.

"Let us turn our attention to this illustration of the top-down structure of a particular programme containing five levels."

Holmes directed their attention to the chart I have included here as Fig. 15.2.

"Observe how individual paths from P_1, as they were designated in our first illustration (Fig. 15.1), are elaborated to produce the individual parts charted in this illustration (Fig. 15.2).

"I imagine that by this time my learned listeners have conceived some applications of the top-down method to their own investigations in various scientific disciplines. As a man acquainted with several branches of natural science, and especially chemistry, I am confident that the principles outlined in this lecture can be of service to investigators in all fields, mundane as well as academic."

As could only be expected, the members of the Royal Society greeted Holmes's lecture with considerable applause and afterwards detained him for nearly an hour with their questions concerning the details of the top-down method. Many of them were delighted to meet the famous detective, whose adventures they confessed to having followed in my modest chronicles; and they pressed Holmes to discuss his latest endeavours in criminal investigation.

Once we were back at our comfortable lodgings in Baker Street, sitting on either side of the fire, Holmes, who was always amenable to flattery, allowed his more sombre and cynical spirit to comment on the evening's course of events.

"Do you realize, Watson, that none of our distinguished company this evening enquired as to my plans for applying the Analytical Engine in my future criminal investigations? If these are the greatest minds our generation can offer, I fear that the world may not yet be ready or deserving of this magnificent Engine. It was indeed a disappointment, for I would surely like to contemplate tomorrow's challenges as well as yesterday's laurels."

Figure 15.2 ● Top-down structure of a programme

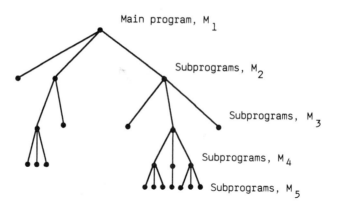

Main program, M_1

Subprograms, M_2

Subprograms, M_3

Subprograms, M_4

Subprograms, M_5

Main Levels = 5

Subprograms = Procedure or Function

"I fear, Holmes, that I am entirely to blame for this," I remarked. "My highly exaggerated accounts of your doings, as you yourself have called them, have given the public a distorted view of the seriousness with which you go about your business."

"On the contrary, Watson. You have given prominence not so much to the many sensational causes in our cases together, but rather to those seemingly trivial incidents that have given room for those faculties of deduction that I have made my special province. For this, I am eternally grateful. As for the Analytical Engine, I offer my work to the next generation of scientific investigators—to those young boys still in boarding school, capsules they are, hundreds of bright little seeds from which will doubtless spring a wiser, and indeed, better England."

Chapter 15

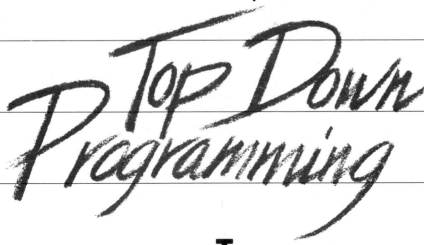

There are many different approaches to a programming problem. The top-down approach is in marked contrast to other methods, including the following ones.

    Linear approach
    Bottom-up approach
    Inside-out or forest approach
    Imitation approach

In the *linear* approach the programmer immediately starts writing code as it will appear when executed, first line first, second line second, and so forth. The drawback with this approach is the need to make specific, detailed decisions with very little assurance that they will be appropriate to the problem at hand.

It is a capital mistake to theorize before one has data, because one begins to twist facts to suit theories, instead of theories to suit facts. It is just so with programming; if one begins to construct a program without sufficient data one must be prepared to accept the consequences. The linear technique may seem obviously poor, but the temptation to use it can be very strong, especially on those problems that appear "easy." But beware of this temptation—the little, easy problems have a way of ending up much more complicated than they first appear.

In the *bottom-up* approach, the programmer designs and writes the lower components first, and the upper levels later. The bottom-up approach is in a sense the inversion of the top-down approach. It suffers severely by requiring the programmer to make specific decisions about the program before the overall problem and algorithm are understood.

In between the top-down and bottom-up approaches, we have the *inside-out* or "forest" approach, which consists of starting in the middle of the program and working down and up at the same time. Roughly speaking, it goes as follows:

1. General idea. First we decide upon the general idea for programming the problem.

2. A rough sketch of the program. Next we write any "important" sections of the program, assuming initialization in some form. In some sections we write portions of the actual program. In doing this, we hope that the actual intent of each piece of program will not change several times, necessitating rewriting parts of our sketch.

3. Programming the first version. After step 2, we write the entire program. We start with the lowest level module. After an individual component has been programmed, we debug it and immediately prepare a description of what it does.

4. Rethinking and revising. As a result of step 3, we should be close to a working program, but it may be possible to improve on it. So we continue by making improvements until we obtain a complete working program.

It is probably fair to say that many programmers, even experienced ones, often work inside out, starting neither very close to the top nor very close to the bottom level. Instead they start in the middle and work outward until a program finally appears on the horizon. The approach is a poor one, for the program may undergo many changes and patches and thus seldom achieves a clear, logical structure.

As another method, consider the *imitation* approach, a method superficially resembling the top-down approach. This approach is discussed in detail because many programmers *think* that the top-down approach is really the way they have always programmed. There are, however, subtle but important differences. The imitation approach is as follows:

1. Thinking about the program. Having been given a programming task, take the time to examine the problem thoroughly before starting to program. Think about the details of the program for a while, and then decide on a general approach.

2. Deciding on subprograms. After having thought about the problem in detail, decide on what sections will be sufficiently important to merit being made into subprograms.

3. Writing of subprograms. At this point write each subprogram. After each is completed, write down what it expects as input, what it returns as output, and what it does. The subprograms should be written in a hierarchical manner: the most primitive first, calling routines second, and so forth. Doing this will ensure

that the subprograms are fully written before the upper-level program structures are finalized.

4. Writing the main program. After all subprograms have been written, write the main program. The purpose of the main program is to sequence and interface the subprograms.

The imitation approach has some important similarities to the top-down approach:

- The problem must be understood thoroughly before writing the program.

- The actual writing of the program is postponed until after certain decisions have been made.

- The problem is broken up into clear, logical units.

However, there are important differences between the two approaches:

- In the top-down approach, a *specific* plan of attack is developed in stages. Only the issues relevant to a given level are considered, and these issues are formalized completely.

- Furthermore, whenever the programmer decides to use a subprogram, the interfaces (arguments, returned values, and effects) are decided *first*. The inputs and outputs are formalized before developing the subprograms; that is, the subprograms are made to fit the calling routine instead of the other way around.

- Most important, at *every step* in the top-down approach, the programmer must have a complete, correct "program."

The disadvantages of the imitation approach are that it is more likely to produce errors, to require extensive program modifications, or to result in a somewhat ill-conceived program. Choosing a partially specified attack may require serious changes to the program. Writing subprograms first may result in confusing program logic if the subprograms do not integrate easily into the upper-level code designed later.

In summary, think carefully about programming technique. The top-down approach may provide the best alternative.

Prelude to Expansion

The Final Programme

W ITH Mr. Sherlock Holmes at Baker Street, one's morning paper presented infinite possibilities. The air of London remains all the sweeter for his absence, but the days of the great cases are past following his retirement to the Sussex Downs.

During this period of my life, Holmes passed almost entirely beyond my ken, save for an occasional weekend pilgrimage I might make to his little villa at Fulworth. I was surprised and delighted, therefore, when one morning in June the maid brought in a small package and a note from my old companion. Removing the wrappings I found a slim volume entitled, *Practical Handbook of Bee Culture, with Some Observations upon the Segregation of the Queen.* The accompanying note read:

> *Watson,*
>
> *As you can see, I have been considering some of the problems furnished by Nature, rather than those of a more superficial character for which our artificial state of society is wholly responsible. Of late, however, I have been tempted to direct my thoughts towards the Analytical Engine. Can you spare me a few days? Air and scenery are perfect.*
>
> *Holmes*

Owing to my experience in the rough-and-tumble camps of Afghanistan, I was quite a ready traveller. My bag was packed and I was rattling out of Victoria station within the hour.

Mrs. Hudson, his old housekeeper, showed me into Holmes's sitting room where I found him engaged in conversation with a distinguished gentleman, vaguely familiar to me.

"Surely you remember Major General Henry Prevost Babbage?" said Holmes.

"Of course," I replied. "We met at the annual meeting of the Royal Society. I am delighted to meet you again, sir."

"Naturally the conversation turned to the Analytical Engine."

"The pleasure is mine, Dr. Watson," he answered, extending his hand. We sat for a while and, naturally enough, the conversation turned to the Analytical Engine.

"As you know, Watson, I am now preparing the *magnum opus* of my career, a comprehensive treatise of my methods entitled *The Whole Art of Detection*, with illustrations from my most noteworthy cases. As you may imagine, this is the longest and most difficult work I have ever attempted, over five hundred pages in its entirety. I have spent countless hours and many sleepless nights verifying minute points and making hundreds of emendations.

"The content and style of this manuscript have so engrossed my attention that I simply have no patience left for the more mundane aspects of its creation, such as typing and proofreading. Yet I dare not entrust the copying and editing of such an important work to just anyone. Do you understand, Watson?"

"Yes, quite, Holmes," I replied, with some apprehension lest he ask me to serve as his scribe. A sudden thought came to me. "Perhaps the Engine can be put to good use here?"

"Precisely what I had in mind, Watson. Now, you may well wonder how the Engine is equipped to serve in this capacity. Imagine, if you will that I have scribbled out a paragraph of my manuscript without observing the conventions of margins, indentation, *et cetera*, as in this fragment."

He placed before Babbage and myself a card with the following inscription:

> While the   criminal investigator
> typically does
> not consider himself a   disciple
> of empirical science,
> his work, like   the chemist's,
> consists in a logical and systematic
> quest   for Truth.

"Obviously I could not submit a collection of such fragments to a publisher. I am trying to design a programme that will, among other things, arrange such fragments of text correctly, as follows."

He thereupon handed us another card on which was written an emendation of the first:

> While the criminal investigator typically does
> not consider himself a disciple of empirical science,
> his work, like the chemist's, consists in a logical
> and systematic quest for Truth.

"Notice here that the words are arranged to fill the line properly," Holmes continued. "You see, the typing and editing process can be made considerably simpler. I can enter the text at leisure; and if a mistake is encountered or a change is deemed necessary, I can simply correct the original version. The Engine can then be commanded to print a perfect, corrected copy. Here I have made an outline of the desired format for my entire manuscript."

I inspected the profferred conventions, which are reproduced here:

1. Page Size (standard 8 1/ 2-by-11 page)
   85 characters per line
   66 lines per page

2. Margins
   Left: 15 characters in from left edge of page
   Right: 10 characters in from right edge of page
   Top: 6 lines down from top of page
   Bottom: 6 lines up from bottom of page

3. Printing Area (standard 10 point spacing)
   60 characters per line
   51 lines per page

4. Page Numbers
6 lines down from bottom margin, centered between the left and right margin, and enclosed by hyphens, for example:

–14–

I immediately thought of my own writings and the great amount of time that could be saved with the implementation of such a scheme. It would sometimes take up to a year for my manuscripts to be edited by my literary agent, Dr. Arthur Conan Doyle, again by *his* editors, and finally appear in their printed form. I noted that in addition to spacing each line of text properly, the Engine would ensure that the margins were observed and that page numbers were correctly incremented.

"Well, Holmes," I said after a time, "this idea of yours will undoubtedly spare you much of the tedium authors ordinarily suffer."

"True, Watson," he replied, "but this is only the beginning of my work. Remember that before approaching the Engine it is imperative to define the problem completely and exactly, using the top-down approach. In particular, one must enumerate every possible detail of the input and output. On these pages I have described the commands for formatting text and worked out a hypothetical input with its corresponding output."

Holmes then showed us the commands as well as samples of the input and output to his programme. I have replicated them here as Table 16.1 and Fig. 16.1, respectively.

"The Engine would also be employed to control the general scheme of the printed page, that is to say, it would handle the paragraphing and indentation patterns. Thus a command such as

:Indent 10

would cause following lines of text to be indented ten spaces. Then if one wished to return to the left margin, the command

:Indent 0

would suffice."

"I beg your pardon, Mr. Holmes," Babbage interjected at this point. "But what exactly do you have in mind when you speak of enumerating every possible detail of the input and output?"

"I am delighted that you asked, Mr. Babbage," said Holmes, "for that is the most difficult aspect of this programme's design. When creating a programme intended for intimate use by a person such as this, we must always ask ourselves such questions as: What sorts of command are useful? What precisely are the actions these perform? What sorts of error might one make while using the programme? What would happen if one incorrectly entered some input to the Engine? And what are all the possible ways of entering input incorrectly?"

Table 16.1 ● Text formatting commands

Commands	Meaning
:Paragraph	Marks the beginning of a paragraph. All following lines of text up to the next command line are treated as a sequence of words without line boundaries. The words are printed with end-of-line markers inserted so that each line (except the last) will be filled with one space between each pair of words. The first line of each paragraph is indented 5 spaces. The right margin is ragged.
	If the paragraph is followed by a blank line or one or more commands (excluding the Verbatim command), then the next line of text will be considered the beginning of a new paragraph.
:Verbatim	Marks the beginning of a series of lines that are to be output exactly as given, except for possible indentation. All lines (excluding command lines) between the Verbatim command line and the next Paragraph command line (or the end of the input) are to be printed verbatim.
:Indent n	Causes all following lines of text to be indented n spaces from the left margin (n from 0 through 60).
:Center n	Causes the following n lines of text ($n > 0$) to be centered between the left and right margins. If n is omitted, then only the next line will be centered.
:Skip n	Causes n blank lines ($n > 0$) to be printed. If n is omitted, then one blank line is printed. Note that a blank line of text in the input is treated exactly as a ":Skip 1" command line.
:Page	Causes the next line to be printed at the top of a new page. This is also done automatically whenever a page is filled.

"But Mr. Holmes," interrupted Babbage, "with all due respect, my first impression is that all this detail and fussing only complicates the problem before one even begins to solve it. My research has trained me to find the shortest possible route to a problem's solution and then take that route without a glance at the more convoluted byways. Does this top-down approach not result in considerable wasted time?"

"On the contrary, my dear Babbage," Holmes replied, as he reclined in his sofa and reached for a cigarette case on a table near at hand. He lit one end of a cigarette and blew a thin cloud of smoke into the room before he continued. "You must know the value of taking pains in any scientific endeavor. It has long been an axiom of mine that the little things are infinitely the most important, and that one must realize the

Figure 16.1 ● Sample
input and output

Sample Input

```
    :Center 2
    THIS IS A TITLE
    ---------------------

    :Paragraph
    The text of a paragraph is adjusted
    on a line to fit on
    a line with at most 60 characters.

    :Indent 10
    One or more lines can be indented from the left margin
    with an Indent command.

    :Indent 0
    One can also specify that lines are to be printed
    verbatim, as in the following short table:

    :Verbatim
    ITEM        AMOUNT
      1           18
      2            6
      3           11
```

Corresponding Output

THIS IS A TITLE

The text of a paragraph is adjusted on a line to fit on
a line with at most 60 characters.

One or more lines can be indented from the
left margin with an Indent command.

One can also specify that lines are to be printed
verbatim, as in the following short table:

```
ITEM        AMOUNT
  1           18
  2            6
  3           11
```

need for analyzing a situation thoroughly before making a single attempt to call upon the Engine.

"You will recall my address to the Royal Society, when we had occasion to meet for the first time, and your own brilliant paper in the Proceedings of the British Association. Keep in mind that we are not merely seeking a single answer to a perfectly defined problem, as an engineer does many times in his daily work. Rather, we must instruct the Engine to deal with an entire host of problems. Our first and foremost task is to define these problems, as it remains impossible to solve them without first grasping an understanding of the general situation and all its ramifications. This procedure may appear very time-consuming at the outset. However, it usually results in an accurate programme requiring few emendations; thus our method will actually save us time."

Holmes then produced yet another chart, given here as Table 16.2. I now began to see that his problem was not a simple one at all. The Engine would have to keep track of many details and even be tolerant to the errors of its employer. He had obviously spent a considerable amount of time thinking about the design of the programme.

"I have asked you out for the weekend, Watson," said Holmes, turning his attention to me, "to call upon your remarkable powers of stimulating genius, which I have, of late, found in short supply. I have been lost without my Boswell. I would appreciate your company also, Mr. Babbage; and, at any rate, there is no return train to London tonight and I have unwittingly condemned you to the horrors of my hospitalities. I have oysters and a brace of grouse, with something a little choice in red wines."

We enjoyed a pleasant meal together and continued our discussion of the Analytical Engine well into the evening, with a bottle of claret among us. When the conversation again turned to the design of a top-down outline of a programme for formatting Holmes's manuscripts, Babbage tried his hand at sketching a preliminary design.

"I am not wholly certain how far to delve into your list of exceptions and details, or where to draw the line," said Babbage. "Perhaps something like this would suffice." He then scribbled on a sheet of paper and handed it to Holmes. It read:

Initialize programme variables

As long as InputFile is not empty, do the following:
   read NextCharacter
   process NextCharacter

Print last PageNum

"Very good," said Holmes. "But there remain some points in need of clarification. In the first place, what programme variables are to be initialized? And the specification for reading characters is not explicit enough. The characters, you see, may be either part of the text or part of a command; and these two categories must of course be treated differently.

"A line of input falls into the command category if it begins with a colon. Otherwise, it is a line of text. Notice that in practice, lines will tend to occur in groups belonging to one category or the other. Thus we may view the input as groups of one or more lines of a given category.

"Notice also that command lines are treated uniformly, regardless of their context, whereas this is not true of text lines. The treatment of a text line depends upon whether the line is part of a paragraph or is to be printed verbatim. Moreover, this distinction depends on the context.

Table 16.2 ● Holmes's list of exceptional conditions

1. An input line beginning with a colon is not followed by a legitimate command.
   Response: The line is output verbatim with five asterisks in the left margin to call attention to the problem.
2. The argument given for an Indent command is not numeric or too large (> 60); the argument given for a Center or Skip command is not numeric or too large (> 99).
   Response: As above.
3. One of the lines to be centered with a Center command is a command line.
   Response: The line is output centered with five asterisks in the left margin to call attention to the problem.
4. A line to be output extends beyond the right margin. This can be a verbatim line that is too long or a word in a paragraph line that is too long (for example, if the indent happens to be 50 characters and a word will not fit in the remaining ten spaces).
   Response: Allow the line to be output up to, but not beyond, the edge of the page. Place five asterisks in the left margin to call attention to the problem.
5. A text line is seen before either a Paragraph or Verbatim command is seen.
   Response: Assume that a Paragraph command has been seen at the very beginning.

When a Paragraph or Verbatim command is entered, the Engine must 'remember' the command so that all following groups of text lines can be treated accordingly. The input mode is initially assumed to be paragraph mode in order to accept input text directly, and is altered when a Verbatim command is entered."

We then waited in silence while Holmes's mind worked uninterrupted. Finally he continued.

"I'm glad you wrote this out, Mr. Babbage, as it has forced me to consider several alternatives. I would now formulate my approach to this problem as follows."

Holmes began to outline a format programme and wrote the following sketch:

```
Assume TextMode is paragraph mode
As long as InputFile is not empty, do the following:
    if next input character is ':' then
        process one or more command lines
    else — next line is a text line
        if TextMode is paragraph mode then
            process one or more paragraph lines
```

```
        else
            process one or more verbatim lines
    Print last page number
```

"Yes, now I see," said Babbage. "Your method is becoming clearer to me. In the first draft of a top-down analysis you want to be very general, yet also account for all the various possibilities as they might logically arise."

"Quite so," replied Holmes. "But I should like to make this analysis even more precise, for no surprises should arise later as a result of initial misjudgment. There are some details this first top-down sketch does not include—for example, the line number on the output page, the page number if a page becomes full, or the possibility of an input line resulting in a change to the indentation."

"Well, Mr. Holmes," said Babbage after some length, "I fear that Dr. Watson and I have been of very little help to you this evening. Perhaps tomorrow will bring more profitable results."

"Nonsense," snapped Holmes. "I cannot agree with those who rank modesty among the virtues. To a logician all things should be seen exactly as they are, and to underestimate oneself is as much a departure from truth as to exaggerate one's own powers. You have both paid me a great service this evening and I am most appreciative."

Here was a different Holmes at work, for historically it had been one of the peculiarities of his proud, self-contained nature that, though he docketed any fresh information very quickly and accurately in his brain, he seldom made any acknowledgment to the provider.

I rose the next morning earlier than usual to find Sherlock Holmes pacing back and forth in his sitting room. He was in excellent spirits. I could see that he had been up the whole night working on his programme and, furthermore, that he had good news to report.

"You have met with success, Holmes," I stated confidently.

"Indeed, Watson, I have," he replied, looking me over curiously. "The top level of the design is completed and sketched in Pascal, but the papers are stored away in my desk. How is it that you knew?"

"Obvious, my dear Holmes. What else am I to assume when I see your right cuff so very shiny and spotted with ink for nearly four or five inches, and left one with the smooth patch at the elbow where it has rested for some length of time upon your desk?"

"I must say, Watson, the faculty of deduction is certainly contagious."

And so I close this account of Mr. Sherlock Holmes and his contributions to the development of the Analytical Engine. A detailed sketch of his final top-down design is reproduced here as Fig. 16.2, and a top-level sketch of the design as written in Macintosh Pascal is here shown as Fig. 16.3.

His decision to test out the programme on a complete chapter from his forthcoming work, *The Whole Art of Detection*, brought to mind my first encounter with Sherlock Holmes in January of 1881. A chance reunion with young Stamford, a dresser at St. Bartholomew's, brought Holmes and me together. How well I recall Stamford, standing there at the Criterion Bar, saying of Holmes, "I could imagine his giving a friend a little pinch of the latest vegetable alkaloid, not out of malevolence, you understand, but simply out of a spirit of inquiry in order to have an accurate idea of the effects. To do him justice, I think that he would take it himself with the same readiness."

Figure 16.2 ● Second version of Holmes's top-level design

```
Definitions:
   TextMode   :   paragraph or verbatim
   Indentation:   the current indentation·
   LineNum    :   the current line for output
   PageNum    :   the current page being printed
Algorithm:
   Set TextMode to ParagraphMode
   Set Indentation to 0
   Set LineNum to 1
   Set PageNum to 1

   As long as InputFile is not empty, do the following:
      if next input character = ":" then
         process commands, possibly updating TextMode, Indentation,
                                           LineNum, PageNum
      else
         if TextMode = ParagraphMode then
            process paragraph lines, using Indentation,
                           possibly updating LineNum, PageNum
         else
            process verbatim lines, using Indentation,
                           possibly updating LineNum, PageNum
   Print last PageNum
```

```
program Format;
  const
    PageSize = 66;        { Number of lines from top of page }
                          { to bottom edge of page. }
    TextWidth = 60;       { Number of columns from left margin to }
                          { right margin. }
    CommandChar = ':';
    { -- remaining constant declarations }

  type
    Mode = (ParagraphMode,VerbatimMode);
    CommandName = (Paragraph, Verbatim, Indent, Center, Skip,
              Page, Illegal);
    IndentRange = 0..TextWidth;
    LineNumRange = 0..PageSize;
    { -- remaining type declarations }

  var
    TextMode : Mode;
    Indentation : IndentRange;
    LineNum : LineNumRange;
    PageNum : Integer;

    { -- Procedures and functions, for example procedures }
    { -- DoCommands, DoParagraphLines, DoVerbatimLines, and the }
    { -- function NextInputChar }

begin { -- MAIN ALGORITHM }
  TextMode := ParagraphMode;
  Indentation := 0;
  LineNum := 1;
  PageNum := 1;

  while not EOF do
    begin
      if NextInputChar = CommandChar then
        DoCommands(TextMode, Indentation)
      else
        case TextMode of
          ParagraphMode :
            DoParagraphLines(Indentation);
          VerbatimMode :
            DoVerbatimLines(Indentation);
        end
    end;
  NewPage
end.
```

Figure 16.3 ● Top-level sketch of text formatting program

Chapter 16

Beyond the Small Program

I t is with a heavy heart that we sit down to our word processor to write these, the last words in which we record the singular gifts by which Mr. Sherlock Holmes distinguished himself as a pioneer in the field of computer programming. His "final programme" is a full-scale application of computers that we may employ in many circumstances and with a variety of computers.

Let us begin with the structure of the entire program. It has the form of a tree, much like that in Fig. 15.2. The root point of the tree is the main program. Each successive point at a level of the tree is a subprogram. The branches emanating from a subprogram point are the subprograms that, in turn, are called from the subprogram.

The individual subprograms are quite straightforward, and we will not elaborate on each. We will describe one subprogram to get a feel for the entire program.

As the sample subprogram, let us look at DoParagraphLines. The procedure performs the actions required for adding input lines to a paragraph. The procedure has one parameter named Indentation, giving the current indentation from the left margin. The body of the procedure begins with

```
Column := Indentation;
NewParagraph := True;
```

These statements set the column position of the next printed word to the indentation, and a new paragraph flag to true.

16.1 ● The Example, Text Formatting

The major work in the procedure is accomplished next in the loop:

```
repeat
  GetWord(Word);
  if Length(Word) = 0 then
    —what to do if the next line is blank
  else
    —what to do for a nonblank line
  ReadLn(InFile)
until (NextInputChar = CommandChar) or EOF(InFile)
```

This loop keeps reading and processing lines until a new command is encountered or the end of the text is reached. The call to ReadLn simply reads the end-of-line marker.

Finally we have

```
if Column <> Indentation then
  NewLine
```

which closes the last line of the paragraph.

Elementary, but keep in mind that when using the top-down approach the main program should be so carefully defined and mapped out that each procedure can be written independently. Thus any subprograms that are true to the behavior expected by the main program will suffice.

The comments shown in Table 16.3 contain information that is useful for any user of the program and would most certainly be needed by anyone wanting to modify it. They should be reviewed and understood before an attempt is made to read the program itself.

Table 16.3 ● Format Comments

PROGRAM TITLE: Format

PROGRAM INTENT

This program reads a text file and formats it according to conventions given below. The text file contains lines of text and command lines. Each command line begins with a colon and must be followed by a legal command.

INPUT AND OUTPUT FILES

Input: A file containing text lines and command lines.
Output: The formatted text.

Table 16.3 continued

GENERAL LAYOUT CONVENTIONS

Page Size

Standard 8½ by 11 page, 85 characters per line, 66 lines per page.

Margins

Left:	15 characters in from left edge of page.
Right:	10 characters in from right edge of page.
Top:	6 lines down from top of page.
Bottom:	9 lines up from bottom of page.

Printing Area

Standard 10 pitch spacing, 60 characters per line, 51 lines per page.

Page Numbers

6 lines down from bottom margin, centered between the left and right margin, and enclosed by hyphens, For example

-14-

COMMANDS

Paragraph

Marks the beginning of a paragraph. All following lines of text up to the next command line are treated as a sequence of words without line boundaries. The words are printed with ends-of-lines inserted so that each line (except the last) will be filled with one space between each pair of words. The first line of each paragraph is indented 5 spaces. The right margin is ragged edged.

If the paragraph is followed by a blank line or one or more commands (excluding the Verbatim command), then the next line of text will be considered the beginning of a new paragraph.

Verbatim

Marks the beginning of a series of lines that are to be output exactly as they are given, except for possible indentation. All lines (excluding command lines) between the Verbatim command line and the next Paragraph command line (or the end of the input) are treated as text to printed verbatim.

Indent n

Causes all following lines to be indented n spaces from the left margin (n from 0 to 60).

Center n

Causes the following n lines of input text ($n > 0$) to be centered between the left and right margins. If n is omitted, then only the next line will be centered.

Skip n

Causes n blank lines ($n > 0$) to be printed. If n is omitted, then only one blank line is printed. Note that a blank line of text in the input is treated exactly as a "Skip 1" command line.

Table 16.3 continued

Page

Causes the next line to be printed at the top of a new page. This is also done automatically whenever a page is filled.

SAMPLE INPUT
```
:Center 2
THIS IS A TITLE
---- -- - -----

:Paragraph
Each line of text in a paragraph is adjusted
to fit on
a line with at most 60 characters.

:Indent 10
One or more lines can be indented from the left margin with an Indent
command.

:Indent 0
One can also specify that lines are to be printed verbatim, as in the
following short table:

:Verbatim
    ITEM      AMOUNT
      1          18
      2           6
      3          11
```

CORRESPONDING OUTPUT:

THIS IS A TITLE
---- -- - -----

Each line of text in a paragraph is adjusted to fit on
a line with at most 60 characters.

One or more lines can be indented from the
left margin with an Indent command.

One can also specify that lines are to be printed
verbatim as in the following short table:

```
    ITEM    AMOUNT
      1        18
      2         6
      3        11
```

Table 16.3 continued

ERROR CONDITIONS

1. An input line beginning with a colon is not followed by a legitimate command.

Response: The line is output verbatim with 5 asterisks in the left margin to call attention to the problem.

2. The argument given for an Indent command is not numeric or too large (> 60); the argument given for a Center or Skip command is not numeric or too large (> 99).

Response: As above.

3. One of the lines to be centered with a Center command is a command line.

Response: The line is output centered, but 5 asterisks are placed in the left margin to call attention to the problem.

4. A line to be output extends beyond the right margin. This can be a verbatim line that is too long or a word in a paragraph that is too long (for example, if the indent happens to be 50 characters, and a word will not fit in the remaining 10 spaces).

Response: Allow the line to be output up to, but not beyond, the edge of the page. Place 5 asterisks in the left margin to call attention to the problem.

GLOBAL VARIABLES

There are two global variables, LineNum and PageNum, which are manipulated solely by the two procedures, NewLine and NewPage. They are used to paginate the formatted text and print page numbers.

As always, the complete, final program comprises the main program and the declarations of all the subprograms, as shown in Fig. 16.4. You may wish to read over the main program and all its subprograms until you are satisfied that they work correctly. While doing this you may note several ways of "speeding up" the program. The fact is, we confess, that efficiency was not a significant design criterion during development.

Figure 16.4 ● Program
Format

```pascal
program Format;
  const
    PageSize = 66;
    LinesPerPage = 51;
    LeftMargin = 15;
    TextWidth = 60;
    MaxLineLength = 70;

    CommandChar = ':';
    Blank = ' ';
    NormalMargin ='        ';
    ErrorMargin = '*****        ';

  type
    Mode = (ParagraphMode, VerbatimMode);
    CommandName = (Paragraph, Verbatim, Indent, Center, Skip,
                        Page, Illegal);
    IndentRange = 0..TextWidth;
    ArgumentRange = 0..99;
    ColumnNum = 0..MaxLineLength;
    LineNumRange = 0..PageSize;
    LineImage = string[121];
    CommandInfo = record
      Name : CommandName;
      Argument : ArgumentRange;
      Line : LineImage;
    end;

  var
    TextMode : Mode;
    Indentation : IndentRange;
    LineNum : LineNumRange;
    PageNum : Integer;
    InFile:  Text;


{ -- Utility Routines }

function NextInputChar : Char;
begin
  if not EOF(InFile) then
    NextInputChar := InFile^
end;

function DigitValue (C : Char) : Integer;
begin
  DigitValue := Ord(C) - Ord('O')
end;
```

Figure 16.4 continued

```pascal
procedure SpaceOver (NumSpaces : IndentRange);
   var
      I : Integer;
begin
   for I := 1 to NumSpaces do
      Write(Blank)
end;



procedure NewPage;
   const
      PageNumColumn = 27;
      PageNumLine = 57;
   var
      LineCount : LineNumRange;
begin
   for LineCount := LineNum + 1 to PageNumLine do
      WriteLn(Blank);

   Write(NormalMargin);
   SpaceOver(PageNumColumn);
   Write('–', PageNum : 1, '–');

   for LineCount := PageNumLine to PageSize do
      WriteLn(Blank);
   LineNum := 1;
   PageNum := PageNum + 1
end;



procedure NewLine;
begin
   if LineNum = LinesPerPage then
      NewPage
   else
      begin
         WriteLn(Blank);
         LineNum := LineNum + 1
      end
end;
```

Figure 16.4 continued

```
procedure GetWord (var Word : LineImage);
begin
  Word :=' ';
  while (NextInputChar = Blank) and not EOLn(InFile) do
    Get(InFile);
  if not EOLn(InFile) then
    repeat
      if Length(Word) < MaxLineLength then
        Word := ConCat(Word, NextInputChar);
      Get(InFile)
    until (NextInputChar = Blank) or EOLn(InFile)
end;


procedure GetCommand(Line : Line Image;
              var Name : CommandName;
              var EndOfCommand : ColumnNum);
  var
    FstWord : LineImage;
begin
  if Pos(Blank, Line) = 0 then
    EndOfCommand := Length(Line)
  else
    EndOfCommand := Pos(Blank, Line) - 1;
  FstWord := Copy(Line, 1, EndOfCommand);
  if FstWord = 'PARAGRAPH' then
    Name := Paragraph
  else if FstWord = 'VERBATIM' then
    Name := Verbatim
  else if FstWord = 'INDENT' then
    Name := Indent
  else if FstWord = 'CENTER' then
    Name := Center
  else if FstWord = 'SKIP' then
    Name := Skip
  else if FstWord = 'PAGE' then
    Name := Page
  else
    Name := Illegal
end;
```

Figure 16.4 continued

```
procedure GetArgument (Line : LineImage;
          EndOfCommand : ColumnNum;
          var Name : CommandName;
          var Argument : Argument(Range);
   var
      Column : ColumnNum;
      NextChar : Char;
begin
   if EndOfCommand = Length(Line) then
      if Name in [Center, Skip] then
         Argument := 1
      else
         Name := Illegal
   else
      begin
         Column := EndOfCommand + 1;
         while Line[Column] = Blank do
            Column := Column + 1;
         NextChar := Line[Column];
         if not (NextChar in ['0'..'9']) then
            Name := Illegal
         else
            begin
               Argument := DigitValue(NextChar);
               if Column <> Length(Line) then
                  begin
                     Column := Column + 1;
                     NextChar := Line[Column];
                     if (Column <> Length(Line)) or not (NextChar in
                              ['0'..'9']) then
                        Name := Illegal
                     else
                        Argument := (Argument * 10) + DigitValue(NextChar)
                  end
            end
      end
end;
```

Figure 16.4 continued

```
procedure GetLine (var Line : LineImage);

   var
      CharCount : Integer;
      TrailingBlanks : Boolean;
begin
   ReadLn(InFile, Line);
   CharCount := Length(Line);
   TrailingBlanks := True;
   while TrailingBlanks and (CharCount <> 0) do
      if Line[CharCount] <> Blank then
         TrailingBlanks := False
      else
         CharCount := CharCount – 1;
   Line := Copy(Line, 1, CharCount)
end;



procedure ParseLine (var Command : CommandInfo);

   var
      EndOfCommand : ColumnNum;
      BadArgument : Boolean;
begin
   GetLine(Command.Line);
   GetCommand(Command.Line, Command.Name, EndOfCommand);
   if (Command.Name in [Paragraph, Verbatim, Page]) and
            (Length(CommandLine) <> EndOfCommand) then
      Command.Name := Illegal;
   if Command.Name in [Indent, Center, Skip] then
      begin
         GetArgument(Command.Line, EndOfCommand, Command.Name,
               Command.Argument);
         if (Command.Name = Indent) and
               (Command.Argument> TextWidth) then
            Command.Name := Illegal
      end
end;
```

Figure 16.4 continued

```
procedure CenterLine;
  var
    Line : LineImage;
    LeadingBlanks : Integer;
    NextChar : Char;
    IsCommandLine : Boolean;
    Column : ColumnNum;
begin
  if not EOF(InFile) then
    begin
      IsCommandLine := (not EOLn(InFile)) and
                    (NextInput Char = CommandChar);
      while (NextInputChar = Blank) and not EOLn(InFile) do
        Get(InFile);
      GetLine(Line);
      if Length(Line) > 0 then
        begin
          if Length(Line) < TextWidth then
            LeadingBlanks := (TextWidth – Length(Line)) div 2
          else
            LeadingBlanks := 0;
          if IsCommandLine or (Length(Line) > TextWidth) then
            Write(ErrorMargin)
          else
            Write(NormalMargin);
          SpaceOver(LeadingBlanks);
          Write(Line)
        end;
      NewLine
    end
end;
```

Figure 16.4 continued

```pascal
procedure DoCommands (var TextMode : Mode;
            var Indentation : IndentRange);
  var
    Command : CommandInfo;
    LineCount : ArgumentRange;
  begin
    repeat
      ParseLine(Command);
      case Command.Name of
        Paragraph :
          TextMode := ParagraphMode;
        Verbatim :
          TextMode := VerbatimMode;
        Indent :
          Indentation := Command.Argument;
        Center :
          for LineCount := 1 to Command.Argument do
            CenterLine;
        Skip :
          for LineCount := 1 to Command.Argument do
            NewLine;
        Page :
          NewPage;
        Illegal :
          begin
            Write(ErrorMargin);
            Write(CommandLine);
            NewLine
          end
      end
    until (NextInputChar <> CommandChar) or EOF(InFile)
  end;
```

Figure 16.4 continued

```
procedure PrintWord (Word : LineImage;
            Indentation : IndentRange;
            var Column : ColumnNum);

  var
    FirstWordOnLine : Boolean;
    EndOfWord : Integer;
begin
  if Column = Indentation then
    begin
      FirstWordOnLine := True;
      EndOfWord := Column + Length(Word)
    end
  else
    begin
      FirstWordOnLine := False;
      EndOfWord := Column + Length(Word) + 1
    end
  if not FirstWordOnLine and (EndOfWord > TextWidth) then
    begin
      NewLine;
      Column := Indentation;
      FirstWordOnLine := True;
      EndOfWord := Indentation + Length(Word)
    end;
  if EndOfWord > TextWidth then
    begin
      Word := Copy(Word, 1, MaxLineLength - Indentation);
      Write(ErrorMargin);
      SpaceOver(Indentation);
      Write(Word);
      NewLine
    end
  else
    begin
      if FirstWordOnLine then
        begin
          Write(NormalMargin);
          SpaceOver(Indentation)
        end
      else
        Write(Blank);
      Write(Word);
      Column := EndOfWord
    end
end;
```

Figure 16.4 continued

```pascal
procedure DoParagraphLines (Indentation : IndentRange);
  const
    ParaIndent = 5;
  var
    Word : LineImage;
    Column : ColumnNum;
    NewParagraph : Boolean;
begin
  Column := Indentation;
  NewParagraph := True;
  repeat
    GetWord(Word);
    if Length(Word) = 0 then
      begin
        if Column <> Indentation then
          begin
            NewLine;
            Column := Indentation
          end;
        NewParagraph := True;
        NewLine
      end
    else
      repeat
        if NewParagraph then
          begin
            Column := Column + ParaIndent;
            PrintWord(Word, Indentation + ParaIndent, Column);
            NewParagraph := False
          end
        else
          PrintWord(Word, Indentation, Column);
        GetWord(Word)
      until Length(Word) = 0;
    ReadLn(InFile)
  until (NextInputChar = CommandChar) or EOF(InFile);
  if Column <> Indentation then
    NewLine
end;
```

Figure 16.4 continued

```
procedure DoVerbatimLines (Indentation : IndentRange);
  var
    Line : LineImage;
    NewLength : Integer;
begin
  repeat
    GetLine(Line);
    if Length(Line) > 0 then
      begin
        NewLength := Length(Line) + Indentation;
        if NewLength > TextWidth then
          Write(ErrorMargin)
        else
          Write(NormalMargin);
        SpaceOver(Indentation);
        if NewLength > MaxLineLength then
          Line := Copy(Line, 1, MaxLineLength - Indentation);
        Write(Line)
      end;
    NewLine
  until (NextInputChar = CommandChar) or EOF(InFile)
end;


begin              { -- MAIN ALGORITHM }
  Reset(InFile, 'SOURCETEXT');
  Close(Output);
  Rewrite(Output, 'Printer:');
  TextMode := ParagraphMode;
  Indentation := 0;
  LineNum := 1;  .
  PageNum := 1;
  while not EOF(InFile) do
    begin
      if NextInputChar = CommandChar then
        DoCommands(TextMode, Indentation)
      else if TextMode = ParagraphMode then
        DoParagraphLines(Indentation)
      else if TextMode = VerbatimMode then
        DoVerbatimLines(Indentation)
    end;
  NewPage
end.
```

16.2 ● Parting Comments

Format is a program of fairly large scale. In the testing of this program, we were faced with the necessity of conserving memory space without sacrificing any of the desired procedures and functions.

Certain steps can be taken to conserve memory space when working with Macintosh Pascal. One very simple step is to remove the windows from the screen before running the program. Should an error occur during the run, the program window reappears and the program is displayed indicating the location of the error.

Another space saver is to output directly to the printer as we have done in Format by using

```
Close(Output);
Rewrite(Output,'Printer:');
```

The Close call closes the standard output file which writes to the Text window. The Rewrite call sets the printer as the output file. Since the internal output file has been closed, the space normally reserved for it is freed for other uses.

To create the input file, a program similar to CreateBreedFile (Fig. 14.1) can be used. Program Format requires a file of type Text where the characters are read in one at a time. The end character can be any character that will not appear within the text, a backward slash ($\backslash$) is usually a good choice. We leave the writing of the program to you.

MacWrite can also be used to create the source text. The text can be entered on MacWrite and then saved as a text only document. The Save As dialog box offers the option of saving the entire document or the text only. Choosing Text Only saves what is needed for a source file; that is, the text is saved without the MacWrite formatting commands. The text can be saved on the Macintosh Pascal disk by choosing Eject and then inserting the Pascal disk before clicking the Save button.

In parting, we would like to underline a few points:

- Like Holmes, we strongly advocate the top-down approach.
- Regardless of the approach a programmer settles upon, we cannot over-emphasize the importance of *thinking*. Recall the great detective's thoughts on human reasoning in earlier chapters, especially *before* attempting to write any code.
- Finally, we should not forget that ultimately computer programs are designed to do useful things, for *human* users.

Sadly, our narrative is all but done. "What is the use of having powers, Doctor, when one has no field upon which to exert them?" inquired Holmes in "The Sign of Four." Indeed. Surely, dear reader, you have some field of your own to address?

Appendix A

Summary of Menus

Listed below are the menus and selections available on the Macintosh Pascal disk. Some of the selections are available only when the Finder is active; others only when the Macintosh Pascal interpreter has been activated. Still others are available from both applications.

The Finder is the Macintosh application that controls the manipulation of the various sets of data on the disk; for instance, the opening and closing of files, the copying and naming of documents, and the displaying of information about the contents of the disk. The selections that are available as part of the Finder are indicated by (F) following the selection or menu name. Those that are available when using Macintosh Pascal are indicated by (MP).

Only the selections that show in bold print can be activated; for instance, Eject will be in bold print on the File menu only if the active item is the disk which is presently in the machine.

About the Finder (F)	Shows which version of the Finder the disk contains, the copyright date, and the authors.	**Apple**
About Macintosh Pascal (MP)	Shows which version of Macintosh Pascal the disk contains, the copyright date, the authors, and the memory usage.	

Other choices on this menu contain information about the Macintosh desk accessories; refer to the owner's manual for information.

File	New (MP)	Available only when a program window has been closed. Creates an untitled window for writing a new program.
	Open (F)	Opens the selected icon or item name into a window displaying the contents of the item.
	Open (MP)	Available only when a program window has been closed. Puts up a dialog box listing the available files and offering the option of opening an existing file, canceling the choice, or ejecting the disk.
	Close (F,MP)	Closes the currently active window.
	Close All (F)	Closes all windows and removes all desk accessories from the screen.
	Duplicate (F)	Duplicates the selected item onto the same disk; labels the item as "Copy of **ItemName**."
	Get Info (F)	Puts up a dialog box with the following information about the selected item:

Type of Item: Disk, document, folder or application.

Size in bytes:

Location: The folder or disk containing the item.

Dates: The date the item was created and the date it was last modified.

Also offers the option of locking the items and a place to enter comments about the item.

	Put Back (F)	Returns selected item(s) to the folder or disk they were last taken from.
	Save (MP)	Enters the changes made to the document onto the disk file.
	Save AS (MP)	Puts up a dialog box requesting a name for the program, a choice of saving the entire document or the text only, and the opportunity to eject the disk in order to save the document on a different disk.
	Revert (MP)	Discards the changes made and reverts to the last version saved.
	Page Setup (MP)	Puts up a dialog box allowing choices of the following details for page setup:

Paper: US Letter, US Legal, A4 Letter, or International Fanfold.

	Orientation:	Tall	— normal printing
		Tall Adjusted	— graphics adjusted to be consistent with that appears on the screen.
		Wide	— wide printing

Print (F,MP)	Puts up a dialog box allowing the following printing choices:
	Quality: High, standard, or draft.
	Page Range: All, From: ____, To: ____
	Copies: ____ Number of copies.
	Paper Feed: Continuous or Cut Sheet.
Quit (MP)	Closes the windows and returns to the Finder.
Eject (F)	Ejects the disk.

Edit

Undo (F)	Undoes the last text editing action.
Cut (F, MP)	Removes the highlighted text and places it on the clipboard replacing whatever was previously on the clipboard.
Copy (F,MP)	Copies the highlighted text onto the clipboard replacing whatever was previously on the clipboard.
Paste (F,MP)	Inserts a copy of the text contained on the clipboard at the location of the cursor; if a section is highlighted it is deleted and the new text is entered in its place.
Clear (F,MP)	Deletes the highlighted test; does not save it on the clipboard.
Select All (F,MP)	Causes all the text in the window to become highlighted.
Show Clipboard (F)	Displays a window with the current contents of the clipboard.

Search

Find	Looks for and highlights the text indicated in the What
to	Find dialog box; starts seeking at the current cursor location.

	Replace	Replaces the currently highlighted text with the text indicated in What to Find dialog box.
	Everywhere	Performs a Find and Replace on the whole current document in accordance with what has been specified in the What to Find dialog box.
	What to Find	Puts up a dialog box allowing you to indicate what text to Find and what to Replace it with.

Run (MP)	Check	Checks the current program to see if it is a valid Macintosh Pascal program.
	Reset	Returns the current program to the beginning.
	Go	Begins or resumes execution of the current program; continues until it reaches a pause, stop, or end.
	Go-Go	Similar to Go except that when execution reaches a stop sign it pauses only long enough to update the Observe window.
	Step	Executes one line of the program; the finger in the left margin points to the next line to be executed.
	Step-Step	Similar to Go-Go except that the finger points to the line to be executed next.
	Stops In	Causes the Stop Signs to appear in the program window. If the stops are already in, this menu choice appears as "Stops Out."

Windows (MP)	Untitled	The name actually appearing here will be the name of the current program; choosing this window causes it to become the active window.
	Instant	Causes the Instant window to become active. Pascal statements can be entered and executed in the Instant window whenever it is active.
	Observe	Causes the Observe window to become active. The values of any variables entered in the Observe window will be displayed as the program is running.
	Text	Causes the Text window to become active. Whatever text is written as output by the program will appear in this window whether or not it is active; activating it brings it to the front of the screen for visibility.
	Drawing	Causes the Drawing window to become active; QuickDraw output will appear in this window.

Clipboard   Causes the Clipboard window to become active displaying its current contents.

Type Size   Puts up a dialog box allowing the selection of small, medium or large type size.

Pause (MP)

This menu appears only when a program is running. Holding the button down on Pause stops the program run temporarily; choosing Halt causes it to stop until a new run command is selected. The program continues at the point where it was interrupted.

View (F)

By Icon   Displays the contents of the disk or file by icon. When items are displayed by icon, the icons can be moved from one location to another; for instance, a document can be moved into or out of a folder, or any item can be moved into the trash or to an alternate disk. Furthermore, the names of items shown beneath the icon can be edited. The heading of the icon display gives the number of items contained, the amount of space used and the space available.

By Kind   Lists the contents of the disk or file and tells whether the item is an application, a file, or a document. For documents, the listing also shows what application was used in its creation. In addition, the size of the item and the latest modification date are shown.

By Name   Lists the same information as above with items arranged alphabetically by the name of the item.

By Date   Lists the same information as above with items arranged by the latest modification date.

By Size   Lists the same information as above with items arranged by size starting with the largest.

Special (F)

Clean Up   Puts the icon display into neat rows and columns.

Empty Trash   Erases the contents of the trash barrel. Until this choice has been selected, items in the trash barrel can be moved back to the screen; however, once the trash has been emptied, the items contained are no longer retrievable.

Erase Disk   Erases the disk.

Appendix B

Syntax Summary of Macintosh Pascal

The following table summarizes the rules for writing the Macintosh Pascal programs given in the text. These rules define much, but not all, of the Macintosh Pascal language. In the table describing our subset, the following conventions have been used.

1. Italicized names appearing in the left column, for example,

   variable-declaration

   give the names of constructs in Macintosh Pascal.

2. The symbol → separates the name of a construct from the form for writing the construct in Macintosh Pascal. The symbol → may be read "is written as" or "is defined as."

3. If a construct has two or more alternative forms, the symbol | is used to separate each alternative. The symbol | may thus be read "or."

4. Braces, for example, the braces in

   { *parameter-part* }

   enclose optional items.

5. An ellipsis symbol ... following a name or an item in braces, for example, the ellipses in

   digit ...
   { *adding-operator term* } ...

   specifies that the preceding name or item can be repeated one or more times.

Programs

program	→	**program** *identifier* {(*file-list*)};
		declaration-part
		begin
		statement-part
		end.
declaration-part	→	{ **uses**
		identifier-list;}
		{ **const**
		constant-declaration; ... }
		{ **type**
		type-declaration; ... }
		{ **var**
		variable-declaration; ... }
		{ *subprogram-declaration*; ... }
statement-part	→	*statement* {;
		statement } ...

Declarations

constant-declaration	→	*identifier* = *constant*;
type-declaration		*identifier* = *type*;
variable-declaration	→	*identifier-list*: *type*;
subprogram-declaration	→	**procedure function**
procedure	→	**procedure** *identifier*
		{ *parameter-part* };
		declaration-part
		begin
		statement-part
		end;
function	→	**function** *identifier* { parameter-part };
		result-type;
		declaration-part
		begin
		statement-part
		end;
parameter-part	→	(*parameter-definition*{ ;
		parameter-definition } ...)
parameter-definition	→	{ **var** } *identifier-list* : *type-identifier*
result-type	→	*type-identifier*

		Statements
statement	→	assignment-statement | if-statement
	|	case-statement | while-statement
	|	repeat-statement | for-statement
	|	procedure-statement | with-statement
	|	compound statement
assignment-statement	→	variable := expression
		function-identifier := expression

if-statement →

if condition **then**
    statement
{ **else if** condition **then**
    statement } ...
{ **else**
    statement }

case-statement →

case expression **of**
    constant-list : statement {;
    constant-list : statement } ... {;
otherwise
    statement }
end

while-statement →

while condition **do**
    statement

repeat-statement →

repeat
    statement {;
    statement } ...
until condition

for-statement →

for variable := expression **to** expression **do**
    statement
\| **for** variable := expression
    downto expression **do**
    statement

procedure-statement →

procedure-identifier
procedure-identifier (expression-list)

with-statement →

with record-variable **do**
    statement

compound-statement →

begin
    statement {;
    statement } ...
end

condition →

expression

Types

type	—→	*type-identifier* | *ordinal-type* | *real-type* | *array-type* | *record-type* | *set-type* | *file-type* | *string-type* | *pointer-type*
ordinal-type	→	*integer* | *longint* | *boolean* | *char* | *enumerated-type* | *subrange*
enumerated-type	→	*identifier-list*
subrange	→	*constant .. constant*
real-type	→	*real* | *double* | *extended*
array-type	→	{ **packed** } **array** [*index-list*] **of** *type*
index-list	→	*index-type* {, *index-type* } ...
index-type	→	*type-identifier* | *subrange*

record-type	→	**record**
		    identifier : type {;
		    identifier : type } ...
		 end

set-type	→	**set of** *ordinal-type*
file-type	→	**file of** *file* | text
string-type		**string** {[*size-attribute*]}
size-substitute	→	*unsigned integer*
pointer-type	→	*dynamic-variable*

Variables and Expressions

variable	→ |	*variable* | *array-component* | *string component* *record-component* | *file-component*
array-component	→	*array-variable* [*expression-list*]
string-component	→	*string-variable* [*expression*]
record-component	→	*record-variable.field-designator*
field-designator	→	*identifier*
file-component	→	*file-variable*
expression-list	→	*expression* { , *expression* } ...
expression	→ |	*simple-expression* *simple-expression relational-operator* *simple-expression*
simple-expression	→	{ *sign* } *term* { *adding-operator term* } ...
term	→ |	**not** *operand* *operand* { *multiplying-operator operand* }...

operand	→	*unsigned-constant* | *variable* | (*expression*)
	|	*function-call*
function-call	→	*function-identifier* { (*expression-list*) }
set	→	[*element* {, *element* } ...]
element	→	*expression* | *expression* .. *expression*
sign	→	+ | –
relational-operator	→	= | <> | < | <= | >= | >
adding-operator	→	+ | – | **or**
multiplying-operator	→	* | / | **div** | **mod** | **and**

---

type-identifier	→	*identifier*	**Identifiers,**
procedure-identifier	→	*identifier*	**Numbers, and**
function-identifier	→	*identifier*	**Strings**
identifier-list	→	*identifier* {, *identifier* } ...	
identifier	→	*letter* { *letter-or-digit-or-underscore* } ...	
constant	→	{*sign*} *unsigned-constant*	
unsigned-constant	→	*number* | *identifier* | *string*	
number	→	*integral-number* | *real number*	
integral-number	→	*digit* ...	
real-number	→	*integer.integer*	
	|	*integer.integer* E *scale-factor*	
scale-factor	→	{*sign*} *integer*	
string	→	'{*character*} ...'	
character	→	*letter* | *digit* | *special-character*	
digit	→	0 | 1 | 2 | 3 | 4 | 5 | 6 | 7 | 8 | 9	
letter	→	A | B | C | D | E | F | G | H | I	
		J | K | L | M | N | O | P | Q | R	
		S | T | U | V | W | X | Y | Z |	
special-character	→	! | " | * | $ | % | & | | { | } | ° | +	
		| , | - | . | / | : | ; | < | = | > | ? | ®	
		| [| |] | ^ | | __ | | { | | } |	

Appendix C

The programming exercises that follow are rather difficult ones, possibly requiring many hours to solve. These problems present a worthy challenge to those who want to really exercise their programming skills. We present them here for use as term projects, or team projects, or simply as good exercise for those who want to improve their mental capacities in the area of programming.

C.1   Drawing a Circle
Many programmers have seen computer-drawn shapes. Here is one that is not too difficult to draw, but does have a little twist to it.

Write a program to read in a real number representing the radius of a circle in inches. The program should print a circle of the given radius, centered on the page. Your program should accept input values up to 4.0 inches, and draw the circle with about 100 points.

Note: You do not have to connect the points, but just print the 100 or so points on the circumference.

C.2   Paying Caesar His Due
When tax time comes around, most of us hate doing the figuring as much as we dislike paying Caesar his due. With the right program and information, the computer can prove to be most useful in figuring out taxes. Although there is much more involved, the last step is to take out final earnings figure and use that to look up the amount due.

So, obtain a copy of a recent tax table and write a problem to read in your earnings and print out the tax. If you feel that this is not enough to flex your programming muscles, include the number of dependents in your calculations.

383

C.3 Word Searching

You may have heard of an automatic indexing program. This is a program that reads in a document, searches for a given list of keywords and keyphrases, and then prints each keyword or keyphrase followed by the page numbers on which the word or phrase occurs. For example, for a text on Pascal, we may have

    addition   16,31,32
    and   35
    array   102-108, 154, 191
    assignment statement   21-25, 104, 252

It is easy to see the merits of such a program.

Unfortunately, automatic indexing has its problems. Should you distinguish between capitalized and uncapitalized words? What about plurals? Shouldn't the first page listed be the major entry? What about words like "assignment" that appear almost everywhere? Should "add" be treated differently from "addition" or "real" be treated differently from "real number"? What about "real world"? Should there be subcategories? Or cross-indexing?

Never mind. For this problem consider the following simplified task. You are to write a program that first reads in a series of keywords, ending with the word STOP, and then reads in a document. For simplicity, use the first page of this chapter as your document and invent your own keywords; the page can be entered with all words fully capitalized.

The program should print the number of occurrences of each keyword.

C.4 Inventories

It is hard to think of many large-scale purchasing operations whose inventory is still done by hand. Enter the computer, of course. For book inventories the problem is not too difficult. Suppose the inventory entries for each book are ordered by stock number, and that each inventory entry contains the stock number, title, author, list price, quantity on hand, and publisher of the book.

For input, such a program is given two files: (1) the file of inventory entries, and (2) a file of purchase entries, also ordered by stock number and each containing the quantity sold. For output, the program prints any inventory entry whose remaining quantity on hand is fewer than 500. The remaining quantity on hand is calculated by subtracting all purchases from the quantity given in the corresponding inventory entry.

Write such a program, along with the design of the appropriate file entries. Test your program with two short input files of your own.

C.5   Computations Based on Physical Measurement

Imagine for the moment that you are trying to calculate the area of a rectangular room. You can only really read your ruler to three digits, for example:

Width = 12.4 feet
Length = 13.6 feet

Now imagine calculating the product of these two numbers, 168.64. Can we be sure that the area of this room is 168.64 square feet and not 168.63, 168.65, or even 169 square feet? No.

It is a law of physical measurement that the precision of a computed result can be no greater than the precision of any measurement needed to calculate the result. For example, all we can say is that the area is accurate to three digits. Thus, we can say that the area of our room is 169 square feet, but we cannot be any more precise than that. The actual area could be 168.83, 168.70, 169.08, or 169.40 square feet.

Write a program to read in two real numbers and print out their exact product and the number of digits of precision. The precision should be equal to the number of digits of the input value with the fewest number of digits. For example, if you input

12.4   9.1

the output should be

THE PRODUCT IS 112.84
PRECISION IS 2 DIGITS

Note: This problem requires reading the input values on a character-by-character basis.

C.6   The Computer in the Kitchen

There are many who believe that it will not be long before the computer will be a household appliance. It's not clear that this will be the case, but here goes.

Imagine a program with the following dialogue:

Computer: Enter recipe name
You   : Truffle sauce a la Michel Guerard
Computer: For how many servings is the recipe written?
You   : 8
Computer: How many servings would you like?
You   : 6
Computer: How many ingredients are there?
You   : 7
Computer: Now for the recipe

```
You        : 1/2   pint  Port
             8     tbs.  Cognac
             1.75  oz.   Chopped truffles
             4     tbs.  Truffle liquid
             1     pint  Demi-glace
             1.75  oz.   Unsalted butter
             --    --    Salt and pepper
Computer:  Ingredients for 6 persons.
           Truffle sauce a la Michel Guerard.
             3/8   pint  Port
             6     tbs.  Cognac
             1.3   oz.   Chopped truffles
             3     tbs.  Truffle liquid
             3/4   pint  Demi-glace
             1.3   oz.   Unsalted butter
             --    --    Salt and pepper
```

It all looks simple, but . . .

Whipping up a truly useful program for this application means dealing with strings in Pascal. In addition, this sort of problem puts you in touch with all kinds of recipes; and you've got to keep in mind that the chef is not always a computer expert, so your final list of ingredients has to make sense. For instance,

        1.750000000   Oz.   Butter

or

        175E–2   Oz.   Butter

would hardly please the cook. And what about reading (or printing)

        1 3/4   Oz.   Butter

instead of

        1.75 Oz. Butter

Hmmm.

In any case, give it a good try and write such a program.

C.7   Justified Text

The text of many manuscripts (including this one) is written with justified text. That is the words of a paragraph are aligned on both the left *and* right margins. Many consider this layout more aesthetic than having a ragged right edge.

Revise the program of Fig. 16.4 to produce justified text. To do this you will need to decide on a scheme for "balancing" lines, and add several new procedures to the program.

C.8   Reservations Please

Have you ever walked up to a ticket counter, asked to reserve some seats, and noticed that the reservations were handled by computer?

For plane reservations the problem is not too overwhelming. Suppose there are 25 rows of seats, six to a row. The rows are numbered 1 through 25, and the six seats in each row are labeled A through F. Assume that seats A, B, C are on one side of the aisle: D, E, and F on the other. Seats A and F are window seats. Rows 1 through 15 are nonsmoking rows.

We can readily imagine a simple dialogue as follows:

```
Computer: Number of seats?
You       : 2
Computer: Smoking or non-smoking?
You       : NS
Computer: Window?
You       : Y
Computer: Reservations OK, seats 10A and 10B
```

In the above dialogue, the following abbreviation are assumed:

```
S  — Smoking
NS — Nonsmoking
Y  — Yes
N  — No
DC— Don't care
```

Obviously, we could consider much more complex situations, but this should suffice for a start.

Now for the problem. Write a program to accept a series of reservation requests for a single plane. On request at any time, the program should display the status of the seats, for example, in the form

```
          A  B  C     D  E  F
          - - - - - - - - - - - - - - - - -
Row 1     X  X  —     —  —  X
- - - -
Row 2     —  X  X     X  X  X
- - - -
Row 3     X  X  —     —  X  X
- - - -
Row 4     X  —  —     —  X  X
- - - -
```

where an X denotes a seat already taken.

The following characteristics are important in the program's design: the ability to handle abbreviations, the ability to respond to typing errors, maximization of the number of seats occupied.

The output of your work should contain:

a) A short but clear guide for using the program. The User's Guide should be suitable for a lay person.

b) Several test runs to show the performance of the program. These may be included in (a).

c) The program itself.

C.9   Fractional Arithmetic

The built-in types in a language almost never include whole fractions. The reason is simple: exact arithmetic with fractions is not easy.

Consider the following expression and the (exact) fractional values.

```
2/6                  — value is 1/3
2/6 + 2/6            — value is 2/3
(1/2)*(1/4)          — value is 1/8
1/2 + 1/3 + 1/4      — value is 13/12
(11/16)*2 + 1/3      — value is 41/24
1/3 – 2/3 + 1/3      — value is 0
(2/3) / (1/3)        — value is 2
```

To make these calculations we have to know about putting fractions in their lowest terms, and other such familiar operations.

Write a program to read in a fractional arithmetic expression, such as the above, and print its exact fractional value. The expression must satisfy the following rules:

a) The results of the expression can be whole numbers (i.e., 1, 2, 3, and so on) or fractions (such as 1/2, 3/2, 1/3, 2/3, and so on).

b) The operators can be $+$, $-$, $*$ or $/$.

c) Fractions or sub-expressions can be parenthesized.

d) Within a parenthesized expression, the operators $*$ and $/$ are applied before $+$ and $-$. Otherwise evaluation proceeds from left to right.

You may add some restrictions of your own if you think they will add to the clarity of the expressions.

Index